The publisher and the University of California Press Foundation gratefully acknowledge the generous support of the Roth Family Foundation Imprint in Music, established by a major gift from Sukey and Gil Garcetti and Michael P. Roth.

Who Hears Here?

PHONO: BLACK MUSIC AND THE GLOBAL IMAGINATION

This series is a dynamic collection of work that explores and documents the long-playing histories of Black musical innovation. The title is a nod to the grooves, play, tactility, and archives produced by the phonograph, which serves as inspiration for a complex series of musical concerns and possibilities. The series title indexes how Black sound, performance, and musical idioms are inscribed in the acoustics of everyday Black life, both local and transnational.

Shana L. Redmond and Tsitsi Jaji, Editors

Who Hears Here?

ON BLACK MUSIC, PASTS AND PRESENT

Guthrie P. Ramsey, Jr.

Foreword by Tammy L. Kernodle
Afterword by Shana L. Redmond

UNIVERSITY OF CALIFORNIA PRESS

University of California Press
Oakland, California

© 2022 by the Regents of the University of California

Library of Congress Cataloging-in-Publication Data

Names: Ramsey, Guthrie P., author. | Kernodle, Tammy L., 1969- writer
 of foreword. | Redmond, Shana L., writer of afterword.
Title: Who hears here? : on black music, pasts and present / Guthrie
 P. Ramsey, Jr. ; foreword by Tammy L. Kernodle ; afterword by Shana
 L. Redmond.
Other titles: Phono (Oakland, Calif.) ; 1.
Description: Oakland, California : University of California Press, [2022] |
 Series: Phono: black music and the global imagination ; 1 | Includes
 bibliographical references and index.
Identifiers: LCCN 2022010756 (print) | LCCN 2022010757 (ebook) |
 ISBN 9780520281837 (cloth) | ISBN 9780520281844 (paperback) |
 ISBN 9780520392182 (ebook)
Subjects: LCSH: African Americans—Music—History and criticism. |
 Popular music—Social aspects—United States. | Musicology—United
 States—History.
Classification: LCC ML3556 .R323 2022 (print) | LCC ML3556 (ebook) |
 DDC 780.89/96073—dc23/eng/20220331
LC record available at https://lccn.loc.gov/2022010756
LC ebook record available at https://lccn.loc.gov/2022010757

Manufactured in the United States of America

31 30 29 28 27 26 25 24 23 22
10 9 8 7 6 5 4 3 2

For my forerunners: Rich, Sam, Rae Linda, and Portia

And to the memory of Auntie Inez Lyles, forever in my heart

This is what pushed me. But as I began to get into the history of the music, I found that this was impossible without, at the same time, getting deeper into the history of the people. That it was the history of the Afro-American people as text, as tale, as story, as exposition, or what have you, that the music was the score, the actually expressed orchestration, of Afro-American life, our words the libretto to those actual lived lives.

Amiri Baraka, *Digging: The Afro-American Soul of American Classical Music*

But then there is life! My own memories of a life lived in worlds different but exciting, full of things to learn, understand, enjoy, dance and listen to, see, and live for. Life as fun but life as mission. To tell it, to make people see, know, and accept all of it at whatever cost; a responsibility to the past but also to the present and to the future. To write oneself back into history, as a continual action, as a responsibility not just to oneself but also to community.

Kellie Jones, *EyeMinded: Living and Writing Contemporary Art*

Contents

Foreword

Tammy L. Kernodle

Speak the truth to the people
Talk sense to the people
Free them with reason
Free them with honesty
Free the people with love and courage and with care for their being
Spare them the fantasy, the fantasy enslaves

Mari Evans, "Speak Truth to the People"

I first met Guthrie P. Ramsey Jr. (who I affectionately call Ramsey) in the early 1990s, when I was navigating graduate study in musicology at The Ohio State University. As a first-generation college student, and the only Black woman enrolled in the MA/PhD program from 1991 to 1997, I often felt unsure and isolated. The isolation I felt was not due to maltreatment or lack of support from my colleagues or professors, but because of how different my perspectives were regarding my identity in a largely white discipline and the work that I wanted to do. I entered graduate school with the express purpose of training to do Black music study. This was concrete in my mind, despite selecting a graduate program whose focus was traditional musicology. I knew that OSU also had a strong jazz program led by William "Ted" McDaniel and an equally strong Black Studies Program. For me this combination ensured that I could develop all sides of my intellectual soul. Beyond this, I really had no concept of what it meant to be a Black musicologist whose work focused on Black expressive culture, and no real understanding of what I was getting myself into, especially given the emerging discussions on "new musicology" and "traditional" musicology that erupted in the 1990s. The discipline was at a crossroads in the early 1990s, and so was I. It was then that I met Guthrie Ramsey at a music conference.

He was confident, and his scholarship was sound and theoretically strong. He genuinely cared about your work, and you. Ramsey came to model many things for me and the generation of scholars that navigated music graduate programs and entered the academy during the late 1990s and early 2000s. We were the generation whose life trajectory had been significantly shaped by the Black civil rights movement, the integration of historically white colleges and universities, and the emergence of Eileen Southern's seminal book *The Music of Black Americans*. We were those who Southern, Samuel Floyd Jr. and other members of the Black music intelligentsia wrote of and dreamed of—or at least that was what we thought. Most of us never engaged directly with that generation of scholars, so for us Ramsey represented a personal, professional, and intellectual bridge to these foremothers and forefathers. He was a picture of what we could be as well as the power that lies at the foundation of our work.

Ramsey showed us that we no longer had to choose Black music as a secondary area of study, subordinate to a primary area or topic that focused on Western European music. He showed us how we could bring our whole selves to the work without compromising integrity, rigor, and strength. He showed us that we did not have to follow the masculinist or "great men" framework of the previous generation in order elevate Black music studies into a field of serious inquiry. We could enlarge our conversations to consider the work and contributions of Black women! He embodied the persona of the postsoul Black music scholar and charted a new praxis of Black and American music study.

The essays in this anthology are important for many reasons. They situate Ramsey within the genealogy of Black music and the American music scholars who inspired new conversations in our music disciplines. They contextualize how Ramsey spoke truth to power, embodying the spirit of the epitaph above—how he challenged existing paradigms and promoted theoretical frameworks that underscore contemporary Black music scholarship and engaged in a type of intellectual activism that can easily be forgotten given the current culture of inclusion reflected in contemporary conference programs, journal issues, symposia, and workshops.

Ramsey's work calls us back into the nexus of tense disciplinary debates that took place in the 1990s and the early 2000s regarding the emergence of "new musicology" and how Black music—and, by extension, the Black scholar—existed within this epoch. "Who Hears Here?," "The Pot Liquor Principle," and "Secrets, Lies, and Transcriptions" remind us of just how bold and radical those working to advance these new conversations were. Most importantly, they reflect how Ramsey trusted his own mind not only to ask the questions that needed to be asked, but also to find the answers. His strategies pushed the methodological scope of Black music studies beyond that of the Black power–era intelligentsia as he looked to cultural theory, feminist theory, and autoethnography. He exploded the model of genre and specialty by writing across the full spectrum of Black expressive culture and expressing himself through different media. He invoked historical tropes and voices of the past while simultaneously challenging the thoughts and ideas of his contemporaries. He forged liberation narratives of new intellectual and cultural worlds that were not unlike those of the Black revolutionaries that preceded him.

I want to end this foreword by offering a personal story about Ramsey and the importance of his presence and work. In 2010 I was asked to serve on the senior editorial board for the revision of the *New Grove Dictionary of American Music*. My primary responsibility was to commission, curate, and edit articles in the areas of gospel, blues, and jazz. I was also tasked with commissioning the large anchor articles on these genres and the long history of African American music. Although many assumed that I would take on this task myself, I knew it was not my time. As a southern-born, southern-raised Black woman, I know the importance of doing things with decency and in order, and I knew it was not my time; this task required the perspective and the voice of an elder, one who came before me.

I was aware that, in the history of these large reference projects, the vanguard voice of a particular generation or epoch was often tasked with this duty. So, in keeping with this tradition, I reached out to Ramsey. I knew that he was busy managing his own record label, composing, and performing, but I thought I would take a chance. After all, by that time our relationship had extended to twenty-plus years.

It took some convincing, but he finally relented, and the resulting essay closes this anthology. Rereading it in preparation for writing this foreword reminded me of its strength and radicalness. It exceeded every expectation I had then and continues to do so even now. It points to how, thirty years after his first work appeared in disciplinary journals, Ramsey continues to ask difficult questions, mediate the tensions that surround them, and challenge us to hear, see, and think more deeply about Blackness and Black expressive culture.

Acknowledgments

It's been miraculous to witness and to participate in the explosion of writing about Black music studies since I joined the field. And I've been supported and inspired by many over the years that these essays were written. The senior scholars and contemporaries who guided me, the journalists and bloggers who keep me up-to-date, and the younger generation of writers charting new and exciting directions have all contributed to my thinking, research, and writing. I'm particularly indebted to the scores of students I've taught throughout my career; their brilliance, ambitions, and curiosities have sharpened me in innumerable ways. Working alongside my colleagues at Tufts University and the University of Pennsylvania—the writers of amazing books, convenors of powerful courses, and composers of remarkable music—has been a profound source of motivation to me. To share students with them always guaranteed an education as their teachings circulated in my courses through osmosis.

I thank Matthew Valnes, Ben DuPriest, Siel Agugliaro, and Vincent Wilson for their assistance in preparing this book for publication. Tamara Nopper, thank you for pushing this book over the finish line. I'm also indebted to the extended Musiqology team for their unwavering and enthusiastic support. Pamela Yau, Mikel Washington, Fredara Hadley,

John Vilanova, Bridget Ramsey-Russell, Shakira King, Nadia Henry, Michelle Zipkin, Jalessa Savage, and Cobbina Frempong, I thank you. Mark Anthony Neal, Lisa Thompson, Michael Veal, and Alisha Lola Jones—you "squad up" very well. Thank you for your examples in these artist/scholar streets. Deborah Thomas, John Jackson, Michael Hanchard, Tukufu Zuberi, and Kenneth Shropshire, our conversations illuminate all the things on campus and beyond.

To my editor, Raina Polivka, I extend my deep gratitude for your expert advice and unfailing support in the projects we've worked on together, especially this volume. You're the best. And to Mary Francis, thank you for your belief in this book from the beginning. Tammy Kernodle and Shana Redmond, I'm constantly energized by your intellects, accomplishments, and support. Thank you both for your brilliant, heartfelt contributions to this book. To the two groups of readers who reviewed this book for the University of California Press, I was humbled by and learned from your insightful comments. You made the book better. In his capacity as a friend and chair of Penn's music department as I prepared this collection, Timothy Rommen provided much-needed guidance and support. I'm grateful. I'd like to also extend my deep appreciation to the estate of the great Jack Whitten for allowing me to use his stunning painting on the cover of this book.

I can always count on my extended family and friends for care, sustenance, stimulation, and good humor. The Ross, Ramsey, Jones, Brown, and Archie clans do family very well. My mother, Celia, lights up the world and sits at the helm of many cherished and connected descendants. And trust me: the music is strong among her folks. My own children and their children (affectionately known as the "spring-offs") continually bless me with a bounty of love and support. I thank you all. To my partner, Kellie Jones, thank you for all the good things. A lady who hums along with a John Coltrane solo, who knows all of Prince's lyrics, and who translates Spanish songs for me in real time is definitely the one for me. A special shout-out to my mother-in-law, Hettie Jones, for a love and editing supreme; and two more to my dear colleague Jim Primosch and to my "bonus mom," Dr. Peggy Brown, two cherished supporters who we lost as I was pulling this book together.

I dedicate this book to my scholarly forerunners Richard Crawford and Portia Maultsby, and to the memories of Samuel A. Floyd Jr. and Rae

Linda Brown. All of you have enriched my life through your teaching, research, service, and pioneering spirits. You clear the way for me.

And to the memory of the beautiful one, my Auntie Inez Lyles, whom we lost to the pandemic, I also dedicate this book. She absolutely had the music in her in a very big way.

Introduction

The question posed by the late musicologist Christopher Small, "Why are these people making this music at this time and in this place?," provided a way to open many of my courses and a number of research projects.[1] I love it because it gave me an easy way to investigate how people make meaning of the musics they made and heard. The four-part equation—people, music, time, and place—covers a lot of territory. Indeed, the identities of musicians, audiences, and critics, the structure and syntax of organized sound, and the historical and geographic contexts of music rarely failed to spur stimulation and provocation.

I'm engaging Small's question once again as I introduce this selection of my writings. Why *did* I write these essays at this or that time and place? How do I make sense of pieces that were written in varied circumstances and times and shaped, as they are, by diverse motivations? Is there some value in suggesting that they have some kind of unity and to anthologize them as such?

I believe that writing (and any act of creating) is "about" self-fashioning. While it certainly encompasses other things, the establishment of Self in writing is always present—even if it's done under the category "objective scholarship." Thus, these essays document, among other things, my

1

dynamic and changing relationship to various topics over the years; I never thought of myself as a writer standing still in a single theoretical or methodological orbit. I'm collecting my "Selves" and these engagements with assorted topics to represent, I hope, a cohesive body of work.

If there's a prominent organizing theme in my writing, it would be my belief in the strength, resilience, and dignity of Black people, who have fought adversities for centuries. I wanted to tell our musical stories and truths. I desired to reveal the lies and misunderstandings, too. I've worked to understand and explain the histories and mysteries of this thing called Black music, something that has been a powerful, energetic, and magnetic force in my life from my earliest recollections.

The politics of writing and lecturing in the academic guild was powerfully addressed by the late filmmaker Marlon Riggs in an essay resembling an extended poem written in the third person. In "Unleash the Queen," Riggs critiques what happens when "Others/Minorities" adopt what he called "dominant discourses" to validate themselves as intellectuals.[2] He wondered if, by participating in those language communities, they were "singing someone else's tune to be heard."[3] While Riggs was speaking from the prospective of a Black/queer identity in the 1990s, his thoughts resonate across time and category. Riggs asks the guild, "My mouth moves, but you hear your own words. What nature of ventriloquism is this?"[4] Did the use of specific kinds of academic language—another tongue, if you will—leave Riggs, in effect, voiceless?

The prospect of invisibility/voicelessness and the perception of "cultural illiteracy" all informed how I eventually came to understand the politics of the guild's words, grammars, writing formats, and theories in the context of my own musical background. During my early years in the field, I realized that the academy was just one (and not the most important) of the many "ways of knowing" I had experienced in my musical life. Some of the academy was unbelievably enlightening and motivating. Other aspects of my training and research journey to become a recognized expert in the field alienated me. Had I been "Negro miseducated," to coin a phrase, or were my citations, references, and stories just different? And did/could they have some benefit to music studies?

I became a writer because I wanted to be a scholar—not because I had a strong drive to write from an early age (as I did to create music). Yet telling stories has been particularly important as I have established a writerly voice in research. As scholar Katherine McKittrick sees it, stories, citations, and references announce one's intellectual history. They also show how we collect ideas, how we know what we know, and what ideas outside ourselves we've adopted to develop a personal, critical voice.[5]

When I wrote the essay from which this book takes its title, I was compelled to make some elbow room for *all* of what I (we) knew to be my (our) intellectual, political, and musical foundations. I wanted to make room for the other experiences I'd lived through. There were, I realized, other stories to tell as I became the "who" in the title.

"Stories," McKittrick writes, can "move us and make place." Clearly, in many of these essays, making place for myself (and others like me) was a central goal. At the same time, as a Black scholar in a nondiverse discipline that had begun to open its gates to multiculturalism, I wanted more. Given the dearth of Black scholars at that time, how could I abide what could only be called antiblackness even as the field increasingly allowed Black musical topics into its array of "legitimate" research topics?

More than creating place for my own voice in the field, the query "who hears here?" invites us all to consider our backgrounds and identifications when writing about a music tradition in which power relationships have been a persistent underlying theme. Riggs expressed my attitude toward the field concisely: "Do you honestly think you can so closely . . . [and] critically examine me without studying or revealing yourself?"[6]

Beyond "outing" and disrupting "the invisible white, critical I," the essays in this collection also document my search for musical meaning via my musicological training and through the other disciplines I engaged. Some of the latter include the other subdisciplines of music theory and ethnomusicology. Add to these Black cultural studies, literary studies, and American studies frameworks. Beyond producing powerful ideas, these other nonmusic disciplines had a much more diverse constituency and provided opportunities for a broader range of insights. Yet over the last thirty years I've witnessed a changing ethos in musicology, and some of that shifting intellectual terrain can be seen in these essays.

Three main impulses run through this work: historiography, cultural criticism, and genre studies. My fascination with historiography—the history of writing history—began with the example set by my advisor and mentor, the eminent musicologist of American music Richard Crawford. His brilliant historiographical ruminations instilled in me a respect for what could be learned from studying the contours, twists, and turns of historical writings. Indeed, asking "Why are these people *writing* music history at this time, in this place?" allowed me to grasp and organize the ideologies of historical writers.[7]

Cultural criticism, the activity that tries to uncover the often-cloaked motivations animating historical and contemporary actors—as well as the rippling, unintentional social impact of the things they do—is an underlying methodological approach of some of the essays. The challenge for my generation of music scholars was to talk about how sound organization itself—how the pitches, rhythms, timbres, harmonies, and so on—could purvey social meanings. As musicologist Susan McClary put it, cultural criticism in music allows us to "investigate the syntactical conventions that grant coherence to our repertories and also to examine the ways music participates in the social construction of subjectivity, gender, desire, ethnicity, the body, and so on."[8]

At that time, some scholars were pushing musicology to broaden the demographics of its rank and file (more on this later), a challenge that has historically vexed the field. Part of my work, as I understood it through the years, was to think about what impact cultural criticism could have on Black music study if the field remained a predominantly white, male endeavor. In other words, what were the implications of achieving a diversity of thought without a diversity of thinkers doing that work?

As a musician I've participated in a wide swath of music, from standard chorale literature to gospel and more. Although I wrote a dissertation on jazz pianist Bud Powell, I've always considered the full range of contemporary and historical African American music my scholarly domain. I argue in some of these essays that the genres of jazz, gospel, hip-hop, and others have established "social contracts" with audiences—agreements that have created expectations of sonic organization, of audience reaction, and in marketing strategies. My goal in this work (as it was for many music scholars) was simple: to explain how social meaning is derived from the sonic details and assorted reception contexts.[9]

Now I'd like to "storify" the provocation "who hears here?" and Riggs's metaphor "singing someone else's tune." If these essays mark different points in my scholarly self-fashioning, I should say what led me to the field in the first place. What musical and political selves arrived at musicology's door?

The whole thing seems like an accident.

"Jesus, Lover of My Soul," "Jesus Wants You for a Sunbeam," "God Gave Me a Song," "Oh, Happy Day." These were the first songs I remember rehearsing as part of the tiny-tot and youth choirs of the church I attended in my youth. Rehearsals were taken very seriously in this setting, a small church founded by southern migrants living in the greater Chicagoland region. The migrants brought things from the South—memories and ways of doing—that they insisted on passing on to the next generation. Music was one of them.

In the mid-1960s our elementary school teachers, many of them Black migrants, taught us spirituals and blues together with lessons in math and geography. (Yes, there were pianos in the classrooms.) Our middle school cheerleaders led a cheer in twelve-bar blues form, "Don't Say Nothing Bad about the Spirit" at every home basketball game. We experienced a social world saturated in symbolic cultural forms—at midnight roller rink sessions, at midnight church musicals, in local college gospel choirs and jazz ensembles, and more. They "made" us; it's who we were at that time, in that place.[10]

In the mid-1970s my musical interests exploded when I attended the racially integrated township high school, which gave me more opportunities to think abstractly about music as I attended music theory classes, sang madrigals and choral literature, learned the repertoire of the American musical theater, and performed in the jazz band. Somehow this all seemed additive to me and not a challenge to my previous musical literacies. Along the way I jammed on rock and jazz with talented high school friends in living rooms and garages. I began to think of myself as a serious musician.

But there were other literacies to encounter and explore. When I discovered the ML 3556 section of the library (the one focused on Black music history) as an undergraduate in the mid-1980s, it took me by surprise how much I loved the literature about Black music of the United States. As a working musician since I graduated high school and an unlikely candidate to become a scholar, I matriculated at Northeastern Illinois University in Chicago in 1981 primarily because the jazz band was hot and I could gig in the city and attend college simultaneously. The band was directed by Aaron Horne, a clarinetist specializing in modernist concert music. He was the first Black "doctor of music" I'd ever met. Doc, as we affectionately called him, was on a mission to see that musicians like me got an opportunity to study and earn degrees. He recruited great players from around the country. I was in luck: the band needed a piano player. And the opportunity changed the course of my life, steering me toward a land called Academia.

"I have to type a paper," I remember telling another student. She happened to be an accomplished pianist for the Black Heritage Gospel Choir on campus, a group that was formed to provide a social network to its participants. While I put a little jazz into my gospel accompaniment, she described herself as "just a hymnal girl." I was in a panic, and she showed me patience and mercy, teaching me how to load the paper into the typewriter and a few other basics necessary to operate a machine I'd never touched with any seriousness. Another beginning began. I don't recall the topic of my paper, but from that point on putting words on a page didn't intimidate me. The finished product, in fact, reminded me of making a recording. Writing was permanent, memorializing a moment in time.

Along the way I encountered books by LeRoi Jones (aka Amiri Baraka), Charlie Keil, Eileen Southern, Dena Epstein, and others—all writers I would get to meet in the next decade. Venturing further into this fascinating world of letters, I learned about academic journals that featured articles by scholars who had become my role models: Portia K. Maultsby, Samuel A. Floyd Jr., Josephine Wright, and Olly Wilson, among others, who laid the foundation for Black music research's contemporary era.[11]

I'll never forget a black-and-white photograph of Maultsby that accompanied one of her articles. She was crowned with a voluminous, perfectly shaped 1970s-era Afro that reminded me of Angela Davis's iconic style. Plus, the article was immensely pertinent to what I wanted to study. I think that photo was at least one of the reasons I decided that a career in music scholarship might be an option for me. It wasn't just the hair, of course, though that helped. It was, more specifically, about the entire message she sent. For me, it was a "welcome" sign.[12]

Who was writing those works and what they were talking about allowed me to think about possibilities beyond transcribing Dexter Gordon solos and my youthful dreams of playing like Oscar Peterson. Could there be a rewarding musical life beyond the gig, beyond trying to play fast rhythm changes and the soulful blues of my Southside of Chicago tribe?

Like many of the striving, hopeful young musicians in my crew, I naïvely and arrogantly thought that "Those who can, do; those who can't, teach." Now, in the autumn of our careers, we've all (predictably) spent time teaching, some more than others. In fact, I've taught in some form or fashion for more than three decades. I often advise young musicians to craft a life that will support your art and not to put the pressure on your art to support your life. I've learned, in fact, that teaching can be an important extension of an art practice and certainly a powerful form of activism. Writing can do the same; it would ultimately become one of my primary pedagogical tools and a way to stay musical.

I learned that representation and being "seen" mattered when I met Samuel A. Floyd Jr. (1937–2016), the genius activist and organizer who founded the Center for Black Music Research, an institution that at the height of its influence "Blackened" (and strengthened) American music scholarship. As I pursued my degrees in music, his name surfaced constantly in Black music literature. It turned out that he also lived in Chicago, which made it easy for me to show up to his office one day unannounced. I'm embarrassed that I didn't know better, but after reading some of his work I felt compelled to meet with him. Sam was a tall, gracious gent with a quiet swag. When we met he was surrounded by books, and my first impression was that he looked like the most learned musician I'd ever seen. And his avuncular attitude toward me felt very much like that of the migrants who had raised and nurtured me.

Sam eventually extended an invitation to work on a research project for the Center that would fulfill a course requirement in my Masters of Music Education program. At the time I was the typical hustling musician, using all of the literacies and skills I had acquired to that point to make a living. I was also teaching general and choral music, giving door-to-door piano lessons, teaching workshops at a community conservatory, and gigging in churches and nightclubs.

It turned out that Sam had a plan. He strongly suggested that I drop the gigging life and think about becoming a music historian. And he knew where I should study. I took the bait, went through the application process, and moved a very young family of five to Ann Arbor, Michigan. It was a gamble for everyone involved.

One of the first things I learned at the University of Michigan's storied School of Music is that my extensive naiveté hadn't expired. The first shock was that Richard Crawford, the preeminent scholar of American music who would become my strongest mentor and guide in the field, wasn't African American. We had only spoken by phone, and Google didn't exist. I wondered why Sam would recommend with such confidence that I study with him if he weren't Black? I called Sam. He assured me through a chuckle that his good friend Rich would be the ideal advisor. He was, of course, right: Rich, who had a number of impressive advisees working on jazz topics, guided me through meeting the high standards of the program. And, what's more, I learned that if I were successful, I would probably be the first Black person to earn a PhD in music history from the institution since nobody could remember any previous ones. No pressure.

There was a lot to learn. One big lesson was appreciating how the field perceived the distance between being a performer and being a contributor to the world of ideas *about* music. Some of my musician acquaintances from back home believed I'd officially elected the "teach and can't do" path. And, from the scholarly side, I experienced the belief that if someone continued to perform they must lack the commitment to become a serious scholar. This was the accepted wisdom at that time, or so it seemed to me.

In the early 1990s, many new ideas were changing the field of musicology as they had reshaped other humanistic disciplines. The turn was branded the "new musicology." Calls sounded at conferences and in publications for the field to become more inclusive in the topics it sanctioned, more open to methodologies from other disciplines, and better attuned to *whose* ideas were heard and valued. A more direct way to put it: scholars began to confront head-on the whiteness, Eurocentrism, and phallocentrism of the American musicology project. It seemed I had arrived on the doorstep of musicology at just the right time.

It never occurred to me that I had the luxury of participating in this conversation solely under the guise of "scholarly objectivity," even though it was at times a cantankerous, high-stakes, and public debate. I put skin in the game, so to speak, when I began to think about how identity informed my analytical conclusions. Anxieties surrounding this new musicology was intense. It felt like a cultural war.

It was at this time that I met the influential scholars Robin D. G. Kelley and Farah Jasmine Griffin. Kelley was teaching at the University of Michigan and, in my view, symbolized all the promise of this moment in Black studies. He was prolific, trained as a historian, and wrote about labor, politics, and culture. When he agreed to be an advisor on my dissertation on pianist Bud Powell, he asked, after viewing some of my initial work, "So, what's your argument?" I'm sure I responded with an expression like a deer in the headlights, which is seared in my memory, but his challenge turned my writing in a new direction: I wanted to make specific kinds of arguments about the facts of Black music history. Kelley's style, expansive musical literacies (from bebop to hip-hop), political focus, and integrity had a tremendous impact on my work.[13]

Griffin and I were fellows at Harvard's DuBois Institute when we formed a writing group with Daphne Brooks, Bill Lowe, and Salim Washington. Griffin's fascinating and groundbreaking work on migration narratives in Black expressive culture cut across multiple texts and media—print, visual, and sonic—and inspired me to make connections outside of musicology.[14] If Kelley's and Griffin's work provided me up-close examples of how to weave around disciplinary gatekeeping, an audacious publication would do the same for the entire academy.

Black Popular Culture (1992), edited by Gina Dent, was a beacon to many.[15] As I was working through my first major scholarly assignment—an MA historiographical essay on gospel music—this book of essays and discussions appeared to much fanfare. It seemed like every young Black academic I knew dropped everything to read it. The book grew from a conference, whose thirty participants included scholars, journalists, art historians, filmmakers, activists, literary scholars, and more. I learned about an entire community of Black thinkers working on integrating diffuse materials, theories, and art making. It was a multimodal, intergenerational, vernacular, theoretical, aesthetically varied, and politically focused project. Knowing about this work and all the insurrections it was attempting to make compelled me to ask, "Guess who's coming to the musicology seminar table?"

No musicologists were included in the landmark *Black Popular Culture*, a fact that wasn't lost on me at the time. Bridging this chasm between

Black cultural studies and musicology has been one of the priorities of my writing through the years, especially as I became more seasoned. The same year that *Black Popular Culture* appeared, Greg Tate's bombshell book *Flyboy in the Buttermilk* was published; Cornel West's *Race Matters* (1993) and Tricia Rose's *Black Noise* (1994) followed.[16] All three of these monumental contributions showed that there was an audience for smart yet accessible Black cultural studies beyond the college classroom. Around this time I also encountered Samuel Floyd's 1991 article on the ring shout, a compelling study that forecasted the use of literary and cultural theory in both jazz studies and popular music studies.[17] I was also part of a cadre of scholars at the University of Michigan who wrote dissertations on (male) jazz musicians.[18] And ethnomusicologist Judith Becker's seminars were particularly eye-opening and provided me many opportunities for intellectual adventure. This was an exciting time for the music disciplines to begin to legitimate the study of all Black music styles on an unprecedented scale.

After publishing the essay "Who Hears Here" in 2001, I began my first book, *Race Music* (2003), with a musical memoir recounting some early experiences within community theaters. One of the things I wanted to establish was how the extended community into which I was born and raised had imprinted my aesthetic sensibilities, and, by extension, the scholarly questions I pursued.[19] My ears heard through the migrant culture I knew as a young person. The institutional terrain—the storefront churches, cathedrals, barber and beauty shops, political machines, sporting cultures, print mass media, radio programming, parades, and radical bookstores—birthed ideologies from traditional notions of uplift to unapologetic militancy. I wanted to drag all of that "who" with me to graduate study and ultimately into my scholarship by adding this "song" to my musicology toolbox.

Not everyone was pleased. As I explored my musicological voice, I began to hear whispers through the scholarly grapevine and in some written responses that I was claiming I could speak about African American music with more authority simply *because* I was Black *and* working on African American music. I didn't agree and interpreted this critique to mean musicology should be new but not *this* new or new in *this* way. Authority and authenticity were battlegrounds.

The "here" in "who hears here?" can stand as a metaphor for the world I encountered in the ML 3556 call numbers. It can also represent the living created in the community theaters. And "here" in these spaces is not always about safety and nurturing; the idea can also acknowledge the negative impacts of power and subjugation. I heard a story in childhood, for example, that informed my notion of home. Back in the late 1960s there was a "Black" bookstore near my home. It was lined with literature, incense, posters, and the ubiquitous colors of "Black liberation"—red, black, and green. Some comrades and I were directed to a wall splayed with maps of our surrounding neighborhood. The intense twenty-something young man with a "statement" Afro directing our tour told his young and rapt audience that "the Man's" plan to extend Interstate 57 through our neighborhood was a ploy to be able to contain us with military force when "the revolution" finally came. With incredulity I told this story to a colleague who studies these things. She said that the ominous plan was at least part of the reason for that highway.[20] Apparently this convenience could also easily bring containment.

Looking back, I guess I've been looking for the possibilities between the call numbers and the highway. I wanted to be a musicologist who combined intellectual life as a reader and researcher, my background in performance, and the cultural literacies I learned within the primarily segregated world of my birth. These essays demonstrate this desire. They give witness as well to how I sought to participate in "project musicology" in ways that would push the field as well as make place in other disciplines in which music was being analyzed and where diversity was more apparent.

In 1998 I began teaching at the University of Pennsylvania in the city where the descendants of Du Bois's "Philadelphia Negroes" comprised a large percentage of the population. Coming to town as a musicologist to work in a highly respected music department could have been an excuse to loosen my ties to these cultural communities. Penn-based musicologists like Gary Tomlinson and Jeffrey Kallberg were mavericks in advancing knowledge in the field. With their provocative insights and analyses, they had a strong impact on my thinking and, frankly, my courage. Fortunately for me, Black Philadelphia—unlike the city of Boston, where I wrote a couple of these essays while teaching at Tufts University—was a place that rivaled Chicago in its demographic and cultural composition and even as a site of ethnographic study.[21] It was rich with Black music traditions. I'd found another "here."

Shortly after arriving I was taken to Natalie's Showcase Lounge, a dive bar situated on the western edge of Penn's urban, protected campus. It was right off 40th Street, which was then recognized as the dividing line between Black West Philly and the fortress campus. Inside the long and narrow nightclub I found yet another community theater, one that took pride in continuing Philly's hard bop, gospel-tinged jazz scene, complete with an informed, let-the-good-times-roll *listening* audience that stood as guardians of their deeply rooted traditions. I found myself in a great house band led by drummer Lucky Thompson.

The bully pulpit of Penn's historic music department with its rigorous traditions of musicology, theory, ethnomusicology, and composition, anchored as it is in one of the most vibrant centers of jazz, gospel, R&B, neo-soul, and hip-hop, was a great place to be "here"—between the call numbers and the highways. I had the best of both worlds. Even my latest adopted home, Brooklyn, New York—the "here" from which I wrote some of this work—allowed me to stay centered. When I walked through the Bedford-Stuyvesant neighborhood of Brooklyn I was always struck by the mosaic of Black musical styles that saturated the public sphere, shaking windowpanes and setting off finicky car alarms.

These writings show, among other things, my participation in the ongoing institutionalization of Black music research over the past thirty years. I began this journey at a moment when the American Musicological Society was forced—by the initiatives of an interracial group of scholars—to confront its exclusionary practices. When the AMS's Committee on Cultural Diversity was formed and began its work to counter sexism and racism in the early 1990s, "women, people of color, and other minoritized members were mostly absent from the organization's power structure, including both its elected leaders and awardees of prizes and fellowships," as pointed out by scholar Carol Oja in her reflection looking back on that moment in the professional society's history.[22]

On the one hand, one could suggest that my career and other indicators demonstrate that inroads have been made regarding musicology's problematic racial history. On the other hand, urgent ongoing calls for equity and fair practices in the field have been instigated by social media hashtags like #AMSSoWhite and highlight the need for more action. Other music disciplines have exploded with similar awkward moments in their racial reckonings. The essays in this book were written in the days before social media up until the present era of activism such as Black Lives Matter, #metoo, #sayhername, and recent efforts to decolonize the music curriculum. (I should add here that I've haven't changed the capitalization of the descriptor "black" in the early essays, as this was the custom at the time they were written.)

These essays carry resonances of the conversations I've had in bars and hotel rooms during professional conferences, in the deliberations published in the pages of journals and blogs, and in the firestorms that occur on Twitter feeds. At the same time, this work primarily documents my engagement with the joys that music making and listening inspire—together with my insistence on the undeniable place Black music holds in global cultures. At a moment when more voices are becoming "unleashed" and adding their songs and stories to the shape of music history, I'm pleased to offer my various takes on the musicians, styles, and topics that have held me spellbound for more than three decades. I hope you find something of value in what follows: the work of an accidental musicologist who wanted to know, among other things, who was doing the hearing, the making, and the explaining.

1 Cosmopolitan or Provincial?

IDEOLOGY IN EARLY BLACK MUSIC
HISTORIOGRAPHY, 1867–1940

Eileen Southern, recently called "a quiet revolutionary," published *The Music of Black Americans: A History* in 1971.[1] The appearance of her book in the wake of the black power movement, the turbulent social upheaval of the late 1960s, links it to an auspicious historical moment. Among other dramatic social changes, the period saw the radicalization of the word "black," a designation standing provocatively, even proudly, in Southern's main title. Furthermore, widespread student protests led to sweeping curricular advances in colleges and universities across the nation, most notably, the addition of courses in black history and culture. Designed to fill a void in the new curriculum, Southern's work broke new ground in its method and scope, inspiring others (both directly and indirectly) to similar inquiry and helping to establish black music as a scholarly specialty. Thus *The Music of Black Americans* stands as an important

"Cosmopolitan or Provincial? Ideology in Early Black Music Historiography, 1867–1940," *Black Music Research Journal* 16, no. 1 (Spring 1996): 11–42. This essay was written for a joint session of the national conferences of the Center for Black Music Research, the American Musicological Society, and the Society for Music Theory. My first major published article, it represents an attempt to identify some organizing themes of historical writings on Black music.

symbol of the epoch in which it first appeared, even as it filled a glaring lacuna in American musical scholarship as a whole.[2]

Work on black music that followed has featured research rich in variety and scope: musical biography and autobiography, archival and oral histories, systematic research on jazz and blues, the compilation of bibliographies and indices, ethnographic studies, critical editions, and much more. In addition, the recent introduction of contemporary cultural and social theory into the field has pointed out new critical directions, stimulating many exciting possibilities.[3] Yet despite its catalytic role and the explosion of literature that followed, *The Music of Black Americans* also belongs to a legacy of previous research that stretches back more than a century.

The black music historiographic tradition began in the latter half of the nineteenth century. I will trace the rise of black music research from that time through about 1940, or to the end of what Meier and Rudwick call the first period of Afro-American historiography.[4] Throughout this period, black musical activity in the United States attracted an impressive array of critics, practitioners, and admirers. From the "origins of the Negro spirituals" debate and the recurring argument, "Is it jazz or isn't it?" to the question of racial "authenticity" in the symphonic and operatic works by black composers, black music has proven itself a fertile subject for commentators from many sectors. (The appearance of rap music suggests that the controversies shall continue to appear.)[5]

Despite this historical interest in black music, its journey to academic legitimization has mirrored the progression of black Americans themselves into mainstream American life: slow, demanding, and sinuous. Once sanctioned in academic circles, however, the "formal" study of black music has flourished steadily and methodically. The appearance of scholarly journals and dissertations and the growing number of reference works devoted to black music speak to the vitality of the field.[6] The early years of this historiographical tradition, however, are difficult to trace because its historical trajectory has not developed solely within academic disciplines such as musicology. Writers have approached the subject from a variety of different perspectives, methodologies, goals, and motivations.

My goal here is to discuss, in more or less chronological order, some key works in early black music historiography. These include book-length studies, pre-1900s journalism, folklore, work from the fields of history and musicology, and literature from the Negro Renaissance of the 1920s. In addition, I consider in the latter half of this chapter some of the dynamic issues raised by early jazz criticism, which I read as an important subfield of black music research, albeit one with its own vital and singular development. Many of the issues raised by early jazz criticism, for example, not only resonated with nineteenth-century black music inquiry, but they have also influenced research activity on black music up to the present. Although all of the literature referred to above cannot be discussed extensively in this context, my purpose in their treatment is to position them within other related discourses: the historiography of African peoples in the United States, the dynamic tradition of black arts and letters in general, and the broad scope of American musical scholarship. In short, this project on black music historiography seeks to draw together common elements in a field that has developed in several disciplines and streams of knowledge.

At first look, the unwieldy nature of early black music research makes the idea of producing a convincing report of all the intellectual issues present appear impossible. But, upon closer inspection, distinct patterns emerge so that something of an ideology takes shape in the literature. Black music historiography, for example, seems to have developed from several impulses from outside and within the discursive world of black music making, including the ideology of race and the attitudes about the art of music in America (such as those reflected in Crawford's "cosmopolitan" and "provincial" model discussed below). Furthermore, the fields of journalism, academic music study, and history and the budding disciplines of anthropology and folklore have also played a crucial role in the development of this literature. The boundaries between these impulses are theoretical; they frequently overlap, and a single document can embody the influences of more than one. Taken together, this varied cluster of discourses forms the ideological basis of the historical study of black music in America.[7]

My work here purposes to uncover—albeit in a preliminary way—some of the conceptualizations that have undergirded the historical study of black musical practice in the United States. Thus, this project in historiography is archaeological in that, like Gary Tomlinson's work on music in Renaissance magic, "it takes us beneath questions of authorial intent and intertextuality to the grid of meaningfulness that constrains and conditions a discourse or social practice."[8] Preceding Tomlinson with this line of thinking in the realm of black culture, Houston Baker writes that "as a method of analysis, the archaeology of knowledge assumes that knowledge exists in discursive formations whose lineage can be traced and whose regularities are discoverable." These discourses, Baker argues, are informed by governing statements, which are linguistic and "materially repeatable" gestures and are regulated "by discoverable principles."[9]

A most striking quality of early black music historiography ideology is how writers—particularly African American ones—negotiated the generally accepted "divide" between Euro-based and Afro-based aesthetic perspectives. Not simply representing a binary opposition, this tension had deep roots in inherited attitudes about American music making and race ideology. Richard Crawford has recently written of two "musical ways of life" in eighteenth-century America that have inspired two prevalent tendencies among historians of American music, which he labels "cosmopolitan" and "provincial." Writers in the cosmopolitan school took their creative and intellectual direction from Europe, extending Old World practices, attitudes, and hegemony. The provincial group, on the other hand, "involved those who resisted, or reinterpreted, or, most likely, failed to receive" the pan-European musical model promoted by the cosmopolitan school.[10] Crawford's formulations are useful as a backdrop and as a starting point in this study. But black music research has developed with important divergences from American music historiography, and thus the cosmopolitan/provincial split is less applicable here, primarily because of the ideology of race permeating the literature and complicating this ideological/cultural model.

Race ideology is of singular importance in writings by African Americans, who have provided what has been called a black perspective to the field. St. Clair Drake defines the black perspective as a point of view that represents "reality as perceived, conceptualized, and evaluated by individuals who are stigmatized and discriminated against because they are designated as 'Negroes' or 'Blacks.'"[11] That sense of perception has given the literature a strain of black nationalistic thought, usually expressed around the notion of black social progress and, as historian Sterling Stuckey has noted about nineteenth-century African American nationalism, in the idea of pan-Africanism.[12] The dynamic relationship of these themes in black music historiography provides a window into the tensions between the "Western" and the "black" of this literary tradition.

Yet, as the final section of this chapter will show, race ideology in black music research took on dramatic new dimensions with the appearance of jazz criticism. With white critics from America and Europe championing jazz, the response of black writers—and, perhaps, the dynamic aesthetic principles that informed the genre itself—forced a shift in the rhetoric, if not some of the underlying "governing statements," of black music research. In fact, some of the issues that surfaced in the literature— namely, white participation and reception, black "authenticity," and the social "pedigree" of jazz, among a host of other important issues—are only beginning to be explained convincingly by contemporary researchers. Together, these shifting ideas about race and Afro/Euro aesthetics provide important ways to understand African American music both as a Western and as a black enterprise. But most important to the present study, these themes provide a way to talk about the beginnings of ideology in black music historiography. As the first book-length study about black musicians in this country shows, these impulses had already crystallized in the work of a nineteenth-century African American writer.

. . . . .

When James Monroe Trotter (1842–92) published *Music and Some Highly Musical People* in 1878, he established himself as America's first African American music historian. Scholars have noted the book's significance, its position as a landmark study, the thoroughness of Trotter's treatment of black nineteenth-century musicians, and the author's position as "not only the first black but also one of the most provocative, most thoughtful, and most courageous American music historians of any color to date."[13] In his own words, Trotter wrote *Music and Some Highly Musical People* "to perform . . . a much-needed service, not so much, perhaps, to the cause of music itself, as to some of its noblest devotees and the race to which the latter belong."[14]

Trotter's racial agenda is clear: he wanted to chronicle the musical activities of African Americans and instill in his people pride in those achievements. Thus the hagiographic tone of the book served to present these musicians in the best light possible. Trotter hoped his work would serve as a landmark and guide for others and establish between blacks and whites "relations of mutual respect and good feeling."[15] Unquestionably, his concerns were more than musical. Trotter's mandate of racial pride and the central position he gave the Western art music tradition formed the basis for an important ideological dichotomy in subsequent black music historiography, especially in those writings by African Americans themselves. In other words, the collision between Trotter's racial politics and his Euro-based aesthetic perspectives formed an important and persistent tension in future work on black music.

Trotter's qualifications to write this book also deserve attention. Although he lacked professional training as a music historian, Trotter's personal, educational, and occupational background provided him valuable experiences, and he drew on many of them while writing his study. Born in Grand Gulf, Mississippi, Trotter was the son of a slave owner, Richard S. Trotter, and his slave, Letitia. He received "a superior education" in a Negro college preparatory school in Cincinnati, Ohio, and studied music there.[16] Trotter held many occupations in his lifetime, from the most menial to the most prestigious, including a cabin boy on a riverboat, bellboy in a hotel, schoolteacher, soldier in the Union Army, manager of opera singer Madame Selika, postmaster of Hyde Park, Massachusetts, and, finally, Recorder of Deeds for the District of Columbia, a relatively high-paying and prestigious appointment that Republican and Democratic presidents had reserved for blacks. Apparently these occupations permitted Trotter firsthand experience with little-known musical activities among blacks, as the following statement taken from an essay titled "The School-Master in the Army," which Trotter wrote for a contemporary newspaper, shows:

> In quite a number of the colored regiments military bands were formed, and under the instruction of sometimes a band teacher from the north, and at others under one of their own proficient fellow-soldiers, these bands learned to discourse most entertaining music in camp, and often by their inspiriting strains did much to relieve the fatigue.[17]

The content and organization of *Music and Some Highly Musical People* provide a revealing profile of Trotter's musical values. He begins his book with a discussion of the music of ancient Greece, followed by a survey of Western European music through the nineteenth century. Insofar as Trotter believed that this was Black classical musicians' legitimate legacy, he gave priority to those musicians and music organizations (such as opera singer Elizabeth Taylor Greenfield, pianist Thomas Greene Bethune, and The Colored American Opera Company) who participated in Western art music. Trotter's appendix includes a 152–page collection of thirteen vocal and instrumental pieces by black composers, for which he offers the following philosophical explanation on its opening page:

> The collection is given in order to complete the author's purpose, which is not only to show the proficiency of the subjects of the foregoing sketches as interpreters of the music of others, but, further, to illustrate the ability of quite a number of them (and, relatively, that of their race) to originate and scientifically arrange good music.[18]

Despite Trotter's emphasis on American composers of Western art music, *Music and Some Highly Musical People* failed to have a significant impact on subsequent American music histories beyond the literature by other black authors. The book was referred to in Frédéric Louis Ritter's *Music in America* but ignored by other early histories of American music.[19]

Because the book was written by a black citizen in the years following the Civil War and during the "Golden Age of Black Nationalism," *Music and Some Highly Musical People* resonates with the prominent racial and cultural politics of its day. A striking similarity exists, for example, between Trotter's views and those of Alexander Crummell, the nineteenth-century pan-Africanist, founder of the Negro Academy, missionary, and statesman.[20] Crummell's stated goal for the academy constituted a "high-brow," though staunchly pro-black, stance: "to aid youths of genius in the attainment of the higher culture, at home and abroad."[21]

Although Trotter's allegiance to Western art music is indisputable, he does show an openness to vernacular music making. Trotter discusses the Fisk Jubilee Singers, the Georgia Minstrels, and minstrel singer Sam Lucas in arguing the case of "orally transmitted racial music."[22] Nevertheless, Trotter apparently believed black participation in Western art music to be a higher calling, arguing vehemently against the hindrance of "the art-capabilities of the colored race" because of "the hateful, terrible spirit of *color-prejudice,* that foul spirit, the full measure of whose influence in crushing out the genius often born in children of [the black] race is difficult to estimate."[23] In summary, Trotter's *Music and Some Highly Musical People* embodies a blend of uncompromised black nationalistic thought and Euro-based aesthetic sensibility.

Beyond Trotter's book-length study, a plethora of literature produced in the nineteenth and early twentieth centuries brought other themes to black music inquiry. Travelogues, diaries, regional and national histories, letters, sermons, and political tracts written before 1860 document aspects of black expressive slave culture. Much of that literature highlights what these observers saw as a hybrid of the emerging African American folk culture, "an amalgamation of African and European elements, overlaid with a predominantly African tone."[24] From today's vantage point, sources from this period mapped out the acculturation process that produced African American expressive culture. Furthermore, the dramatic rise of professional American journalism and the accompanying explosion of media publishing during the antebellum era produced a voluminous literature. The black slave received much attention in these writings, particularly the socioeconomic and moral matters surrounding the issue of slavery.[25] These writings (along with those found in novels and slave narratives) included descriptions of slave festivals and black church services, which contain a wealth of information on black music. Thus, these historic journalistic activities have proven invaluable to black music research as a discipline. But, ultimately, they seemed to work against certain assumptions and goals of the strain of black music inquiry pioneered by Trotter.

While Trotter gathered information for his book, for example, other writers were busy collecting materials of their own. The latter work also sought to document the music of black Americans, but not those who sang arias nor those who composed works for the pianoforte. With the rise of journalistic interest in slave culture, there also came a heightened curiosity about black vernacular musical practices. Travelers, teachers, and other collectors gathered the songs of slave culture. What these writers contributed should clearly be considered a forerunner to work conducted later within the disciplines of ethnomusicology and folklore, for these collectors concerned themselves primarily with issues of repertory, preservation, transcription, and performance practice. And the repertory that attracted most of their attention was the spiritual, on which these researchers conducted, between the years 1860 and 1890, what would today be called fieldwork.[26] The literature abounds with vivid descriptions of these folksongs because the vocal quality and improvisational performance practices held continual fascination for white listeners.

Published collections soon appeared. The first of these to reach press was the landmark *Slave Songs of the United States* (1867) by William Francis Allen, Charles Pickard Ware, and Lucy McKim Garrison. The book comprises melodies and lyrics of 136 spiritual and secular songs. That James Monroe Trotter avoided reference to this book, one that he would surely have known, should come as no surprise. While *Slave Songs of the United States* and *Music and Some Highly Musical People* both sought to show "the musical capacity of the Negro," as William Allen put it in the introduction to *Slave Songs of the United States*, each took a different route to do so.[27]

Allen, Ware, and Garrison were all graduates of Harvard University, with varying degrees of musical training, and their families were connected with the abolition movement and to various aspects of New England aristocratic culture. The nineteenth-century racialist and Eurocentric language that one might expect does appear throughout the text. These authors believed, for example, that the beauty of the songs in their collection provided evidence that Negroes held the potential to become more like the "cultivated race." Of course, with the anthropology of culture available today, such views should certainly be considered naive, whether they were written by James Monroe Trotter or by William Francis Allen. Instead of spending time upbraiding these authors on political grounds, however, I chose here to concentrate on what they achieved. As Dena Epstein has argued, the authors of *Slave Songs of the United States* "displayed a concern for a music that they could not fully understand, but that they recognized as valuable, attractive, and eminently worth preserving from the hazards of time and historic change."[28] Furthermore, similar efforts that succeeded *Slave Songs of the United States* led the way for collections of concertized or arranged spirituals, which, as we shall see, appeared later during the Harlem Renaissance era. Future collectors also included introductions to their anthologies, providing discussions about historical contexts and performance practice.[29]

The tensions surrounding *Music and Some Highly Musical People* and *Slave Songs of the United States* raise important historiographic issues. On one hand, Trotter, an educated black man, believed that putting the race's best foot forward meant proving that they could master the Western art music tradition. On the other hand, the authors of *Slave Songs of the United States* found abolitionist currency in the power of the vernacular spiritual, even though many of its performance traits, as they learned, could not be captured by their transcriptions.[30] The cultural politics of ethnic or racial identity, the idea of what would best improve the collective social position of African Americans, the dynamic aesthetic conventions of black expressive culture, and the idea that these authors believed that music was central to understanding these ideas would become an important theme and creative inspiration in subsequent black music research.

Like Trotter before them, turn-of-the-century African American journalists usually promoted the advancement of the race. The *Negro Music Journal* (a "Monthly Magazine Devoted to the Educational Interest of the Negro Race in Music") documents such an attitude. The journal's publication run lasted a little more than a year—from September 1902 to November 1903.[31] The magazine's editor, J. Hillary Taylor, possessed musical taste embedded in high culture, as the almost evangelistic zeal of his magazine's mission statement attests: "We shall endeavor to get the majority of our people interested in that class of music which will purify their minds, lighten their hearts, touch their souls. . . . It is the music of . . . Bach, Handel, Mozart, . . . S. Coleridge Taylor, Grieg, Chaminade, Saint Saëns, Paderewski, McDowell, Mrs. Beach and others."[32] As Riis has noted about *Dwight's Journal of Music* before it, the *Negro Music Journal* sought to influence and mold musical taste. But, unlike Dwight's readership, Taylor's target was African Americans, whose homes he wanted to become "cultured . . . with only the purest and best in music."[33]

During the first decades of the twentieth century, the academic fields of history and musicology saw developments that influenced how American music and African American culture would be studied in the future. A trend toward the use of scientific (or systematic) methodology can be noted in each of these specialized areas. Scholars began to advance methods of inquiry that not only imposed order on these fields but also helped them progress toward recognition as legitimate areas of academic study. (Each, however, still struggles in many ways for respect in the academy.) Black music research has strong connections to each of these areas—American musicology and African American history—and has profited from and contributed to developments within them.

The field of American music scholarship experienced systematic research most notably in the work of Oscar G. Sonneck (1873-1928), called "the first serious student of early music in America." In 1902 Sonneck was appointed chief of the Music Division of the Library of Congress. When he had begun his research on early American music two years earlier, "he found himself heir to no strong tradition of historical inquiry." By 1905, when Sonneck published his first books, he launched "a new phase in the writing of American music history."[34] In 1915 Sonneck became the founding editor of Schirmer's *The Musical Quarterly*, America's first scholarly music journal. In 1916 Sonneck delivered an address on American musical historiography to the Music Teacher's National Association, wherein he argued for "more neutral, more impartial, more disinterested—in brief, more scientific" research on American music, echoing similar exhortations in other fields of American studies.[35] Finally, when Sonneck resigned from the Library of Congress in 1917 and joined the music publishing house G. Schirmer in New York as director of the Publication Department, he ceased his work in "objective" research. Oscar Sonneck played a crucial if not singular role in creating a space for literature by American writers whose concerns went beyond that of music journalism and criticism. Moreover, Sonneck's career had a direct and early impact on black music historiography. Maud Cuney-Hare's treatment of black music in *Negro Musicians and Their Music*, a book I'll discuss more thoroughly later, for example, relies on research conducted at the Library of Congress Music Collection, which Sonneck had established as an important research archive. In addition, *The Musical Quarterly* published articles on black music during its first years.[36]

Systematic research's manifestation in early African American history is, perhaps, best represented by the groundbreaking work of Carter Godwin Woodson (1875-1950).[37] Like other black writers who preceded him, Woodson's work carried a distinct political import beyond its stated goals of objective, disinterested scholarship. Woodson, the second African American to earn a doctorate in the field of history, founded the Association for the Study of Negro Life and History (ASNLH) in 1915 and a year later launched the *Journal of Negro History*. These activities made him almost solely responsible for establishing African American history as an academic field.[38] Woodson's goal, the popularization of Negro history, had dual purposes reminiscent of Trotter's earlier sentiments: the building of pride and self-esteem among blacks and the lessening of prejudice among whites. What remains remarkable is that Woodson's scholarly efforts, together with his constant appeals for philanthropic assistance, succeeded during what Meier and Rudwick refer to as "the apogee of popular and scientific racism in Western thought."[39] As a rule, Woodson and other members of the black intelligentsia sought to counter racism's effects among African Americans by championing the systematic study of black history. Woodson's and his contemporaries' work took place in the context of other related developments: the professionalization of the field of history and the establishment of graduate departments in history that emphasized the scientific method. Thus, Woodson's work represented "the convergence of two distinct streams of historical publication: the long tradition of writing on the black past on the part of black intellectuals and polemicists, on the one hand, and the professionalization of American historical study and the triumph of 'scientific' history, on the other."[40]

To summarize, developments in the fields of history and American musicology provided an atmosphere in which serious writing on black music history could take place. These two impulses—the historical and the musicological—are both present in early black music historiography, though none of this literature, I believe, subscribes to either tradition unconditionally. For example, as we have seen, "Afro-American history, almost from the beginning, was an enterprise promoted jointly by those who wrote history and those who viewed the study of history as a way to raise the level of Negroes in American life."[41] As we shall see below, the musical writings of philosopher Alain Locke, pianist/critic Maud Cuney-Hare, and others certainly fit this pattern. During the first two decades of the twentieth century, writers on black culture syncretized their advanced educational backgrounds with their nationalistic political goals. Woodson's most important contemporaries, for example, belonged to "a small band of blacks who were able to obtain doctorates during the 1920s and 1930s . . . [most] at some of the most prestigious graduate history departments."[42] But given their strong commitment to "the elevation of the race" and to black cultural nationalism, none of these early writers could be considered neutral, impartial, or disinterested about their subject matter, although many shared Sonneck's "musical patriotism" as well as his belief in systematic scholarship.[43] All of these ideals coalesced into a complex strategy I call the "rhetoric of the New Negro," which was especially prevalent in literature on black music written during the years of the Harlem Renaissance.

The legacy of the rhetoric of the Harlem (or Negro) Renaissance, the literary and artistic movement that arguably reached its height during the 1920s, influenced not only black music inquiry during the early decades of the twentieth century but subsequent work as well. In 1925 Alain Locke (1885–1954) published his important anthology *The New Negro*, and many soon recognized the book as a definitive statement. In this collection, Locke and other Renaissance architects advanced the ideals and goals that characterized their movement—chief among them, economic, social, and cultural equity with white citizens—to be achieved through the creation and dissemination of great works of literary, musical, and visual art. Vernacular expressions such as jazz and blues, however, received little attention from these writers.

> Renaissance leaders aspired to create a "New Negro," one who would attend concerts and operas and would be economically and socially prepared to enter an ideally integrated American society. . . . He would not frequent musical dens of iniquity, for he would then tarnish the image that was to be presented to the world as evidence of his preparedness. So, at first, the "lower forms" of black music were frowned upon by those of this outlook.[44]

Thus, the sociopolitical views of many Renaissance writers, together with their narrow notion of "great art," prevented them from unequivocally (or perhaps just publicly) embracing the music of the cabarets, theaters, and speakeasies. Nonetheless, such pre-Renaissance black music, as Floyd argues, unquestionably set the climate for the New Negro movement.

The particular strain of black musical nationalism promoted in the New Negro rhetoric participated in the American music nationalism of the 1890s. The Czech composer Antonín Dvořák (1841–1904), as is well known, inspired the idea of a national school of serious composers in the United States by extolling the use of African, Native, and Anglo-American folk music as basic materials.[45] Black writers on music, such as James Weldon Johnson, saw great strategic promise and vindication in Dvořák's statements and adopted what they thought his ideals to be into their own philosophies and literature on music. They also continued to build on the work of Trotter as well as nineteenth-century journalism and folklore activities.

James Weldon Johnson's and J. Rosamond Johnson's two collections of concert spirituals, *The Books of American Negro Spirituals* (1925 and 1926; reprinted in a single volume in 1989), offer a good example. In their introduction the authors not only cite *Slave Songs of the United States*, but they also offer useful information on the spiritual's history and their views on the aesthetics of these songs.[46] The brothers' arguments about the cultural specificity *and* universal appeal/accessibility of the spiritual show how their ideas embodied the politics of race ideology of this time. James Weldon, for example, acknowledged a noble African origin for the spiritual. By promoting racial pride through "the glories of the racial past," Johnson's philosophy resonated with a more militant strain of black nationalism from this period and, consequently, with some of the considerable baggage of this position.[47] When black writers did discuss an African legacy, their work showed how much of the racial pseudoscience of the day they had unknowingly internalized, especially read from a current point of view. In the preface of his compilation of arranged spirituals (which could be considered the New Negro "art song"), for example, Johnson states with a mixture of confidence, apology, and what could be read as essentialist rhetoric, "The Negro brought with him from Africa his native musical instinct and talent, and that was no small endowment to begin with.... Many things are now being learned about Africa. It is being learned and recognized that the great majority of Africans are in no sense 'savages'; that they possess a civilization and a culture, primitive it is true but in many respects quite adequate; that they possess a folk literature that is varied and rich; that they possess an art that is quick and sound."[48]

Johnson drew scholarly authority and inspiration from music critic and historian Henry E. Krehbiel, whose position is clear from the opening sentence of his influential work *Afro-American Folk-Songs:* "This book was written with the purpose of bringing a species of folksong into the field of scientific observation and presenting it as fit material for artistic treatment."[49] But again, this science carried flaws. Krehbiel, like Johnson and many others, seemed to believe that blacks possessed an innate, natural ability for and love of musical activity. Despite these shortcomings, the rhetoric of "African musical genius" and the linking of those musical gifts to African American culture served a larger goal for the Johnsons and other Renaissance writers: racial equality through the arts.[50]

The fulfillment of Trotter's hope that *Music and Some Highly Music People* would serve as a guide for future work did not occur until the appearance of another book by a black author that was devoted to African American music: Maud Cuney-Hare's *Negro Musicians and Their Music* (1936). As revealed by Stevenson, Cuney-Hare used Trotter extensively when dealing with pre-1878 musicians; thus, one gets the sense that a formal historiographical tradition in black music begins to emerge with *Negro Musicians and Their Music.* Cuney-Hare's background prepared her well for such a task.[51] A concert pianist, Cuney-Hare (1874–1936) studied at the New England Conservatory. After settling in Boston, she established the Musical Art Studio and served for many years as musical editor of *Crisis,* the primary organ of the National Association for the Advancement of Colored People (NAACP). Like Trotter, Cuney-Hare had a long list of accomplishments, interests, and expertise that extended beyond the musical world. She cultivated an interest in folklore, building an impressive archive of artifacts and materials; she wrote a biography of her father, Norris Wright Cuney, an important nineteenth-century Texas politician; and she was a recognized playwright and compiled an anthology of poems.[52]

Despite Cuney-Hare's debt to *Music and Some Highly Musical People,* at least two facets of *Negro Musicians and Their Music* distinguish it from the former work. Cuney-Hare begins her study with Africa and speculates on the continent's relevance to Western culture. She opens the first chapter with the following statement: "Negro music traced to its source, carries us to the continent of Africa and into the early history of that far off land. We may even journey to one of the chief sections said to hold the music of the past—that of Egypt, for it was the ceremonial music of that land as well as that of Palestine and Greece, which was the foundation of at least one phase of modern musical art."[53] Another prevalent theme in the book is Cuney-Hare's hope that an American national symphonic, operatic, and ballet tradition based on black musical idioms would develop in this country; she discusses musicians "working toward this end."[54] In other words, her outlook was well formed by her formal musical training and grafted onto the ideals of the New Negro rhetoric: racial equality, black cultural nationalism, and American musical nationalism based on black musical idioms.

In the same year that *Negro Musicians and Their Music* appeared, Alain Locke, a nonmusician, published *The Negro and His Music*, advancing many of these same ideas. Like other Renaissance thinkers, Locke shared Cuney-Hare's philosophy about the potential of black folk music and encouraged its use as the basis for "great classical music."[55] Furthermore, he argued for African Americans developing into "a class of trained music lovers who will support by appreciation the best in the Negro's musical heritage and not allow it to be prostituted by the vaudeville stage or Tin Pan Alley, or to be cut off at its folk roots by lack of appreciation of its humble but gifted peasant creators."[56] The vindication of black music and culture remained an important theme throughout all of Locke's writings on music.[57] Locke's treatment of Africa in *The Negro and His Music* is especially telling in this regard. It showed his desire (and that of other Renaissance thinkers) to understand their cultural past in more scholarly, scientific terms, on the grounds that better understanding would ultimately lead to the elevation of black citizens' social standing. While Locke recognized in African American music a "wide and distinct influence of African music especially through rhythm," he also believed that African music begged interpretation through "scientific study rather than by sentimental admiration for its effects."[58] Locke—like Trotter some fifty years before him—still saw limited opportunity as the primary obstacle hampering the progress and future development of Negro music.[59]

By today's standards, Renaissance writers like Cuney-Hare and Locke seem engaged in a precarious balancing act by promoting black achievement and carefully discouraging backlashes from white society, whose negative reactions could collectively frustrate African American social advancement. Despite any shortcomings produced by the negotiation of this tension, however, the ideals set forth in Locke's *The New Negro* (and other literature) succeeded in defining a Renaissance, a cultural movement, which, in the words of Arnold Rampersad, laid the "foundation for all subsequent depictions in poetry, fiction, and drama of the modern African-American experience," including music.[60]

But conformity to New Negro standards necessarily meant an unfavorable attitude toward the lifeblood of African American music making: blues, jazz, and other vernacular idioms. That attitude manifested itself profoundly in the New Negro rhetoric and literature. Locke, for example, excluded extensive consideration of the blues in *The New Negro*, recommending that composers transform the spiritual more fully into symphonic dress. In an essay titled "Jazz at Home," J. A. Rogers depicts jazz's origins as vulgar and crude. Rogers tersely regards Bessie Smith and other blues and jazz performers as inimitable, inventive, and skilled artists. Throughout the rest of the piece, however, he values their work primarily as source material—as something to "lift and divert ... into nobler channels."[61]

There were dissenting voices. Writer Langston Hughes, an important voice during the Renaissance, was one of the few who championed jazz and blues, believing that these vernacular idioms were legitimate expressions in their own right. In his well-known essay from 1926, "The Negro Artist and the Racial Mountain," Hughes levels red-hot criticism at the "Nordicized Negro intelligentsia" who, while working diligently to dispel prevalent stereotypes about the race, compromised themselves and denied their racial identities. He reserved praise chiefly for "the low-down folks, the so-called common element":

> These common people are not afraid of spirituals, as for a long time their more intellectual brethren were, and jazz is their child. They furnish a wealth of colorful, distinctive material for any artist because they still hold their own individuality in the face of American standardizations. And perhaps these common people will give the world its truly great Negro artist, the one who is not afraid to be himself.[62]

Hughes's argument, the de facto musical preferences of the black masses and to a growing extent the musical tastes of Americans at-large, may have made some, albeit small, impact on writers on black music like

Locke and Cuney-Hare. Although neither shunned their Euro-based aesthetics entirely, signs did exist that each writer's position softened. Locke, for example, held firmly to his conviction that he would better serve the advancement of his race by promoting European models of music making among African Americans. But Locke did discuss jazz and black musical theater in *The Negro and His Music,* albeit with the following qualification: "What we have said and quoted in defense and praise of jazz is by no means meant for the cheap low-browed jazz that is manufactured for passing popular consumption."[63] In a similar light, Cuney-Hare's *Negro Musicians and Their Music* includes a chapter on black musical theater, conceding that a "large number of Negro entertainers in light and popular music, now too many to include in a work interested primarily in music as an art, are men and women of diverse gifts and of decided talent. They are successful on both the vaudeville stage and the radio network."[64] Apparently, Renaissance writers had to acknowledge that musical success of any stripe could not be ignored in their struggle for racial equality.

Like Langston Hughes, writer and folklorist Zora Neale Hurston fashioned an Afro-based aesthetic response to concertized spiritual collections. Hurston highlights, and even celebrates, improvisation as a distinguishing element of black vernacular music. In that regard, her views are linked with some jazz writers. In her essay "Spirituals and Neo-Spirituals," she differentiates the aesthetic conventions of "authentic" spirituals and pieces based on the spirituals. Included in the latter group, according to Hurston, were the spiritual arrangements of composers Harry T. Burleigh, J. Rosamond Johnson, Nathaniel Dett, and Hall Johnson. While these settings possessed craftsmanship and beauty, Hurston argued that the former were new creations every time, stressing improvisation and "unceasing variations around a theme."[65] While Hurston does not explicitly state that the qualities she valued in authentic spirituals came from an African sensibility, the pan-African theme unifying Nancy Cunard's *Negro: An Anthology,* the book in which her essay first appeared, supports that notion.[66]

Renaissance theorists did succeed in some important ways. The rhetoric of the New Negro, as expressed by Cuney-Hare and Locke, sought to elevate the lot of African Americans specifically; it also urged America toward a new spiritual vision through artistic maturity, an American literature, and a national art and music. And as Rampersad observes, despite the movement's trappings (such as the Eurocentric notion that African American culture evolved from infancy to adolescence to maturity), the writers who contributed to *The New Negro*, as well as the musical writings of Cuney-Hare and Locke, managed to mount a frontal attack on contemporary white supremacist pseudoscience:

> For a movement such as the burgeoning renaissance, however, the deepest challenge, in many respects, lay in the poisoned intellectual and cultural climate of ideas in the United States concerning the origins, abilities, and potential of people of African descent. Race, and the idea of white racial supremacy, enjoyed the lofty status of a science at the turn of the century and down into the 1920s. *The New Negro* would have to accept this lofty status even as it sought to dispel the prevailing notion among whites of blacks as not only physically and culturally inferior but without much hope of improvement.[67]

In summary, the work of the New Negro writers made inroads in the following areas: the documentation of the activities of black musicians, especially those whose bent was toward Western European art music; the promotion and the use of black music as a basis for an American nationalistic school; and exploration of the African sources of African American music. The presence of Crawford's "cosmopolitan" outlook can certainly be found in these writers' approaches; yet each recognized in varying degrees the merits, power, and success of black vernacular music. Furthermore, insofar as these writers were black, each could "claim a share of common experience with the musicians" they studied, and thus, they wrote from perspectives unique to their historical and social positions.[68] From a repertory standpoint, the publication of collections of folksongs and art songs and the discussions they inspired (such as the Hurston essay) set the stage for future scholars of black music. Taken together, these studies helped to establish black folksongs as a distinctive body of song with a dynamic set of performance practices and sociocultural history that is worthy of serious study in academic disciplines. Moreover, the journalistic and black nationalistic impulses that expounded black social equality successfully grafted the politics of race into the field and became a crucial, and one might argue permanent, factor in black music historiography.

If the literature by early twentieth-century black intellectuals valued the cultural significance of the spiritual, then as a whole, these works were also notable for their lack of serious consideration of jazz and other secular musics favored by the black masses.[69] Nevertheless, jazz made a significant, though perhaps indirect, contribution to Renaissance culture and thinking. As Long points out, "the development of jazz, the spread of the dance hall, the continual growth of vaudeville (later to be checked by the talking film), and the exploitation of black music by the recording industry" all contributed significantly to the "heightened consciousness of music among the black writers of the Harlem Renaissance."[70] Jazz, for whatever reasons, was problematic for these writers, just as black vernacular music had been for Trotter. But during the 1920s jazz began to attract another group of writers on both sides of the Atlantic who gave the music and its unique qualities their close attention. In fact, the contrast between these writers' interests and those of the Renaissance recalls some of the ideological divisions apparent in *Music and Some Highly Musical People* and *Slave Songs of the United States*. At the same time, however, jazz literature began to amend some of these divisions. It did so by arguing for the artistic merit of a music created by black musicians and comprised of obvious African- and European-derived aesthetic principles. Jazz criticism played a crucial role in elevating international perceptions about the value of indigenous American music making. Moreover, this shift in attitude ultimately helped bring to center stage the role of vernacular music (and issues of socioeconomic class) in future discourse on African American cultural politics.

.   .   .   .   .

Early jazz literature, for the most part, developed along its own trajectory from the earlier, more academic strains of black music research discussed above. In America, during the 1920s and slightly before, writers of various stripes—composers, journalists, music critics, musicians—published books and articles about jazz in many magazines. In fact, "between 1917 and 1929," James Lincoln Collier observes, "leading American magazines . . . [ran] over 100 articles on jazz, only a small minority of them hostile to the music."[71] These early writers include James Reese Europe, Gilbert Seldes,

R. D. Darrell, Paul Whiteman, Virgil Thomson, George Antheil, Carl Van Vechten, and Henry Osborne Osgood. Jazz impressed these writers in a variety of ways—some favorably, others not. It is important to remember that in the 1920s the word "jazz" was used to describe what we now consider to be a range of different styles; thus, writers were not always referring to the same thing when they wrote about jazz. Their personal biases notwithstanding, writers of the 1920s made it their business to grapple openly with the aesthetic underpinnings of this music. Most important, Africanisms were discussed in early jazz literature in an unselfconscious way but often from an essentialist perspective.[72]

Henry Louis Gates Jr. argues that race "has become a trope of ultimate, irreductive difference between cultures, linguistic groups, or adherences of specific belief systems which—more often than not—also have fundamentally opposed economic interests."[73] Given the historical relationship of African Americans to the United States economic system and the profound influence of jazz, it is not surprising that the nation's racial consciousness has been embedded in American jazz criticism from its beginning. As the social boundaries that had separated black and white citizens by law began to relax, expressive culture (such as jazz) emerged as an area of confrontation, especially to those invested in keeping those boundaries intact. As a conspicuous public activity, jazz emerged as an important arena in which racial ideology was articulated and contested.

A notable point of contention lay in both the jazz aesthetic and the music's formal qualities. Black classical musicians like Roland Hayes, Jules Bledsoe, and Marian Anderson, for example, built successful concert careers and emerged as important symbols of progress for African Americans; but jazz musicians raised the stakes in racial progress. Contemporary reviews for Hayes's, Bledsoe's, and Anderson's concerts often hailed their unique talents but at the same time marveled at their lack of black musical idiosyncrasies. Jazz musicians, on the other hand, featured and even flaunted these qualities as a fundamental aspect of their music and threatened the status quo on many levels (e.g., they asserted the racial aspects of their performances as the strength of the whole enterprise). Therefore, heightened interest in jazz as an artistic pursuit posed a serious challenge to one of the central tenets of America's caste system: racial inferiority. In fact, the politics of race has continually mediated jazz's advance toward international prestige. A few examples will show how the trope of race has shaped jazz writings.

A notable theme in early jazz literature is that a race—not individuals—excelled in jazz, as if playing the music were natural and biological. In "A Negro Explains 'Jazz'" (1919), musician and bandleader James Reese Europe (1881–1919) makes the techniques employed in "jazzing" a piece sound almost like a racially specific primal urge:

> The negro loves anything that is peculiar in music, and this "jazzing" appeals to him strongly. . . . It is natural for us to do this; it is, indeed, a racial musical characteristic. I have to call a daily rehearsal of my band to prevent the musicians from adding to their music more than I wish them to. Whenever possible they all embroider their parts in order to produce new, peculiar sounds.[74]

Although Europe's observations may be viewed as an early statement on black aesthetics—a theory that emphasizes culture rather than race—his comments also resonate with theories designed to make distinctions on a racial basis. Perhaps Europe's views represent a survival technique: conformity to white beliefs about blacks. Of course, no one would deny the distinctiveness of the indigenous music by those who "share the juridical characteristic of American citizenship and the 'racial' characteristic of being black."[75] But the statement presents an unqualified essentializing of supposed racial musical characteristics.

Europe's racial essentialism notwithstanding, some African Americans believed that his musical contributions could serve as a formidable cultural weapon for the cause of racial equality, despite the misgivings by some of the black intelligentsia. As early as 1919, the notion was proposed in a *Chicago Defender* editorial titled "Jazzing Away Prejudice." While reviewing a concert by James Reese Europe's orchestra, the writer links the swing of Europe and his band to progressive social action:

> The most prejudiced enemy of our Race could not sit through an evening with Europe without coming away with a changed viewpoint. For he is compelled in spite of himself to see us in a new light. It is a well-known fact that white people view us largely from the standpoint of the cook, porter, and waiter, and his limited opportunities are responsible for much of the distorted opinion held concerning us. Europe and his band are worth more to

our Race than a thousand speeches from so-called Race orators and uplift-
ers. Mere wind-jamming has never given any race material help.

Europe and his band are demonstrating what our people can do in a field
where the results are bound to be of the greatest benefit. He has the white
man's ear because he is giving the white man something new. He is meeting
a popular demand and in catering to his love of syncopated music he is jazzing away the barriers of prejudice.[76]

In his foreword to *So This Is Jazz*, Henry O. Osgood claims to have written "the first attempt to set down a connected account of the origin, history
and development of jazz music." Although other writers were thinking
about jazz in the late 1920s, Osgood provides a telling contemporary view
of the music. He saw himself as part of a "little group of serious thinkers"
taking up "jazz in a serious way," and Africa figured prominently in his
concerns. On the compelling kinetic aspects of black jazz players' performances (he called them "contortions"), he writes, "They are purely negrotic
in themselves and come direct from the 'ring shout', the dances of religious
frenzy or ecstasy, without question of African origin."[77] He also believed
that the word "jazz" itself came from Africa. Despite his interest in jazz's
roots in black culture, Osgood gives considerable attention to Gershwin,
Ferde Grofé, and the merits of symphonic jazz. Nonetheless, he offers a
brief, remarkable statement about the character of jazz that continues to
ring true more than six decades after he wrote it: "Jazz, in truth, is a wild
bird, free to flap its wings in any direction. It defies all attempts to cage it,
however liberal in size the apiary. It is the spirit of the music, not the
mechanics of its frame or the characteristics of the superstructure built
upon that frame, that determines whether or not it is jazz."[78]

In Europe, and especially in France of the 1930s, jazz was noticed by a
number of writers. In fact, enthusiasm for jazz in France led to the establishment in 1935 of the periodical *Jazz Hot: La Revue internationale de
la musique de jazz*. French interest in jazz coincided with the establishment of the "primitivist" movement there during the first decades of the
century. Both Ted Gioia and John Gennari have discussed the "primitivist
myth" and argue convincingly that the strain of essentialism present in
early French jazz writing influenced later perceptions of the music.[79]

Gioia takes a firm, if somewhat misguided, stand against what he calls
the primitivist myth. While discussing the work of three early jazz critics—

Hugues Panassié, Charles Delaunay, and Robert Goffin—Gioia argues that these writers were "limited in their understanding of the musical under-pinnings of jazz . . . [and] focused instead on the vitality and energy of the 'hot' soloist. Jazz, for them, was an intense experience, and a purely musi-cological approach to it, they felt, would only confuse matters."[80] Yet Gioia (perhaps unconsciously) endorses the dichotomy early critics created between the intensely emotional aspects of great jazz performances and the intellectual aspects of the art: "[Jelly Roll] Morton, like most of the Creole musicians of his day, was familiar with the European tradition in music, and his own compositions and performances show a sense of bal-ance and formal structure which is anything but primitive."[81] The jazz aes-thetic had as much to do with its emotional power and spirit as it did with its "balance and formal structure." What moved these early jazz writers is what still requires musical and cultural explanation: the intellectual rigor involved in being hot, that elusive quality in jazz that places it squarely within the domain of African American expressive culture. These foreign writers, Hugues Panassié and Charles Delaunay, sought to come to terms with an important issue in jazz music: those qualities informed by its African heritage. So while Renaissance writers seemed more than a little edgy about the ecstatic basis of black vernacular music like jazz, these enthusiasts publicly celebrated its "hotness" as essential to the spirit of the music and as its definitive and most-treasured quality.

In America, interest in jazz produced the first generation of important critics, including Marshall Stearns, John Hammond, Paul Eduard Miller, George Hoefer, and Roger Pryor Dodge. The early jazz criticism of *Metronome* and *Down Beat*, two magazines that regularly featured these writers, has been characterized by Ron Welburn as primarily for a white readership and "by and about white musicians, with a few blacks present here and there."[82] By the end of the 1930s, literary interest in jazz had escalated, and book-length studies by American authors began to appear. As with the French literature, these writers noted Africanisms but with varying degrees of essentialism, cultural insight, methodology, and philo-sophical motivations.

Winthrop Sargeant's *Jazz, Hot and Hybrid* (1938) stressed the mixed pedigree of jazz. Sargeant wrote in the preface of the third edition that when his book first appeared, it represented "the only serious musicological study of its type," a departure from the "mostly ecstatic" personality- and discography-centered jazz writings.[83] For Sargeant, jazz was neither strictly European ("completely lacking in the intellectual and structural features that sustain the interest of a cultivated 'highbrow' musical audience") nor African ("very few of these influences can be given documentary proof").[84] Jazz was something unique to Sargeant, and he set out to explain why, using detailed musical analysis.

Sargeant leads his reader through twelve chapters of scalar, rhythmic, harmonic, and melodic analysis of jazz, complete with musical examples. In chapter 12, titled "Influences from the Dark Continent," he answers an important question posed at the beginning of the book, "Did the Negroes invent jazz?":

> When one examines the musical structure of these arts in detail, ... it becomes apparent that they represent a fusion of musical idioms in which both White and "African" contributions play indispensable roles. It is safe to say that virtually no Afro-American music today is wholly without White influence; and it is just as obvious that all jazz, from the most primitive hot variety to the most sophisticated, is heavily influenced by Negro musical habits.[85]

Sargeant seems on the verge of grasping an important idea in black music study, one that would begin to blossom in the 1940s, primarily through the work of anthropologist Melville Herskovits: the transformation of African cultural practices into American ones. But not all jazz writers were sensitive to that notion. For example, in *Jazzmen*, authors Frederick Ramsey Jr. and Charles Edward Smith only mention that "The Negroes retained much of the African material in their playing."[86] For these two writers the uniqueness of jazz, especially during the New Orleans period, was the result of musical illiteracy, a condition these authors considered a virtue.

Through a survey of jazz literature from the nineteenth and early twentieth centuries, historian Lawrence Levine has documented the emergence of a cultural hierarchy, a paradigm firmly in place by the 1920s. These fixed "high" and "low" categories point out that, culturally speaking, the United States remained "a colonized people attempting to define itself in the shadow of the former imperial power."[87] Jazz, positioned at that time in the lowbrow category, was condemned by both black and white writers, including Cuney-Hare, music editor of *Crisis;* bandleader Dave Peyton of the otherwise militant *Chicago Defender;* and the *New York Age's* Lucian White. In fact, in one place Peyton advised aspiring pianists to "put two or three hours a day on your scale work, [and] stay away from jazz music."[88]

Levine posits that jazz, "a central element in American culture," and "Culture," a category used to identify selected expressive cultural endeavors, had a reciprocal relationship and defined one another. But as jazz began to move laboriously toward acceptance as art, such boundaries weakened. "Jazz musicians," Levine writes, "helped revolutionize our notions of culture by transcending the adjectival cultural categories and insisting that there were no boundary lines to art."[89] Thus, jazz played a crucial role in transforming Americans' sense of what constituted art and culture by bridging "the gap between all of the categories that divided culture; [it was] a music that found its way through the fences we use to separate genres of expressive culture from one another," especially after World War II and the appearance of bebop.[90] The dialectic relationship of jazz and the notion of the "high culture" produced an interesting result as jazz crossed the "great divide" separating mass and high culture; the "upward mobility" of jazz ultimately challenged the cosmopolitan/provincial divide.

The ascendancy of jazz raises other questions and points to certain tensions, especially concerning the role of black intellectuals in the construction of the new jazz aesthetic discourse. Of course, identifying who these intellectuals are would be the first priority. One could start with African American writers; there were no small number of black writers engaged in producing novels, short stories, and essays about myriad topics for a wide array of publications throughout the 1920s and 1930s. Yet, on the surface, many of these writers appear largely unconcerned with serious study of jazz—especially the improvised, "hot" variety. Was jazz still somewhat of an embarrassment as it seems to have been among many of the early Harlem Renaissance writers? Why, with jazz's move into the concert hall (certainly a sign of growing prestige), did these writers who were absorbed in the cultural politics of integration not immediately seize the moment and promote jazz enthusiastically? After all, as David Levering Lewis pointedly observes, when Roland Hayes in the 1920s took "spirituals into the concert hall, cultured Afro-Americans were suddenly as pleased as southern planters to hear them again."[91]

These questions point to several issues ignored or merely touched upon in jazz literature. Without question, class tensions in the African American community were partly responsible. For instance, since middle-class jazz musicians like Fletcher Henderson were moderately accepted by Harlem Renaissance intellectuals, what class issues (or, better, tensions) among African Americans are suggested by the intellectuals' lukewarm engagement with jazz? Surely the answer cannot simply be, as LeRoi Jones once put it, that "jazz was collected among the numerous skeletons the middle-class black man kept locked in the closet of his psyche, along with watermelons and gin."[92] Du Bois, after all, counts among America's most formidable social thinkers, and his pioneering courage is self-evident. Lewis claims that even Du Bois would occasionally visit the Savoy Ballroom. But he, like many "who felt responsible for Afro-American public behavior could comfort themselves with the fact that success could not have come to a more responsible middle-class musician" than Henderson. "Somehow, under Henderson's baton," Lewis speculates sardonically, "the funkiness and raucousness of jazz dissipated—not altogether, certainly, but enough so that an Afro-Saxon college-trained professional man might leave the Dark Tower and thoroughly enjoy himself at the Savoy without being downright savage about it."[93]

The evidence suggests that many black intellectuals accepted jazz as an art when America at large began to do so. Singer, actor, activist, and "hero of the race" Paul Robeson, like many of the Harlem elite, had generally eschewed jazz. But his biographer states that during the 1940s, Robeson frequented jazz clubs like the Apollo, Café Society, and Manhattan Casino "to hear Charlie Parker and get 'twisted around' trying to dance to those 'off beat riffs.'" "And Thelonious Monk," Robeson once stated, "really floored me." By 1958 Robeson, perhaps reflecting the growing if still moderate acceptance of jazz into the realm of high culture, stated that "modern jazz is one of the most important musical things there is in the world."[94]

One fact remains clear: early jazz literature shows that writers could not celebrate or criticize this music without coming to terms with the fact that the cosmopolitan/provincial split did not hold up well. It would take a future generation of scholars and critics to develop tools suitable to the musical, cultural, and social content of the genre. Much of this work has brought jazz and black musical traditions in general into the scholarly "mainstream," with work being produced by scholars from a variety of academic fields, including musicology, sociology, ethnomusicology, history, and American studies. The discursive world of jazz, beginning with this early literature and its attendant attitudes, played a crucial role in this cultural shift.

·   ·   ·   ·   ·

Early black music historiography forms a scholarly tradition with a cohesive and dynamic ideology. Furthermore, much of this literature—especially the book-length studies and the anthologies and collections by African Americans—can be read as a sustained project in canon formation. As Gates and others have observed about black literary anthologies, there was an added goal at work, namely, the "political defense of the racial self against racism."[95] The early years of this historiographical tradition culminated in the rhetoric of the New Negro and the "aesthetics of jazz" discourse. These impulses still permeate black music research. Jones's *Blues People*, Southern's *The Music of Black Americans*, and Floyd's recent study, *The Power of Black Music*, may all be read as reactions to and extensions of works that preceded them in the field.

Black music historiography helps us understand the historical role of music in the emergence and rise of black nationalism in America. Furthermore, this exploration of black music research's early ideology can, perhaps, play a role in promoting the field's continual growth and future critical directions. For only by understanding the field's history can scholars plan effective strategies and consolidate useful methods that will encourage the academic study of black music. "A scholarly field," as Richard Crawford argues, "forms a tradition of historical study when earlier writers on the same subject are recognized as predecessors, when their work is studied closely, when the questions they raise are identified, discussed, and debated, and when their findings are assimilated."[96] As we have learned, black music research has through the years developed with an additional political agenda. As this scholarly field continues into the twenty-first century and beyond, not only will America's black musical

past and present be brought into sharper relief, but we will also understand America's musical landscape as a whole. Moreover, work in this field
may become one of the avenues through which we achieve James Monroe
Trotter's more humanitarian goals, which seem just as urgent today as
when he first wrote them more than a century ago: equality for all and
"mutual respect and good feeling" between the races.

2 Who Hears Here?

BLACK MUSIC, CRITICAL BIAS, AND
THE MUSICOLOGICAL SKIN TRADE

As more and more scholars—male and female, black and
non-black—take up the task of reading the work of African-
American women writers, *who* reads these texts may have a
direct bearing on *how* they are read. In a best of all possible
intellectual worlds, where we all had equal access to each
other's cultures, the race, gender, and historical experiences
of the critic might be irrelevant.

Ann duCille, "Who Reads Here?" (1992)

You got tuh go there tuh know there.

Zora Neale Hurston, *Their Eyes Were Watching God* (1937)

The late twentieth century has witnessed a shift in both the mystique and
the outlook of the "ivory tower." Much of this shift involves connecting
academic work with "everyday life" in the larger society or "the real world."
Musicians in the tower continue to experience various repercussions of
these changes. As a case in point, the political ramifications of musicology
are becoming more and more evident. Writing in 1996, Phillip Gossett,
then president of the American Musicological Society, expressed "a sense

"Who Hears Here? Black Music, Critical Bias, and the Musicological Skin Trade," *Musical
Quarterly* 85, no. 1 (Spring 2001): 1–52. In this essay I wanted to call attention to the need
for more Black scholars to enter the discipline of musicology at a time when multiculturalism, cultural studies, and diversity became important interventions in the field.

of hope for society at large" following the group's 1995 annual meeting in New York City. One of the reasons Gossett believed that the meeting represented "a further step in the coming-of-age of the discipline" is because it convened in conjunction with the Center for Black Music Research and the Society for Music Theory. Gossett experienced the feelings generated by the diversity of scholars and topics represented on the conference's program as a welcome counter to "the sense of racial crisis engendered during the O. J. Simpson trial."[1] While Gossett's passing reference to O. J. and racial strife may have seemed innocently anecdotal, I believe that it resonates with some important challenges facing the musicological project of the millennium.[2]

In this chapter I provide a preliminary critique of one of those challenges: identity politics in black music inquiry, an important issue about which very little ink has been spilled. Although the relationship of black musicians to their musical output is routinely deconstructed and analyzed, the relationship of scholars to the work they do in this area is rarely addressed in a sustained manner. While in this chapter I certainly raise more questions than give definitive answers, I believe that we cannot move forward with the collective project of musicological diversity until the silence surrounding this topic has been shattered in print; we need to take a pause for the cause of collective self-reflexivity.

Before moving ahead, I need to qualify my argument a bit. I am limiting my discussion to research on black musical topics and identity politics in this body of scholarship. While the latter enjoys a nascent though exciting literature in musical studies, scholars have not dealt extensively with African American music in this regard.[3] In addition, I should make clear that while I am interested in the implications of "colorizing" the ranks of the field, I cannot and do not assume that these black scholars will automatically be drawn to the study of African American music. Nor do I think that they *should* be directed to do so. But for the sake of streamlining this discussion, I am focusing on the potential of the perspectives of black scholars working on black musical topics. I nonetheless hope that these preliminary thoughts carry implications beyond this prescribed limit: they might speak to or for the African American medievalist, the white blues scholar, or the Native American specialist in the music of Trinidad.

COUNTERING ARRESTED DEVELOPMENT: MUSICOLOGY
AND THE CULTURAL DIVERSITY INITIATIVE

A friction has always existed between an uneasiness with what is known as "the black vernacular," the black presence it evokes, and America's otherwise insatiable appetite for such.[4] The formal study of black vernacular music in the academy underscores some of this history. While scholarly journals and academic presses now seem to welcome studies on the topic of black music, this has not always been the case. Journals such as the *Black Perspective in Music, Black Music Research Journal,* and the *Journal of Black Sacred Music* were created to address the gap between populist interest in black music and its scholarly study.[5] Published and edited by African American scholars, these journals were seen ostensibly as "black" projects, although nonblack scholars contributed to them in large numbers.[6] Now that scholarly interest has accelerated in this area, many of the major music journals publish articles on black musical topics. It looks like the battle has been won: black vernacular music inspires a literature growing in size, reputation, and sophistication.[7]

Recently, for example, the *Chronicle of Higher Education* declared that enthusiasm for jazz, rap, and other popular music styles had reached fever pitch in the academy.[8] The field of cultural studies and other clusters of contemporary theories have helped to create a highly specialized "speech community" (some would disparagingly call this speech "jargon"; I call it "scholarly slang") among writers from numerous disciplines. Yet for all of its sophistication and the enthusiasm it inspires, a deafening silence exists in this literature, one that I believe threatens its healthy development in the present century. That silence is directly linked to the lack of black scholars in the academic music disciplines.

The lack of black scholars in musicology and other related fields has not gone unnoticed in recent years. Many of the concerns I raise here are related to my work on the American Musicological Society's Committee on Cultural Diversity and the Society for American Music's Minority Issues Committee during the last few years.[9] Courageous, politically committed, and well-meaning scholars initiated this work to attract minorities into the fields of academic music scholarship. In the mid-1990s they developed and circulated widely an attractive (and, to my knowledge, unprecedented) brochure explaining the requirements for planning a career in musicology, along with other information that might attract minority students to the field. A diverse group of musicians graces the cover of the brochure: the rappers Queen Latifah, Salt-N-Pepa, and Speech from the group Arrested Development; the composers Duke Ellington, Florence Price, and Tan Dun; and the icons Wynton Marsalis and Seiji Ozawa. And the establishment of the Cultural Diversity Travel Fund has assisted dozens of potential scholars to attend our annual conferences.

Efforts such as these have performed an important service to our respective professional societies. My personal involvement in this diversity work certainly has been gratifying. But over the last few years several issues have become apparent to me. One of the most difficult aspects of this work is that it is not directly linked to a conspicuous scholarly agenda in our field. No matter how noble our desires to diversify, the project will remain a marginal effort if it is not tied to the traditional modes of "real work" in our discipline: the production of new knowledge in books, articles, and, to a lesser degree, public talks.[10] No matter how many phone calls we make to locate, persuade, recruit, and cajole interested minority students into our ranks; no matter how efficiently we coordinate their travel plans or how many "programs" and special panels we mount for their edification, a fundamental problem remains. If minorities are not linked to the larger issues of race, racial politics, and ultimately the politics of authorship in the research we produce, I fear we might be unwittingly and ironically calcifying their marginal status in the discipline.

As an African American musicologist, I have responded to "the call" to attract other potential black scholars to the field. After all, to borrow a phrase from a charismatic preacher I once knew, "sheep beget sheep." I, along with other colleagues, have taken this role seriously, participating in many telephone marathons to locate students, late-night "we can make it" rap sessions, panel discussions, and streams of seemingly endless email correspondences too voluminous to remember. But as a junior professor I could not shake the feeling that I was expending precious time and energy away from my "professional" work. Other complications existed. The topic was for me a personal issue, one that because of the color of my skin and my choice of profession would nag me beyond my tenure on whatever service committee to which I happened to be appointed.

What is more, the fact that our field is challenged with a surplus of recently graduated, already trained and qualified white scholars adds to my list of concerns. The suspicion of some of these young scholars (and others) regarding the diversity effort is sometimes palpable. After all, if our efforts to attract minority scholars are successful, this swarm of still-imaginary scholars will hold the PhD "union card" *and* "race card," giving them an "unfair" advantage in an already overcrowded playing field.[11] Despite the many quite thorny and politically charged complications of this discussion, I still wish to argue here for the importance of black scholars in the field of musicology, with special attention to the role (and not the cards) they can play in the specific endeavor of black music scholarship.

CLOGGING THE PIPELINE: QUALIFICATIONS, ESSENTIALISM, AND THE MARKET

The color of the PhD pipeline was a hot topic in the 1990s throughout the academy. Two articles written by humanities professors touch on important points raised over and over again in the various debates that arose in the decade. Writing in *Black Music Research Journal* in 1993, the musicologist Doris Evans McGinty considered the special contribution that black scholars could make to the field of black music studies.[12] She saw contemporary efforts to bring black scholars into the academic fold as tied to historical efforts to document black achievement in the late nineteenth century. McGinty pointed to James Monroe Trotter's survey of black musicians, *Music and Some Highly Musical People* (1878), and to the American Negro Academy, founded in 1897. These historical efforts strove to "combat stereotypical ideas and misapprehensions" about African Americans. The "imperative necessity" of the American Negro Academy was to counter "anti-Negro" propaganda during Reconstruction and to provide what McGinty called "an unbiased view of black culture."[13]

McGinty's call for "unbiased views" is a tricky one because she also argues that while black scholars "speak for themselves . . . they also speak as participants in the culture, who have been exposed to it over a period of time and have learned much of the explicit and implicit truths that surround it. The black scholar is a trusted insider."[14] This sounds like a very strong and persuasive case for bias—a productive bias based on experience, one that can be a powerful writerly space and source of authority. As participants in black culture, African American scholars are able to "identify, and explain, and make a reader or listener understand and feel black music's special qualities."[15] McGinty cautions against cultural chauvinism, however, and asserts that black scholars must strike a balance between the ideals of "scholarship and advocacy."[16] Informed nonblack scholars, in McGinty's view, can also bring nuance and insight to the subject of black culture.[17]

So what is the role of the white scholar in all of this? The African American literature scholar Nellie Y. McKay has taken up this issue forcefully. In a recent essay she traces the root of "the problem" of identity politics in the professorate to a historical resistance to the value of black literary production and to black studies in general.[18] For much of the 1970s and 1980s, many white faculty members dismissed and ridiculed black studies and even "warned white graduate students away from the [African American literature] courses, and discouraged and sometimes even refused to supervise Ph.D. dissertations that focused on black writers."[19] McKay lists three consequences of this attitude in her field: an ineffectual black PhD pipeline, the discouragement of white graduate students from exploring black culture and literature, and underqualified white scholars doing scholarship on black topics.[20]

McKay argues that the paucity of black scholars in the PhD pipeline has had a domino effect. As the demand among students for courses in black cultural areas increases, university departments are not finding enough scholars to fill the positions. Institutions pass over nonblack candidates in favor of the black one who might appear in the future. "Many," McKay writes, "reject well qualified white applicants for these positions in hopes that a black candidate will appear next time. If not this year, runs the unspoken anxiety, then maybe next year."[21] Positions go unfilled awaiting the next black superstar of African American studies. In perhaps her most incisive attack on the academic race-numbers game, which I quote at length below, McKay levels what I am sure many will read as an anti-affirmative action statement:

The reason offered for directing white graduate students away from African American literature returns us to the problem of making particular groups of people the targets for particular positions and relegating candidates' qualifications to a secondary role in the hiring process. We discourage these students from their preferred choices on the grounds that "the market" offers no jobs for them in that area because of who they are. But who is the market? As faculty members who make appointments to vacant positions in our departments, we are the market. In short, when we reject the nonblack candidate for a position in African American or another minority literature on the basis of the candidate's ethnicity, we create a problem, which we then attribute to a faceless entity we conveniently call "the market." What passes unnoticed in this linguistic dance is the real cost to students, black and otherwise, and to the future of our discipline. The alternative to having a black professor of African American literature should not be not having a professor of African American literature.[22]

Before we of liberal cause and persuasion clasp hands and sing "I'd like to teach the world to sing in perfect harmony," I submit that McKay's argument should not be read simply as advocacy for a color-blind professorate and scholarship. She levels criticism at white scholars who are *not* trained in African American literature but who write about and teach it. In addition, McKay also has a "hook" for black scholars whose "angry rhetoric associated with ideologies of essentialism"[23] argues in favor of territorialism, mysticism, or, if I might use a vernacularism here, "it's a black thing, you wouldn't understand" sloganism. No white people allowed. Although she offers no definitive answer to these problems, McKay argues that one necessary step is the demarginalization of black literature and black cultural studies in general. McGinty and McKay stress equal (and mandatory) access to graduate-level training in black cultural areas as partial remedies to these problems. I am encouraged that these issues concerning black studies are being addressed in public forums, though I admit harboring more than a little envy that they are discussed more frequently and openly in the literary fields and in anthropology than in music studies.[24]

African Americans' access to graduate study will remain a crucial concern in the decades to come. The dynamic nature of black cultural production in the United States has attracted scholars from all backgrounds, and that pattern has accelerated with both the legitimizing of the field and the recent development of new critical and theoretical tools. The case of black music is telling. What was once primarily the domain of black scholars is now becoming a field in which they have minority status. Since the number of black music scholars is so pitifully minuscule, especially when compared to that of black literary specialists, the productive bias I mentioned above is needed even more critically, the politics of authorship a more pressing concern. If black scholars have been "trusted insiders," as McGinty suggests, then how will the new demographic configuration among scholars shape that status? Do the "race, gender, and historical experiences of the critic" no longer matter? Will black scholars find themselves countersubjects, audible but secondary, in the polyvocal, multiracial fugue of this emerging criticism of African American music? Whose "truth" will ultimately be told in this research?

Our confronting these difficult pipeline questions is a necessary step in building an effectual criticism of African American music. Social identities, historical experiences, and cultural perspectives are familiar points of inquiry for students of culture, especially in how these factors apply to what and whom we study. But how these ideas play out for the "studiers" is quite another thing. As we bring these considerations into black music inquiry, the benefits of a critical and productive bias (on the part of *all* scholars) become clear. As one scholar recently put it, "the perspective of the critic is not the extraneous, extratextual trivia our anti-essentialist inclinations might like it to be."[25]

In the remainder of this chapter, I review two broad developments that inform the contemporary positions of black scholars in black music study. I engage critically, and perhaps much too selectively, some suggestive works in black music research since the 1960s. The first group of writings encompasses the years of the civil rights and black arts movements. The second belongs to the postmodern era, so called for lack of a better rubric. I call this period the contemporary era of black music inquiry. Notwithstanding the specific case of jazz literature, the relative lack of consideration of the "generational shifts" in black music historiography is striking, especially when compared to fields such as black literary and black feminist studies.[26]

What becomes clear below is that, since the 1960s, the praxis of African American music study has undergone a gradual shift, moving from an

almost exclusive emphasis on the historical and practical to the more theoretical and critical.[27] This generational—or, better, paradigm—shift has
generated among many black music scholars (and some white ones) a
degree of suspicion and anxiety, although this grumbling has taken place
outside the arena of printed scholarship. Each development in the cultural
politics of "blackness discourse" has informed not only musical creativity
but also the various approaches to talking about the music.

My discussion of the new critical turn in academic interpretations of
expressive culture in the 1990s, for example, shows some pertinent implications for the study of black musical culture. Moreover, these new inter-
pretative strategies, in my view, highlight why this area of music studies
seems overripe for a "politics of interpretation" critique. Indeed, these new
theoretical interventions have shaped how race and the "vernacular" are
understood by a growing number of students of black musical culture.
Whether this new "critical condition" represents a healthy turn or a turn
for the worse greatly depends on whether we are successful in recruiting
black scholars to join the project, a project that for reasons I will explain
below might be called "Operation Signify."

SAYING IT LOUD: MUSIC STUDIES AND THE NEW POLITICS OF BLACKNESS

The present-day idea of an ideologically charged blackness is linked to earlier historical developments in post-1950s American society. This radicalized black identity inspired a varied expression in music literature, among
other arenas. It is helpful to discuss some of the social energy circulating
in these discourses in order to understand at least some of what is at stake
in today's politics of interpretation in black music scholarship. The music
of a southern-bred soul singer provides a fitting segue into this part of my
discussion. If any artist announced that a "New World" in black identity
politics wasn't just a-comin' but was indeed here already, this performer
did. And his musical critique of culture is certainly suggestive of larger
developments in the ongoing definition of African American culture.

We cannot underestimate the intense public and scholarly interest in
black culture and the "Negro problem" during the 1960s, approximately

one hundred years following the Emancipation Proclamation. Against the general tone of radicalism sweeping the country, issues of governmental policies toward poverty-stricken African Americans, a growing black militancy, and a strong sense of cultural nationalism dominated the social landscape. With a sense of urgency, policy makers, cultural critics, artists, scholars, and the public at large mulled over various questions concerning black culture. Some scholars questioned aloud whether black culture was, in fact, myth or reality. Researchers stormed inner-city ghettos in search of "authentic black culture," while others wondered aloud whether recognition, let alone research, of such was "essentialist" and would ultimately work against the civil rights agenda of integration through assimilation. The rhetoric of origins and pedigree percolated within many discussions: was the culture of United States blacks African, Afro-American, or simply American? Was the nature of that culture monolithic, diverse, or hybrid? Who were its most important bearers, males or females? Which cultural practices were best suited for the liberation agenda, the written and literary or the oral? Were the "best" expressions, such as jazz, better thought of as "art for art's sake," as propaganda, as universal, or, as LeRoi Jones (Amiri Baraka) argued, as blacks' response "to the psychological landscape that is his [*sic*] Western environment."[28]

"*Uhh!!, wit-cha badd self.* Say It Loud, I'm Black and I'm Proud." With these lyrics, the preeminent soul singer James Brown seemed to declare (in the popular sphere at least) that a new day had dawned in the world of African American cultural politics.[29] Or better: the renewed thrust of black sociopolitical progress during the post–World War II period seems to erupt in this song's candid strut. J. Rosamond Johnson and James Weldon Johnson's hymn, "Lift Every Voice and Sing," written in 1900 and originally sung by schoolchildren in Florida, had found a new and unlikely rival as the "Negro (or Black) National Anthem," as it was dubbed informally in black communities.[30] But "Say It Loud" was no hymn. Released in 1968, it became emblematic of this era's new expression of black pride. Brown was christened "Soul Brother no. 1," "the Godfather of Soul," and "the Hardest-Working Man in Show Business." Indeed, Brown personified these sobriquets, especially soul, work, the show, and the business.

In a string of hit recordings throughout the 1960s and 1970s, Brown's decidedly southern-flavored musical rhetoric galvanized African American communities, linking urban with rural, the North with the South, black revolutionaries with schoolchildren, militant avant-garde artists with audiences possessing more mainstream tastes. Brown's star rose during turbulent times. Just as post-1970s rap music registered the shifting socioeconomic and cultural landscape of late capitalism, postmodernity, and the postindustrial, Brown's musical language, lyrical subject matter, public presentation, and cultural politics were saturated with the new consciousness of the late 1960s. Brown stood at the crossroads between the civil rights and black power movements, between the celebration of black sensuality and wholesome, Afro-styled family values; he stood between an urbanized Afro-modernism, which took definitive shape around the time of World War II, and the blight associated with the postindustrial inner city after the 1970s.[31] He was the 1960s version of a "race man," a determined black capitalist who fought for artistic and financial control over his career. He often spoke out publicly on behalf of those living in impoverished African American communities like the ones in which he had been born and raised. Brown lived a difficult, Depression-era childhood in the South, working numerous odd jobs to help his family make ends meet. One of the ways he earned extra money was by performing for trains loaded with troops, who would throw spare change to young Brown as he danced, no doubt with the unabashed fervor that would one day define his energetic stage shows.[32]

Brown always remembered the struggles of his early life, and this quality endeared him to working-class audiences. In December 1968 he even in one recording entreated Santa Claus to "go straight to the ghetto."[33] That kind of down-home sentiment characterized many of Brown's recordings. The lyrical narrative of "Say It Loud" does not invoke, for example, the respectable, high-toned sentiments of "Lift Every Voice and Sing," which states in its second verse:

Stony the road we trod, bitter the chastening rod
Felt in the days when hope unborn had died
Yet with a steady beat, have not our weary feet
Come to the place for which our fathers sighed?

Like the Johnson brothers, Brown reflects on past struggles and stillborn hopes, but he depends on an entirely different sense of poetic rhetoric. In

one passage from the second verse, for example, Brown references a spiritual's text, mother wit, and colloquial expression:

> We've been 'buked, and we've been scorned
> We've been treated bad, talked about
> as sure as you're born
> But just as sure as it takes two eyes to make a pair
> Brother, we can't quit until we get our share

In another verse Brown seems to speak of his personal experiences with
manual labor. The lyrics could also refer to his earlier struggles for artistic
control and an equitable financial relationship with his record company,
the King label: "I've worked on jobs with my feet and my hands / and knew
all the work I did was for the other man." Even the word "black" in "Say It
Loud" represents a shift in African American sensibilities. During the
1960s it was radicalized and embraced as a politically charged designation
for African American ethnicity. As a dark-skinned African American,
Brown spoke to racial prejudice and to the "color-struck" element in
African American communities.[34] So as Brown tropes the ideas of social
justice and racial uplift that characterized "Lift Every Voice and Sing," he
updates the message for his late-1960s audience. From Brown's opening
trademark, "Uhh," to his half-spoken call, "Say it loud," and the response of
a chorus of (white and Asian American!) children shouting "I'm black and
I'm proud," we are drawn into a world that is, as one writer has described
Brown's lyrical artistry, "far removed from the poetry of Western art song,
the urbane witticisms and sentimentality of Tin Pan Alley, and the folksy,
anecdotal narrative of country-western music."[35]

The musical rhetoric of this piece also breaks with and exploits "tradition." Brown does not sing but speaks the lyrics of each verse, a gesture
that both foreshadows the non- and semimelodic oral declamations of
rappers in the next decade and recalls black "folk" preaching performance.
The form of the piece comprises verses, a chorus, and a bridge section. The
verses and choruses (the "say it loud" refrains) are each performed within
the same choppy, repetitive "cut" groove, which features an angular, prominent bass line and situates the piece firmly in B-flat.[36] The bridge, which
is heard twice in the recording, moves to E-flat (IV) for a few measures;

this summons blues form and is also reminiscent of similar harmonic gestures in gospel music.

Authorship of the piece is attributed to Brown and the woodwind player and arranger Alfred "Pee Wee" Ellis. As performers and composers, Brown and Ellis adorn the simple design of "Say It Loud," which constitutes shifts between what can be heard as two discrete tonal centers—relational but independent because of the repetitive quality of each. Brown and Ellis satisfy what Zora Neale Hurston calls the "will to adorn" in a number of inventive ways.[37] The small horn section almost competes with the bass line with melodic patterns that move between percussive unison lines and chordal passages. The guitarist adds yet another competing pattern to the groove that (like the horns) alternates between single lines and chordal punches but fills in a different part of the rhythmic time line. All parts of this instrumental tableau fit together like the pieces of a puzzle, and each supplies sonic variety within the mix. Audiences and musicians loved it. This division of sonic labor became the foundational element of the funk genre, an approach to sound organization extending from the pronounced glorification of the strong backbeat in earlier R&B practices.

In my view, funk, or the "in the pocket" groove (explained earlier as the funk recipe), rivals for importance the conventions of bebop's complex and perhaps more open-ended rhythmic approaches. Each imperative—the calculated freedom of modern-jazz rhythm sections and the spontaneity-within-the-pocket funk approach—represents one of the most influential musical designs to appear in twentieth-century American culture.[38] The "James Brown sound" inspired admiration, piqued the imaginations of black cultural nationalists interested in "African origins," and inspired contemporary dance crazes that swept the country. One writer working at the time declared with utter sincerity that James Brown's horn section was "the most deadly and earthy music section in the history of American music." He writes further that "the James Brown band represents the quintessence of an African-directed movement in black music expression from the popular idiom, and it has influenced the latest dance styles."[39]

On this latter point, Brown celebrates dance verbally in "Say It Loud," declaring at the end of the piece "and we can do the boogaloo," referring to an immensely popular African American dance of the late 1960s. His statement occurs in the context of the bridge, in which, earlier in the song, he had also broken from the lyrical narrative of the verses by performing various stock but culturally rich phrases such as "ooo-wee, you're killing me, you're all right, and you're outta sight." This narrative respite, together with the harmonic move to E-flat and the rhythmic shift occurring in each bridge, was, in my own experience, often accompanied by kinetic intensification by dancers or roller skaters, who often helped themselves to their own verbal declamations. Thus, in terms of a typical in-the-moment musical experience, audiences freely participated in the recomposition of "Say It Loud." "*Go, girl!*," "*Look out!*," "*Don't hurt yourself*," and "*Hey!*," one might hear on a crowded dance floor. "*Wall!*" one might hear at the roller-skating rink if a skater wanted a slower skater to yield the fast lane near the wall so that he or she could get on with a more intense dance step. This collaborative act among dancers, skaters, listeners, and the mass-mediated musical text mirrors how James Brown's band members created many of his funky grooves from the late 1960s to the mid-1970s. Part of Brown's reputation for being hardworking derived from his relentless touring, rehearsal, and recording schedules. Within this context and under Brown's direction, his bands forged innovative approaches for complementing the singer's virtuoso improvisations. In the process, they laid the musical groundwork for funk, jazz-fusion, numerous hip-hop idioms, and other styles of popular music.[40]

NOT JUST JAZZ, SPIRITUALS, OR MEN: BLACK WOMEN CRITIQUE BLACK POWER

At the height of the black power movement, African American women novelists, scholars, and critics also seized that explosive moment. Writers such as Alice Walker and Toni Morrison published novels that won the Pulitzer Prize. In the 1970s the black female critics Mary Helen Washington, Barbara Smith, and Barbara Christian, among others, worked diligently to define and institutionalize not only black feminist studies, but also the broader field of African American literary studies. Inspired in part by the "discovery" of black female writers such as Zora Neale Hurston, African American women writers have become, in the

words of the black poet and literary scholar Ann duCille, "politically correct, intellectually popular, and commercially precious sites of literary and
historical inquiry." DuCille, with more than a hint of asperity, likens the
fashionable interest in theorizing race, class, and gender in the work of
black women writers to standing in a dangerous and suddenly busy three-
way intersection with the likelihood of being run down by the oncoming
traffic.[41] (She calls this trend "Hurstonism.") The contributions of black
female writers have over the last twenty-five years institutionalized a
dynamic body of literature and, perhaps more importantly, championed
sophisticated frameworks that help us enjoy and understand it.

During the 1960s, populist black nationalism comprised various and
sometimes competing ideologies that, taken together, articulated a desire
for varying degrees of cultural, political, and economic separation from
the dominant culture. Within this historical context, black feminists
fought against two kinds of invisibility. One involved distinguishing their
concerns from those of white feminists. The other entailed exposing and
critiquing the masculinist emphasis of black nationalism, even as these
women drew energy from it. This second goal is instructive for our understanding of one aspect of Eileen Southern's work. The literature that grew
out of the freedom movement, while struggling and waging war against
black stereotypes, erected others, the most notable of which centered the
black male as the true subject of black culture, an attitude that marginal-
ized African American women. Furthermore, the discourse of the black
aesthetic privileged certain genres, preferring drama and poetry because
of their direct, immediate, and oral impact. Black feminist (and "woman-
ist") literary scholars mounted creative and theoretical strategies in their
fiction, poetry, and criticism that, according to one contemporary literary
scholar, sought to "both restructure and supplement the ideological program of black cultural nationalism." In this artistic milieu, black feminists
employed a "double gesture." They continued their "appreciation of the
cultural history that has produced the black writer's strong investment in
the model of a whole, cohesive self" and gave "vigilant attention to the differences within the black experience that confound any totalized, unitary
definition of black identity."[42]

It is within this historical "redefining blackness" context that Southern,
one of the country's first African American female musicologists, published

The Music of Black Americans: A History in 1971. Southern should certainly be considered a "race woman." The appearance of her book in the wake of the black power movement, the turbulent social upheaval of the late 1960s, links it to an auspicious historical moment. As it does in "Say It Loud," the word "black" stands provocatively, even proudly, in Southern's title. The book reflects some of the dramatic social changes of its day, such as the widespread student protests that led to sweeping curricular advances in colleges and universities across the nation and, most notably, the addition of courses in black history and culture. Designed to fill a void in the new curriculum, Southern's work broke new ground in its focus, method, and scope, inspiring others (both directly and indirectly) to similar inquiry and helping to establish black music as a legitimate scholarly specialty. In a 1987 interview Southern explained that attitudes expressed by her colleagues as she prepared to offer a course in black music fueled her resolve. Some of them contended that there was nothing to learn about the subject because it constituted "just jazz and spirituals."[43]

Southern's study resonated with and challenged classic 1970s black cultural nationalism and its feminist response. In the preface to the 1971 edition of *The Music of Black Americans* she writes, "The black musician has created an entirely new music—in a style peculiarly Afro-American."[44] This statement clears a space for her exploration of a musical legacy that countered in scholarly terms sentiments like the "just jazz and spirituals" attitude or the notion that a distinctive African American musical culture did not exist at all. Southern's scholarship reflected the notion of a unified, cohesive, and essentially male "blackness," using terms such as "the" black community and "the Black man" often. Other black female literary critics were intensely debating such representations in their work. Southern was, of course, not alone in this characterization. Many African American writers who contributed to academic discourse during the high years of the black aesthetic referred often to black male composers and performers to illustrate their rhetorical, musical, and polemical points. Aretha Franklin was a notable exception to this unspoken rule. Writers mentioned her music (along with that of James Brown and Mahalia Jackson) no doubt because of the contemporaneous and symbolic currency of "soul music," an important idea in black-nationalist discourse.[45]

There was at the same time a considerable critical gap between Southern's work and that of the black aesthetic (or black arts) project, although, unlike other female writers, she did not discuss this difference in print. As a black female academic in an overwhelmingly white and male professional setting, Southern experienced racism, sexism, and even "the hostility of black male professors."[46] But she did not directly address these discriminatory practices in her work. In fact, as Floyd notes, her research "seems benign" because, methodologically speaking, "she works squarely within the musicological tradition, cherishing its modes of inquiry and its scholarly products, with no desire to undermine or reject the accepted tenets and practices of the profession."[47] Southern recognized a discrete Afro-American musical tradition, but she traced its historical trajectory in relation to Western music traditions, an untenable position for the black aesthetic program. If some black cultural nationalists valorized musical styles such as jazz for their rhetorical immediacy in the liberation struggle, Southern valued historical distance and exercised deliberate caution in her discussion of jazz: "We are yet too close in time to this music to be able to view [jazz] in proper perspective."[48] If the black arts movement embraced a radicalized self-definition for black culture, Southern did not believe that her musicological project should venture into such a contentious, ideologically charged arena. She left that project to future scholars: "Since the immediate purpose of the present work is to record the facts of history, which must precede esthetic and stylistic evaluation, I have not tried to make explicit a definition of black American music. . . . I have tried to provide a solid and useful basis for discussion of the question of its definition."[49]

THE INSIDE-OUTSIDE BLUES

Southern's work contrasts sharply with an earlier book that fits squarely within the ideology of the black arts movement. Many recognize LeRoi Jones's *Blues People* (1963) as a watershed publication in both black music historiography and American cultural studies.[50] Jones (who later changed his name to Amiri Baraka) understood well that an important relationship existed between black music's development and the historical trajectory of African American social progress. *Blues People* represents the first book-length study by a black author to theorize extensively about this connection.[51] As an African American writer, Baraka had an insider's viewpoint that was a novelty to jazz letters at that time. (However, it is also important to emphasize that Southern was just as much a rarity in musicological circles.) If one could sum up Baraka's concerns into one research problem, it would be to trace the political economy of African American music from slavery to freedom. That emphasis makes *Blues People* an important work in itself, a book that, because of the fundamental—not to mention controversial—issues it raises, one writer called "the founding document of contemporary cultural studies in America."[52]

Baraka's attention to the political economy of black music (and numerous related issues) was laudable. But his skepticism of the ever-evolving "modernist" profile of African American musical culture, of which he paints a rather static picture, is plainly, and even painfully, obvious. (By way of comparison, Eileen Southern celebrates this same modernist drive.) Baraka regretted key processes in black music culture, such as commercialism, urbanization, migration, and professionalization. He believed that they corrupted the "real" or authentic black aesthetic. That corruption thesis, as Ralph Ellison pointed out in an eloquent review of *Blues People* in 1964, thins out African American culture, fails to provide a full accounting of its historical influence on mainstream American culture, and ignores the "intricate network of connections" that bind them together.[53] Moreover, I might add that a critique of commercialism, migration, urbanization, and professionalism should also show how these processes figured into what made these styles meaningful for African Americans and the larger American populace. Baraka sought to translate his idea of a collective and communal black experience into a cohesive aesthetic and political theory within an environment saturated with new interest in urban black culture.

The forcefulness of Baraka's critical writings resounds in his 1963 essay "Jazz and the White Critic." Baraka discusses identity politics in jazz criticism and in so doing addresses many of the concerns that future writers would take up some thirty years later but with less political focus. Baraka distinguished "criticism" from the research of historians, whose work he praised. He argued that class and race in the American context should be central to jazz criticism and that writers on black music need to "set up standards of judgement and aesthetic excellence that depend on our [Negro] native knowledge and understanding of the underlying philosophies and local cultural referents that produced blues and jazz in order to produce valid critical writing or *commentary* about it."[54]

Despite Baraka's stringent critiques and his belief that the personal identity and politics of the critic mattered, the notion did not, for the most part, appear to influence white writers, who continued to offer cultural translations of their own during the 1960s and 1970s. Consider, for example, four very important works, Charles Keil's *Urban Blues* (1966), Gunther Schuller's *Early Jazz* (1968), Dena J. Epstein's *Sinful Tunes and Spirituals* (1976), and Lawrence W. Levine's *Black Culture, Black Consciousness* (1977). In *Urban Blues,* Keil, an anthropologist, used social science methodology to explain "an expressive male role within urban lower-class Negro culture—that of the contemporary bluesman."[55] One cannot call *Urban Blues* unpolitical: it is, after all, dedicated to Malcolm X and is steeped in the imperatives of black cultural nationalism. But for unstated reasons, Keil believed it best to suppress the personal, although his instincts pressed him otherwise: "I have restrained a strong impulse to write a soul baring autobiographical preface for the simple reason that much of who I am comes out in the book; how I got that way is probably irrelevant."[56] In the afterword to the latest edition of *Urban Blues* (1991), however, Keil wanted to correct a misunderstanding among some of his readers concerning his racial background. He confesses "I AM WHITE" in one of the postscript's subtitles. He gets even more specific in this glib portrayal: he is "German and Yankee blue-eyed . . . an Aryan from Darien, Connecticut (no blacks or Jews allowed), who served time at Yale (a few of each allowed) and could afford to choose a deep identification with Afro-American values and aspirations."[57] These words are not exactly soul baring, but they do suggest a new attitude for a different time. I will return to this a little later.

Keil also compared the work of white and black writers on the blues. "White writers . . . tend to be folklorizing, documenting, defining, and social scientific: let's pin it down."[58] In his study *Early Jazz,* for example, Gunther Schuller transcribed recordings in order to bring improvised jazz into the realm of written scores, notated musical examples, and stylistic analysis. Schuller listened to "virtually every record made, from the advent of jazz recordings through the early 1930s."[59] The book can certainly be considered a key work in the contemporary era of jazz analysis—many scholars consider it a kind of standard for certain kinds of work in jazz research. Schuller could not have disagreed more with Southern's assessment that jazz was still too new to study in proper perspective. He did share her objective stance, but he threw in a dash of the personal—this *is* jazz, after all. *Early Jazz* combines "the objective research of the historian-musicologist with the subjectivism of an engaged listener and performer-composer."[60] However, the listener, performer, and composer are not historically, culturally, or socially situated vis-à-vis the musical materials under discussion. Like Schuller, Dena J. Epstein mentions her "occupational identity" (she is a librarian) but discusses no other aspect of her background in *Sinful Tunes and Spirituals,* a definitive, indeed monumental, study of black slave music in America. Lawrence W. Levine's *Black Culture, Black Consciousness* treats music extensively, although it is not the primary focus of the study. Levine's book addressed a pressing question being taken up by the popular press and by black cultural nationalists, humanists, and social scientists of the day: did a black culture exist? Interestingly, Schuller, Levine, and Epstein each stressed the time and effort invested in their prospective projects, confirming the "let's pin it down" sensibility. Schuller listened to "virtually every record made, from the advent of jazz recordings through the early 1930s"; Levine "worked [his] way carefully through thousands of Negro songs, folktales, proverbs, aphorisms, jokes, verbal games, and ... 'toasts'"; Epstein's copious research took some twenty years.[61]

By way of contrast, "black writers are more inclined to celebrate blues as a core metaphor in process, the center of a worldview that incorporates jazz, literature, aesthetics, philosophy, criticism, and political strategy."[62] Albert Murray's *Stomping the Blues* (1976) is such a book, bringing a different set of concerns to the table than the white writers discussed above. He argues for an understanding of blues culture as a tradition associated with a variety of attitudes, social customs, personalities, secret rituals, discrete venues, social functions, and vibrant dance forms. Murray's insights are presented from his perspective as a participant-observer. Yet Murray also claims membership in a larger community of American thinkers and writers. He zigzags between the mystical and the philosophical—between mojos and Hamlet. Thus an underlying theme of *Stomping the Blues* represents yet another translation: the universal implications of this specific blues-culture ethos. It is instructive to compare Levine's thinking to that of Murray. Levine writes, "I am aware that many of the materials I analyze have their origins or parallels in the folk thought of other peoples, and whenever it was relevant to my purposes I have explored these avenues, but for the most part I have assumed that once these materials made their way firmly into the network of Afro-American thought and culture they could be used to shed light upon black consciousness without constant reference to their existence in other cultures."[63] Unlike Schuller's, Epstein's, and Levine's heavily documented studies, *Stomping the Blues* contains no scholarly apparatus to speak of; Murray's cultural experience is his "authority," although this sentiment is not addressed specifically. His elegantly written, explicitly musical discussions in the chapters titled "Singing the Blues" and "Playing the Blues" sketch out important conventions of the blues and jazz aesthetic. Murray's musical discussion (based on recordings and live performances), coupled with his extensive use of illustrations (including "action" and publicity shots of musicians and the actual record labels of commercial recordings), gives the impression that he wanted to celebrate—not decry, as did Baraka—the commercial status of blues-based art musics.

Black religious music attracted its share of scholarly attention in the 1970s. Portia K. Maultsby, an African American scholar, played an instrumental role in raising black music's visibility in the fields of ethnomusicology and black studies.[64] Maultsby's work was primarily historical in content and method rather than ethnographic or critical; it reflected the nascent status of black music study in academia and the practical needs of the field. The music theorist Horace Clarence Boyer, also an African American, provided his field with its first extensive look at the compositional, vocal, and instrumental traditions of the black church.[65] Significantly, he published some of his early work in *Black World,* one of the revolutionary periodicals of the black arts movement.[66] The African American ethnomusicologist Jacqueline Cogdell DjeDje combined the historical and theoretical with fieldwork in her 1978 book *American Black Spiritual and Gospel Songs from Southeast Georgia: A Comparative Study.*[67] Importantly, the work focused on her hometown of Jesup, Georgia, and included transcriptions. Maultsby and Boyer both had significant experience as performers in gospel music, and their cultural backgrounds, like Murray's, informed their work.[68] Two other black scholar-performers working in the 1970s deserve mention here. The composer Olly Wilson and the virtuoso pianist Pearl Williams-Jones each discussed the relationship of African to African American music, which many scholars pondered at the time primarily because of populist interest in the topic generated by the black power movement.[69]

Although it is quite varied, all of the work discussed above—from the "academic" to the nonacademic, from Southern to Murray and beyond— laid out important groundwork, structure, and themes for future research. Because of these pioneering endeavors black music became a truly open field of inquiry, attracting scholars from a variety of personal and discipli- nary backgrounds. For the most part, the literature concerned the histori- cal and the practical; writers outside the academy addressed the political import of black music. Ethnographic work represented a small portion of the studies. Whether writers chose to "say it loud" like Baraka or revolu- tionize quietly like Southern, the work made possible today's growing criticism of African American music. I think that Keil's turnabout in spelling out his identity for readers is a telling example of how radically different identity politics have become in recent years. But, as I hope to demonstrate below, music scholarship (especially in the realm of black music) has yet to reap the full benefit of this shift.

A NEW DANCE CRAZE: THE PARADIGM SHIFT

In the 1980s scholars working in black literary studies forged new theo- retical directions for that field, distancing their thinking from the black arts movement. Their writings ultimately became the foundation and van- guard for other disciplines' work on black expressive culture, including music. The body of criticism that emerged used interpretive strategies that included semiotics, structuralism, rhetorical analysis, feminist cri- tique, Marxism, poststructuralism, and symbolic anthropology, among others. Taken together, these methods ushered black cultural studies beyond a somewhat narrowly defined (but powerful) sense of the political.[70]

Contemporary music scholars have taken note of what was called the "reconstructionist" moment in black literary criticism, and recently a new black music criticism has emerged. A criticism of black music, which I distinguish from much of the work discussed in the first part of this chapter, attempts to explain the cultural work the music performs in the social world. This musico-cultural criticism ultimately seeks to explain what these various styles and gestures mean and how they generate and achieve their signifying affect. It exposes some of the critical spaces left by earlier models and analytical methods, first by identifying a work's significant musical gestures and then by positioning those gestures within a broader field of musical rhetoric and conventions. These musico-narrative conventions can then be theorized with respect to broader systems of cultural knowledge, such as the historical contexts in which a musical text or style appeared and the lived experiences of audiences, composers, performers, dancers, and listeners. Thus, black music criticism leaves no aspect of the musical process—creation, mediation, or reception—untouched, frustrating anyone's claim that a single study can provide the definitive account of a musical topic. This analytical project provides alternative ways for scholars of black music history to access and discuss some of the historically and socially contingent meanings generated by a musical style and its surrounding practices.

Some recent studies have advanced various theories of interpretation appropriate for and specific to African American musical theory and history. These works signal a paradigm shift in research on black music topics that is related to similar goals of scholars working in other fields of academic musical study. It should come as no surprise that the studies below draw considerable inspiration from developments in black literary studies, cultural studies, and various strains of poststructuralism. I, too, have found it necessary to join other methods to my musicologist's toolbox. This observation should not be read as an indictment of the discipline but as a simple statement of fact. Moreover, I believe that it becomes a matter of conscience and principle to acknowledge the limits, and indeed try to expand the boundaries, of what is considered the musicological tradition, especially with respect to the study of African American musical culture. We need to couple the sophisticated analytical tools developed in musicology with others in order to reveal the layers of meaning that listeners respond to and find compelling.

The new approaches suggested in the following studies have begun to make an impact on subsequent scholarship, but they have not generated the sharp, critical debates typical of those in the field of black literary criticism. Nor have these works caused the energized, public, and sometimes pointed disagreements that have marked, for example, the introduction of feminist criticism into the fields of musicology and music theory. For present purposes I only discuss a selective list of research that either accounts for music's formal procedures or seems to be written from the perspective of one of the academic music disciplines.

Black musical studies are clearly at a critical juncture, as is witnessed by an intense level of activity by a community of music scholars. David Brackett, Samuel A. Floyd, Kyra D. Gaunt, Ingrid Monson, Ronald M. Radano, Timothy D. Taylor, Gary Tomlinson, and Robert Walser, among others, analyze black music with a combination of tools from musicology, ethnomusicology, and contemporary cultural theories.[71] Broadly speaking, they each suggest alternatives for modernist aesthetics, taking issue with formalist explanations of musical texts. They question the idea of autonomy in musical works and emphasize instead the historical and social contingency of knowledge, and, thus, musical values, by making explicit the links between black music and society. Monson wants to demonstrate "a deeper understanding between musical practice and cultural meaning." Walser discusses the "links among the impressions of listeners, the techniques of musicians, and the actual sounds that result." Brackett wants to understand the "relationship between the musical object and the evaluative discourses used by people who produce and consume music."[72]

Although I have referred to the scholars above as a community, I should say exactly what I do and do not mean by the term. Although they all treat black music in similar ways, one does not get the sense that they conceive of themselves as building a cohesive (if sometimes contentious) project in the same way that feminist musicologists do, for example. Writers in the latter group talk about turning points and *collective* moments of empowerment in the field; they recognize, for example, "the critical mass of feminist contributions that debuted at the 1988 Annual Meeting of the

American Musicological Society."[73] While they acknowledge diversity among their rank and file, they define themselves as forwarding a concerted project: identifying "gender as a distinct social force . . . to examine its ramifications within musical culture, and [to ask] new questions about musical practice."[74] A possible reason for this relatively unified front is that, for the most part, this group primarily comprises white women (both straight and gay) working with other white women who have similar professional and political concerns and who, for the most part, discuss the musical works of white women and men. I do not point this out to be cavalier or insensitive, nor has this fact gone unacknowledged by some of the women in this movement. At any rate, it must certainly be exhilarating to have found a voice within a field; it is certainly gratifying to witness.

The multiracial, mixed-gender composition of the emerging "school" of contemporary critics of black music, together with the aggressive, individualist attitude that the academy fosters, makes building a sense of unity among these and other scholars a more difficult task. Join all of these problematics to the most important issue here—the combustible issue of black identity, which all of this work addresses to some degree—and it becomes clear why the territory feels somewhat constrained. I should make my comparison between the feminist musicological project and black music criticism more explicit. Although great enthusiasm surrounded the 1988 AMS meeting, I have read few references to and rarely heard mentioned casually, for example, the importance of the 1993 National Conference on Black Music, sponsored by the Center for Black Music Research and featuring an interracial slate of scholars. Few have called this conference an awakening in the black critical project, although the whole point of the meeting was to spawn the type of research these scholars do. (In fact, one black scholar has all but dismissed the conference as a Johnny-come-lately project.)[75] Why does the project seem rather disconnected? Could it be that the paucity of black music scholars— indeed, the lack of a critical mass—undermines the effort to lay a foundation upon which unity within this collective could be achieved?

These scholars draw heavily on the work of black literary theorists such as Houston Baker and Henry Louis Gates, especially as this body of scholarship relates to European cultural theorists like Bakhtin, Bourdieu, and Foucault. By combining musical analysis with these other theories, scholars of black music seek to decipher the codes and gestures present in black vernacular music and show how the music acts as a kind of public forum for the practice of African American identity. I want to briefly explore some of this work because I believe their collective analyses are important. It may indeed lay the groundwork and patterns for future theoretical excursions into the relationship between black music and African American identity; it begs critique in the interest of the development of this important line of inquiry.

Finally, these writers address a scholarly audience about African American music and its meanings. Inherent in their positions is the almost inevitable stance of a cultural translator who is explaining "blackness" to the academy. The white scholars in this group (Brackett, Monson, Radano, Taylor, Tomlinson, and Walser) surely understand the problematics involved in that role, especially given the intense conversation about authority, race, and identity politics in the academy over the last few years.[76]

SIGNIFYIN(G) WITH MILES: COMPLICATING BLACKNESS IN THE 1990s

Shelley Fisher Fishkin, an American studies and English professor, has identified the early 1990s as "a defining moment in the study of American culture."[77] Two simultaneous trends in scholarship marked the moment, in which "our ideas of 'whiteness' were interrogated, our ideas of 'blackness' were complicated, and the terrain we call 'American culture' began to be remapped." Indeed, she surveys more than a hundred books and articles from numerous disciplines in which these two agendas are rigorously pursued. I am particularly interested here in the "complicating blackness" part of this equation. Fishkin sees many of the activities in which black scholars engaged in the field of literary studies in the 1970s and 1980s as operating within an "essentialist paradigm" that gave way in the 1990s to a more inclusive or "complex" view of African American culture. This complexity manifested itself, according to Fishkin, in how critics sought to explain the "white side" of things—the interplay of the cultures within American letters and life.

While I remain skeptical that every aspect of this "new complexity" should be viewed as the thoroughly innovative moves that Fishkin suggested— in fields such as anthropology and music, for example, the syncretic nature of African American culture has been an enduring field of debate—a shift, nonetheless, did occur. This development can be clearly seen in the jazz studies wing of black music inquiry. The life, career, and, indeed, the complexity of the jazz trumpeter and composer Miles Dewey Davis (1926–91) has provided scholars with plenty of grist for the complicating blackness mill.

If James Brown emerged as a musical symbol of black power during the 1960s, then Miles Davis became in the 1990s a compelling figure for the-orizing among contemporary cultural critics in the academy. The reasons for this interest are many. It is difficult, for example, to identify one area of Davis's life or work that did not attract some degree of controversy. Born in St. Louis to a middle-class family, Davis moved to New York City in the mid-1940s, just as bebop was emerging as the avant-garde voice of jazz. After spending his apprenticeship years in that scene, Davis went on to compose music and spearhead many of the stylistic shifts that occurred in jazz, including the cool jazz, hard bop, modal jazz, and jazz fusion movements. His signature sound—a lamenting, sighing muted trumpet— arguably became one of the most recognized "voices" in jazz history. Furthermore, Davis's apparel became legendary fashion statements, and his image became among the most photographed in jazz history. In spite of these (and many other) lofty accomplishments, Davis is also remem-bered as one of the more controversial figures of jazz, and perhaps even of twentieth-century American music in general.

I turn now to critiques by two scholars who discuss some of the more controversial issues touching Davis, his jazz-rock experiments and his solo rhetoric. Each scholar uses various contemporary critical tools to shed light on controversial elements of the "Miles mystique." These interventions are excellent examples of an important critical turn in African American music inquiry. They also bring into high relief some issues regarding the politics of identity in contemporary black music scholarship.

Gary Tomlinson goes right to the heart of the matter, subtitling his engaging essay "A White Historian Signifies."[78] Tomlinson is not speaking negatively about anybody's mother here, a key rhetorical practice of signifyin(g). Rather, he finds interpretive value in the more academic concerns of Henry Louis Gates's theory, signifyin(g), which outlines a way to discuss, among other things, the repetition and revision practices prevalent in many black artistic forms, including literature, the visual arts, and music. Tomlinson wants to show the implications of Gates's work for postmodern theorizing and its benefits for black musical studies. Specifically, his essay treats Miles Davis's jazz-rock experiments in the late 1960 and early 1970s as models of cultural dialogics. To its credit, the article painstakingly delivers a point-by-point explanation of how the characteristics (tropological, archaeological, and dialogical) of signifyin(g) relate to the major postmodern theories that have reshaped the human sciences in recent years. Praise comes easily for Tomlinson's work, for it is among the first of its kind in black musical studies. It seems headed for canonical status: it is cited often and has appeared in a subsequent anthology in revised form.

But as students of African American culture know (or should know), every public act of signifyin(g) necessarily invites a response. It is an irresistible antiphonal call begging response, in fact. (Any black scholar worth his or her weight in citations—especially those of us who grew up participating in and witnessing these verbal rituals of wit and virtuosity—relishes such challenges.) As I work out my ideas on paper, I cannot help thinking about the Signifying Monkey tales that Gates's theory and Tomlinson's riff and revision implicitly reference. In those oft-revised oral poems, the monkey, through his signifying instigation, tricks an unsuspecting and, importantly, much more powerful lion into a physical confrontation with an elephant. The fight occurs and the elephant goes "to town ... [and] whup[s] that lion for the rest of the day." The monkey finds the scene hilarious and chides the lion:

> The monkey got to laughing and a' jumpin' up and down,
> But his foot missed the limb and he plunged to ground,
> The lion was on him with all four feet
> Gonna grind that monkey to hamburger meat.
>
> The monkey looked up with tears in his eyes
> And said, "Please Mr. Lion, I apologize,
> I meant no harm, please, let me go
> And I'll tell you something you really need to know."[79]

This signifyin(g) tale is about power relationships; its lesson seeks "to achieve or reverse power, to improve situations, and to achieve pleasing results for the signifier."[80] Tomlinson's varied and daunting accomplishments in musicology have established for him an impressive profile. To personalize and extend my metaphor (signifyin(g) is, after all, *always* personal), and to illuminate just one aspect of the power relationships at hand, I write these passages as a junior faculty member seeking tenure at an Ivy League institution at which Tomlinson holds a named professorship in the humanities. I would not even think about instigating a fight here, especially given our lack of "elephants"—black scholars whose position in the field of musicology is similar to Tomlinson's.[81]

Tomlinson is careful not to claim expertise either in black literature or in the black vernacular languaging upon which signifyin(g) is based. His authority derives from what he calls his own vernacular: "My Signifyin(g) and the theorizing that results from it will manifest my own vernacular as it intersects with other vernaculars. I make no presumptuous claim to blackness in my presentation, but at the same time I do not undervalue the potential dialogical richness of my interlocutions with African-American culture from a position outside it."[82] Despite this statement, we get only a glimpse, near the end of the essay, of Tomlinson's personal investment (dialogic richness) in defending Davis's fusion style against the damnation of jazz critics. He discloses, parenthetically, that he was one of many "venturesome white rockers" who found Davis's interethnic musical dialogue formative to his own musical and cultural identity during college.

Tomlinson's insights would have been even more penetrating had he theorized a bit more about why he, a musician who would ultimately become a preeminent scholar of Renaissance music, found a controversial black jazz musician mixing jazz and rock idioms so compelling in the first place. (How many of us read patiently through Tomlinson's dense theoretical positions just because we were eager to witness a white Renaissance scholar "do jazz" and jazz-rock—in public, no less?) I personally found myself wanting to learn more about Davis's cultural dialogue with "the white historian" in the title of the essay. *That* cultural interchange begs greater visibility in this article, especially given Tomlinson's speculations about Davis's "vernacular"—a black "middle-class ambivalence," a suggestion for which Tomlinson himself admits Davis's autobiography provides slim evidence.

He should be applauded for calling our attention to the nexus of identity, class stratification, and jazz culture, because it is a useful and sorely underinvestigated site of analysis in African American music studies. But Tomlinson misses the possibility that Davis's fellow black musicians may have been gratified to meet the classically trained, middle-class Davis at Minton's. Or perhaps they could not have cared less. On another level, a more important missing theoretical perspective is the specific "vernacular" Tomlinson promised in the beginning of the essay. Did he bring those vernacular sensibilities—the adventuresomeness of a young, white jazz rocker—to his future work? As influential as this article is becoming, it would have been that much more so had even *some* of the complexity of the white historian been theorized into the authorial voice of the essay.

Robert Walser, another scholar who writes on an impressive range of topics in American music, also exhibits a small degree of "trouble in the critical jungle" when issues of audience, authority, and identity intersect. In his essay " 'Out of Notes': Signification, Interpretation, and the Problem of Miles Davis," Walser seeks to square Davis's undisputed position in the jazz canon as a bandleader and innovator with what some heard as the "glaring defects" in his trumpet playing.[83] For Walser, the "problem" of Miles Davis is one of critical assessment. In order to begin setting the criticism straight, Walser provides a transcription and analysis that illustrate specific details of Davis's musical rhetoric in a recorded solo, "My Funny Valentine."[84] This essay, in both its subject matter and its approach, presents an exemplary case study for talking about some pertinent issues raised by black music inquiry's new critical turn.

Walser takes few prisoners as he clears space for his interpretation. If I might extend my signifyin(g) metaphor, he establishes his critical authority (powers of interpretation) by positioning his work against the previously circulated ideas of a rather diverse group of lions: jazz critics, scholars, and musicians. Whether a writer ignored altogether Davis's "missed notes" and "technical flaws," noted and accepted them as part of the allure of his artistic profile, or accepted them as evidence of his technical inadequacy, Walser upbraids him or her for being out of sync with "the actual reception" of the music. His objections and antidotes cluster around two mutually exclusive notions. On the one hand, we have "modernist attitudes" and "modernist aesthetic theories," which, he argues, have dominated jazz studies.[85] He is especially skeptical of what he calls "classicizing strategies": calls for the legitimating of jazz, especially through comparisons with classical music. Some of the other modernist attitudes include belief in the autonomy of the artwork with respect to everyday life, art's separation from mass culture and social content, and the critic's reliance on "certain standards of performance quality and authenticity, the latter encompassing technical accuracy, appropriateness to the style, and originality."[86]

On the other hand, Walser finds a solution for "critical classicizing" in Gates's theory of signifyin(g), which "is opposed to the perspective of modernism."[87] He uses Gates as a way to explore "cultural difference on its own terms" and as "an antidote to theoretical assimilation."[88] While Walser's detailed analysis of the solo is illuminating—fun, even—I did not experience his transcription and lucid explanation as the dramatic departure from previous analyses that he claimed it was. Essentially, Davis's solo, including the missed or cracked notes ("spleaches," "clams," and "fracks," in trumpet players' parlance), is interpreted by Walser against the previously circulated versions of "My Funny Valentine" known by the listener or the performer. Most fundamentally, though, Walser argues that

> Davis is in dialogue with the basic features of the song itself, as jazz musicians would understand them, and as listeners would recognize them. The whole point of a jazz musician like Davis playing a Tin Pan Alley pop song could be understood as his opportunity to signify on the melodic possibilities, formal conventions (such as the AABA plan of the 32-measure chorus), harmonic potentials, and previously performed versions of the original song.[89]

These observations should not be greeted as news. I do not quibble, of course, with the basic point itself—that jazz is a "performance-centered" art; I disagree only with the idea that this analysis takes us (forgive the pun) miles beyond the critical assessments of previous work. The dialogic dissin'—indeed, the serious signifyin(g)—taking place throughout this essay promised as much. I could elaborate further on this issue, but I want to move now to Walser's understanding of signifyin(g) as pointing to "performance, negotiation, and dialogue with past and present as features of this mode of artistic activity."[90] Here I seek to pull the act of scholarship itself into the realm of cultural practice, to consider it as "performance, negotiation, and dialogue." Let us focus specifically on Walser's critique of the jazz pianist and educator Billy Taylor, because it raises several issues related to African American cultural politics, which I read as a fundamental concern in both signifyin(g) and in Walser's essay.

In 1986 Billy Taylor characterized jazz as "America's classical music," believing that within a jazz performance, an individual musician forwards what amounts to a musical "Self," an ideal that demonstrates "the concept of individual freedom."[91] Walser counters Taylor by arguing that

> characterizing jazz in this way effaces both its complex cultural history, including the myriad effects of racism and elitism on the music and the people who have made it, and the dialogue that is at the very heart of the music. Taylor praised individualism. But what of collaboration—in collective improvisation, in composition, in the ongoing collective transformation of the discourse of jazz?[92]

Walser correctly detects, as I am sure other cultural critics will, more than a hint of the modernist sensibility shaping Taylor's views as represented here. The impulse of vindication, indeed the imperative necessity I discussed earlier, certainly rings loud and clear in the "jazz as classical music" chorus. But I could not help being struck by the critical leap of faith we are asked to take in order to accept Taylor's so-called attempt to erase racism, elitism, dialogue, transformation, and collective sensibility from jazz's history. Although I am not advocating that we rescue wholesale Taylor's "classical" ideals, when we consider them in context and in relation to Taylor's broader work, to his subject position, and even to Walser's critique, a familiar pattern emerges.

Billy Taylor did not originate the idea that jazz was America's classical music. An earlier version of the notion, for example, appears in the work of the late Ralph J. Gleason. As a critic of jazz and rock (he was one of the founders of *Rolling Stone* magazine), Gleason, in his book *Celebrating the Duke*, credits the rock organist Ray Manzarek of the Doors with the jazz-as-classical-music idea.[93] Despite Gleason's pronouncement, he is abundantly clear: he is not, by any means, claiming that jazz had no social content. To the contrary, he maps its history against integration, civil rights, race politics, and art discourse. "Art," he writes, "precedes social change as well as mirroring the society from which it comes and the turbulence and strident tone that accompanies some of the black struggle for true freedom is found in modern jazz."[94] Nor does Gleason claim a separatist position for jazz away from other blues-inflected musical styles such as blues, rock, and soul.

That said, it is difficult for me to believe that a black jazz musician, one who has performed throughout the last fifty years—roughly half of jazz's "complex history"—would not himself be aware of the cultural politics behind the jazz-as-classical-music ideal. In fact, some of his writings, while promoting the comparison of jazz to classical music, reveal this understanding. In his book *Jazz Piano: History and Development*, Taylor frustrates the particular point for which Walser chides him: individualism.[95] Taylor, engaging in some signifyin(g) of his own, seeks to distinguish his work from "white 'authorities' who have either ignored or misrepresented important aspects of the history and evolution of various styles of jazz." He writes that

> such writers trace the history of jazz as the impact of one individual upon another; but that kind of historical treatment is fallacious. Jazz began as music created out of the black consciousness to fill needs basic to black existence in a repressive society. Though individuality rates high in its expression, in jazz the musical vocabulary and repertoire quickly becomes [*sic*] the common property of many musicians. The evolution of jazz styles does not progress only from one great individual artist to another . . . but rather from generation to generation.[96]

With these last words in mind, and with all due respect to Walser, I wonder whether the desire to create critical elbow room resulted in his collapsing too many subjectivities, criticisms, and cultural imperatives into a simplified "modernist attitude." Would acknowledging some of the details of Taylor's subjectivity and background (he earned a doctorate in education from the University of Massachusetts) have helped Walser reveal a quite powerful dialogic at work in this black musician's philosophical (albeit legitimating) stance?

What is more, I find puzzling this aversion to the idea of individual voice in jazz, especially in the context of an article that wonderfully accounts for Davis's singular artistic statement in this solo. Walser provocatively describes Davis's solo in terms that ironically support Taylor's (and modernism's) vision of artistic individualism in jazz, a description that contains a hint of what he critiques in Gunther Schuller's work: the "modernist dual answer." He writes that "Davis does not present his audiences with a product, polished, and inviting admiration; we hear a dramatic process of creation from Davis *as from few others*. And as we listen, we can experience these feelings of playfulness, complexity, struggle, and competence as our own" (emphasis mine).[97] In fact, every critic or musician referenced by Walser proclaims how individualistic and singular he or she found Davis's music. Whether we agree or disagree with these critical assessments is not the central question. We must take such ideas seriously because they constitute a part of the actual reception of Davis's work. Can we afford to silence (ironically) in the name of dialogics those who do not dance our paradigm shift—those who hear, believe in, and experience, to use a limited example here, artistic individualism?

I read with interest Walser's actual analysis of the solo: his careful attention to detail, his insightful accounting of the technical challenges of trumpet playing, and his insistence that the rhetorical power of some musical styles often escapes Western notation are laudable. But the aggressive signifyin(g) surrounding it—and I return here to the notion of scholarship as performance, negotiation, and dialogue—serves to undermine the contribution. Voices are censored in the "dialogue." The history of an idea such as "jazz is America's classical music" is drained of the variety and nuance of the political imperatives driving it. The imperialist march of modernism is projected onto the pens of critics, who are then treated as caricatures, as honorary "dead white men" of the postmodernist imagination. This projection ultimately calls attention to a larger issue: the political and personal import of black cultural criticism.

While negotiating the tricky waters of academia, those of us interested in lending our interpretations a certain power and distinction cannot fall into the traps I have identified. I should point out that Walser censors himself along with Taylor and the other critics. We are never told, for example, that he is himself an accomplished trumpeter and therefore brings to the table a particular kind of ear, experience, and culture when he analyzes Davis's solo rhetoric. Missing as well is whatever personal investment he might have in using the recently developed tools of black cultural critique in this context. Perhaps interrogation of and grappling critically with this issue would have allowed him to avoid what I experienced as a kind of displaced hostility onto other analysts. The mere use of Gates's signifyin(g) theory is not enough to fill this critical gap (where is "the actual reception" of Davis's music within African American audiences, for example?). Nor is "the personal" a sign of a lack of rigor; it is an unavoidable consequence of criticism. As Walser himself notes, "reactions to art feel personal, but they nonetheless reflect the ways in which even our most personal feelings are socially constituted."[98] Once we open the door for the personalized critical voice in scholarship, we of course make room to understand the positions of others. This move may help us to understand, for example, why a black jazz musician would make claims for his life's work being seen a statement of "individual freedom." Or why audiences and even musicians still clamor—despite our academic claims to the contrary—for "authenticity" as *they* understand it.

And what happens when this sense of authenticity is challenged? Pearl Cleage expresses outrage in a 1990 essay after learning in Davis's autobiography that, in her words, *"he is guilty of self-confessed violent crimes against women such that we should break his albums, burn his tapes and scratch up his CDs until he acknowledges and apologizes and rethinks his position on The Woman Question."*[99] Cleage tries to reconcile her strong feelings of betrayal toward Davis because she had used his music, particularly his watershed recording *Kind of Blue* (1959), as background music for romantic interludes. In fact, Davis's music became the soundtrack for an important transitional moment in her life as a recent divorcée enjoying her freedom. "For this frantic phase," she writes, "Miles was perfect." As she eloquently explains, Davis's work became a metaphor for the "messages of great personal passions" she wanted to convey to her conquests.

> Restrained, but hip. Passionate, but cool. He became a permanent part of the seduction ritual. Chill the wine. Light the candles. Put on a little early Miles. Give the gentleman caller an immediate understanding of what kind of woman he was dealing with. This was not a woman whose listening was confined to the vagaries of the Top 40. This was a woman with the *possibility* of an interesting past, and the *probability* of an interesting future.[100]

I find Cleage's critique one of the more profound testaments to the power of musical experience, one that I will deal with explicitly in some future forum. Throughout the essay, Cleage attempts to come to terms with her subject position as a black female and the ways in which she perceived that Davis's muse had "made" or shaped a most cherished aspect of her subjectivity. How could she accept Davis's "genius," she ponders, without becoming complicit in his self-confessed violence against women?

THE POLITICS OF WRITING BLACK CULTURAL POLITICS

I acknowledge that since I am a black scholar working in a field that is primarily nonblack, some of the observations that I forward here will have a specific kind of import. Therefore, I want to begin this next section with some qualifications. I believe that all of the scholars whom I am situating in this "new critical school" are indeed working against the notion of racial essentialism.[101] They believe in principle that African Americans possess multiple, complex identities that cannot and should not be flattened out into familiar stereotypes. The composer and musicologist David Brackett, in response to an uninformed critique of "romantic authenticity" in black music literature by Philip Tagg, argues that "simply admitting that a concept such as 'black music' exists need not mean that the music is any more or less 'authentic' than any other music."[102] That Brackett needed to make such a statement at this moment in African American history speaks volumes. This is especially true given the mountain of historical and "living" evidence that black music "exists." It points to one of the more fascinating aspects of African American blackness: the need to re-dress, re-announce, and reprise a definition of blackness in American culture. Terms such as "freedmen," "New Negroes," "colored," "black," and "African American" represent just a few examples of this sociopolitical imperative. And theorizing about this blackness does, in fact, present a special kind of writerly and professional problem. Writers must find a way to explain "blackness" in "black music" and somehow account for it as a tangible, material, and manageable presence.

Writing about music presents a formidable challenge to music scholars, and constructing a nonessentialized yet "authentic" and fluid yet "real" blackness in print, no less, may even surpass that challenge. While the notion of authenticity in African American cultural studies has attracted much attention, far less has been granted to how scholars authenticate and authorize their work in this field. We find two overlapping strategies for authentication in the new critical school, but they are cloaked in how these writers represent or, better, construct blackness in their literary texts. We might call these writerly strategies "professional" and "confessional" blacknesses.

Professional blackness emerges in this literature through writers' strikingly consistent use of sociolinguistic models for representing African American presence, sensibilities, and identity—a sociolinguistic blackness, if you will. The kind of scholarly (and personal) authority it grants comes by virtue of its claim to have been homegrown, cultivated and harvested from indigenous black vernacular culture. Inspired by the radicalized conception of blackness promoted in the 1960s, the work of the anthropologists and sociolinguists William Labov, Roger Abrahams, and Geneva Smitherman, among others, investigated speech patterns among African Americans and discussed how the rules and roles of syntax, performance, and social context contributed to black group identity.[103] Contemporary black-music critics have found these literary studies compelling. In fact, Gates's theory of signifyin(g) exerts an almost hegemonic presence over this research.

I refer to this mode of sociolinguistic influence as professional blackness for several reasons. It consists of complex theoretical explanations of identity and culture that many of us—African Americans and non–African Americans—learned to untangle through, or in some cases in spite of, our professional training. Still others of us taught these theories to ourselves, either through trial and error or with the help of knowledgeable, widely read, and willing colleagues. I believe it is correct to assume that many of us working in this relatively new area would not have been introduced to this "black literary vernacularism" without the privileged access that our specialized training offers. Once this baptism by theoretical fire has occurred, sociolinguistic-literary blackness allows scholars to plunge headfirst into the depths and wonders of black identity, cultural politics, and subjectivity. I want to discuss briefly how this activity calls into question different sets of issues for African American and non–African American scholars. The cleft existing between these constituencies is overripe for analysis, and I hope my attempt at analysis will not be read as brute cultural chauvinism or territorialism. But the door has been opened for this kind of critique because many of the scholars I mention here not only recognize the significance of race but theorize it aggressively in their writings.

The black literary critic Henry Louis Gates's explanation of why he found contemporary theory useful for his graduate training at Cambridge University during the years of the black power movement provides a helpful beginning: "It was a device that enabled me to communicate with my professors in a more or less common language, even if I was attempting to speak in a critical dialect of Afro-American literature."[104] Gates believed that contemporary theory, in addition to its translating function, gave him a critical distance, the ability to "defamiliarize the texts of the black tradition, to create distance between this black reader and our black texts, so that I may more readily see the formal workings of those texts."[105] Many of us who have weathered the storm of rigorous graduate training can relate to Gates's desire to learn how to speak to his professors. And those who found themselves speaking (or, perhaps more appropriately, hearing) across social divides caused by ethnic, racial, gender, or even musical differences can relate to Gates's problematic. Can we assume, then, that the white and black scholars under discussion are similarly motivated to develop a common language with the disciplinary authorities? Are both groups seeking to achieve the critical distance—the defamiliarization—of which Gates is speaking here?

I want to make it clear that I share with both my black and my white colleagues a rejection of racial essentialism. And I realize that since my argument has speculative dimensions, I am skating on pockets of theoretical thin ice, certainly with regard to nonessentialist ideals. But I think it is important to recognize the body of academic work under discussion as a powerful social discourse in itself. This scholarship can be analyzed with respect to the cultural work it is performing for its creators and its audience, thus rendering it not unlike the black musical discourses, musicians, and sensibilities it explores. It is also important for me to emphasize that black music does not exist as the sole territory and private property of African Americans. "Others" have flowed rather freely (pun intended) in and out of this music and have done so at all stages of the creation, mediation, and reception processes. As Ann duCille has argued about intertextual influence in black literature, "Intertexuality cannot be defined as movement solely from black text to black text, from one black author to another. Rather, such resonances must be viewed as cutting across racial identities, cultural spaces, and historical moments."[106] Furthermore, since these are American scholars working on American music, it is unnecessary for these white scholars to mask how intimately the "blackness" of African American music has inspired their admiration, attention, and professional involvement.

But therein lies a key problematic. Given the intense attention to African American cultural identity and politics in these studies, one would expect much more theorizing on how their own subjective, complex identities dialogue with their representations of blackness.[107] The absence of such speculation in work that seems to argue that "race matters," as Cornel West put it, is curious. I am not advocating that white (or black) scholars present autobiographical detail as a matter of course in black music research; sometimes that information is not relevant to a specific project. But in work that seems pressed to deconstruct and decode African American identity and its politics, white and, no doubt, black scholars' claims of access to such sensibilities need to be theorized more often and rigorously. And it should be done with the same enthusiasm that has made the intersecting of gender, race, and class at the corner of blackness and the academy such a busy intersection indeed.

TRUE CONFESSIONS: THE BLACK CRITICAL "I"

Samuel A. Floyd and Kyra D. Gaunt, two African American scholars in this new critical school, raise provocative issues with respect to this topic. They also use professional blackness in the ways that I have discussed above. Floyd's work is based on Gates's sociolinguistic-literary theory, signifyin(g). If Eileen Southern believed that she could not (or should not) venture into a categorical definition of black music, Floyd's interdisciplinary study *The Power of Black Music* (1995) aims directly at that question.[108] Addressing the "absence of a thorough and specific aesthetic for the perception and criticism of black music," Floyd gives you a sense for the capacity of black music to circulate social energy, to embody cultural work, and to express the "struggles and fulfillments of existence."[109] Like that of Southern and Baraka before him, Floyd's thinking for the most part reflects the cohesive, unified black cultural nationalism of the 1960s, which shaped the views of a whole generation of writers and scholars. He explores how music has registered social developments among African Americans, writing, for example, that "a large part of Afro-America made a more or less gradual shift from a cosmos controlled by black mythology and African-American community to one dominated by individual determinism."[110] Floyd monitors this and other shifts—the African American journey from the African continent to slavery to freedom, their move from an African-based cosmology to a distinctly African American one—by tracing how musical values and approaches have transformed yet reproduced certain myths, rituals, and performance practices. Black music, in Floyd's view, can be defined not only by understanding what conceptual traits shape a musical work or style, but also by questioning why certain musical gestures are considered significant.[111]

To bolster his claims with musical evidence, Floyd puts forward a theory of musical and cultural interpretation that he calls Call-Response (not to be confused with the technique call-and-response). Call-Response, he argues, is the master trope of the African American musical tradition. Within this master trope Floyd subsumes the foundational and conceptual elements (or tropes) of African American vernacular music, including call-and-response, the heterogeneous sound ideal, musical individuality within collectivity, a dynamic approach to rhythm, oral declamation, and constant repetition, among other techniques. His theoretical model offers a useful vocabulary with which to talk about the cultural transaction occurring between black music and listeners knowledgeable about its signifying gestures.

But Floyd also establishes authority through a writerly-political strategy we might think of as "confessional blackness." For example, he states that his work is shaped not only by the tools of poststructuralism, but more fundamentally by his childhood experiences in southern African American culture during the 1940s and early 1950s. He describes himself as "a member of perhaps the last generation of African Americans whose parents and grandparents were intimately familiar with Br'er Rabbit,

Legba, the Signifying Monkey, Stackolee, John the Conqueror, and other black folk characters and practices."[112]

Gaunt's work, although still in its formative stages and less widely known than Floyd's, discusses girls' games and their influence on the creation and reception of rap music by a *specific* community of listeners. I stress the word "specific" here because that goal distances much of the professional-blackness work discussed above: for all the talk of "meaning" and "reception," these writers do not often specify who, beyond the musicians, is interpreting the "black" codes within the music.

Gaunt foregrounds her study, for example, by outlining how multiple facets and practices of her own identity—gender, ethnicity, consumerism, academic pedigree, and intense musical involvement—influence her work. She writes, "As an African American woman who adores hip-hop music, my experiences as a purchasing fan began in 1989 as a burgeoning student of ethnomusicology, although rap songs have dotted my musical tastes since 1979."[113] Gaunt's "confession" springboards the reader into broad identity issues and formal explanations of musical processes. As evidenced in the following passage, Gaunt gives weight to the role of gender and black female subjectivity in this study, adding a much-needed gauge of difference *within* the black cultural nationalist sensibility that has predominated in black musical studies. Thus she engenders the black critical "I" and signifies on Floyd and other black writers who have given gender short shrift in their critical work:

> I began to think about my own everyday experiences as a girl within the sphere of girls' musical games. In thinking about games that involved music, I thought of hand-clapping and double Dutch (jump-rope) game songs. The game-songs we performed beyond the public or mass-mediated realm resemble the music of hip-hop in various ways. For example, the sing-song, declamatory nature of the vocal line, the emphasis on rhythmic punctuation and style, the use of the musical break (or interruption of sound but not musical line), the emphasis on narration and linguistic play, and more. Rap music might be seen as a site for revisiting girls' play for African American women fans and performers, in addition to conventional uses of rap as dance music and as a site for cultural and nationalist impulses.[114]

I, too, am offering my own version of the confessional-blackness mode, in a larger study.[115] I explore some of the historical implications of my own subject position—especially my experiences during the 1960s and 1970s—through the oral histories of my extended family of origin. I try to make explicit how these experiences inform my interpretations of the music treated throughout the book.

My mixing the confessional and professional modes of blackness constitutes a kind of double gesture, one that seeks to capture the critical distance but also the familiarity that I am reluctant to even pretend to surrender for the unachievable cause of scholarly objectivity. The purpose behind this critical move can be seen in much recent scholarship in the humanities and social sciences, in which scholars have moved toward a new self-reflexivity, recognizing the ways in which their own experiences shape their studies even in work portrayed as objective.[116]

KNOWING THERE: NATIVE KNOWLEDGE AND PRODUCTIVE BIAS

On the lecture and professional conference circuit I have been accused more than once of not being "theoretical" enough when voicing concerns about some of the current strategies that some scholars use to explain black vernacular music. Yet few, if any, have noted what is missing in these theoretical dialogues. Because *all* the fields of musical studies are overwhelmingly made up of white scholars, we can observe an unconscious interpretive pattern even in research on black music. The white "vernacular" is "understood" as always-already present and therefore requires little explanation, theoretical or otherwise. We take for granted the white critical "I," and it operates as a familiar, naturalized voice in scholarly discourse. Scholars rigorously defend this transparent though powerful space of authority. One defensive tactic assumes that attainment of a PhD erases a black subjective lived experience, varied as these experiences are. The only profit that such thinking might carry, however, is frustrating the development of a "musicology of experience," a development that can only benefit our illuminations of the wonder and power of musical experiences, which constitute, of course, the center and seat of our work as musicologists.

Yet verbal duels at lectures, conferences, and hotel bars are not lasting scholarly discourse and never will be. What counts most (at least to our professional work) is what debates take place in print. One African Americanist distinguishes between postmodern theoretical "discourse" and something she calls (quite sarcastically) "dat-course." Her comparison is instructive for my argument. Discourse stands for all the postmodern, postcolonial, poststructuralist, "sophisticated" methodologies to appear in academia in recent years. "Dat-course," on the other hand, refers to that which is deemed "methodologically sloppy anti-intellectual identity politics."[117] African American critical perspectives will remain marginal in the field and not be given their just due until they move out of "dat-course" and into printed discourse. Many African American critical perspectives are little known, and they will not circulate outside of "dat-course" and into discourse until the demographics and thus the knowledge base of our discipline expands well beyond the status quo.

The theoretical turn in black cultural studies has witnessed black scholars' inclination to write themselves into their criticism. I encourage this trend beyond this group because it can invigorate academia with fresh perspectives and political imperatives. The black law professor Patricia J. Williams notes her desire to search her own legacy and to write her family history into her scholarship: "I decided that my search was based in the utility of such a quest, not mere indulgence, but a recapturing of that which had escaped historical scrutiny, which had been overlooked and underseen. I, like so many blacks, have been trying to pin myself down in history, place myself in the stream of time as significant, evolved, present in the past, continuing in the future."[118] Her work recognizes that not only does race matter, but the critic matters, too. Black music criticism can benefit from this imperative. As others have warned, we cannot kill the critic along with the author. We have not yet arrived at the best of all possible intellectual worlds.

Other disciplines can provide models for the kind of theorizing I propose here. The anthropologist José E. Limón's work on working-class *mexicanos* of south Texas represents an excellent model, and a brief description of it is helpful because so many of his concerns overlap with my own. Limón explores brilliantly the notion of the "native anthropologist" in his work on the expressive cultural practices of the *mexicanos*.[119] An anthropologist working in the cultural and geographical space of his birth and upbringing, Limón provides a deft critique of the interplay of his combined birthrights: *mexicano* and "child of the Enlightenment, of high literary modernism, of classical anthropology."[120] Limón interprets historiographical (previous and selective work on south Texas Mexican American culture) and his own ethnographic research on a number of expressive practices through his multiple lens, and the result is extremely useful for my larger project.[121]

In much the same way that I have discussed recent development in black music research, Limón does not simply provide a review of the literature. He discusses the works "as symbolic action, as cultural practices in themselves, as expressive culture about expressive culture."[122] He is especially concerned with how these previous ethnographies influence his own views—how he struggles against reproducing some of their underlying assumptions. Thus, Limón's historiographic work offers an interpretive history of the "writerly" (or written) culture about the *mexicanos* of south Texas.

Limón's ethnographic case studies are equally helpful. Though his topics of choice can hardly be considered an exhaustive list, he wants their study to gain him access to "large cultural patterns" in the same way that the Renaissance literary scholar Stephen Greenblatt does with his important work.[123] Limón borrows from Greenblatt the term "cultural poetics," an idea meaning "acts of cultural interpretation focused on aesthetically salient, culturally imbedded textualities and enactments."[124] Limón's cultural poetics of south Texas *mexicanos* considers a wide range of literary, folkloric, popular, economic, political, and his own cultural memories "in one interpretive universe."[125]

Black, white, and other scholars are similarly positioned to achieve this kind of work in black music criticism; we can all fashion a cultural poetics specific to our own scholarly and personal *productive* biases. But as Janie Crawford, Zora Neale Hurston's black female protagonist in *Their Eyes Were Watching God*, admonishes, "You got tuh go there tuh know there."[126] In other words, our experiences and productive biases *do* matter. We should not bury them nor disregard those of "others." Through such efforts we might continue to transform America, this house that race built. We can, as the novelist Toni Morrison suggests, "convert a racist house into a race specific yet non-racist home" and encourage "race specificity without race prerogative."[127]

We will never attain these ideals within the realm of black music studies, however, without interracial cooperation. And that cannot be achieved
without a dramatic increase in the number of highly trained black scholars who have been there and know there. And, of course, there is no single
black "there." As black music research continues to cut the academic rug
with its paradigm shift, we will need many more black scholars on the
dance floor, saying it loud and intensively taking it to the bridge. Without
African American critical perspectives we remain trapped in a familiar
pattern, one in which "black culture is more easily intellectualized (and
canonized) when transferred from the danger of lived black experience to
the safety of white metaphor, when you can have that 'signifying black difference' without the difference of significant blackness."[128]

The stakes are high. As different sensibilities, knowledge bases, and
intellectual interests join in the musicological project, and as the safety of
white metaphor makes room for not only the black lived experience but
the white as well, we will all benefit, intellectually and morally. "Racial
constructs," as Toni Morrison argues, will be "forced to reveal their struts
and bolts, their technology and their carapace, so that political action,
legal and social thought, and cultural production can be generated sans
racist cant, explicit or in disguise."[129] If we undertake this important
project together, all this revelation will no doubt carry with it some
uncomfortable moments. Such critical self-reflection never comes easily.
As more vernaculars reveal themselves in the new black music criticism,
the language through which we communicate will certainly be altered,
and this shift carries with it the risk of misunderstanding. I will never
forget when a senior, well-respected white colleague asked me at a conference if I thought that *I* was a "trickster figure" because of an observation I
had made concerning a well-known black composer.[130] I hope I misunderstood. Where are the elephants when you need them?

WHO WILL HEAR?

This chapter, although wide-ranging, has focused on two main concerns.
The first addressed the need for more black scholars in the academic
music fields generally and black music research specifically. Since we have

decided that an increase in cultural diversity is desirable in the professorate, I questioned exactly what that might mean for the kind of work created from this demographic shift. One result might be something that I
am sure some readers may have found disconcerting: my traversing the
various vernacularisms reflected in my own admittedly complex background, an identity that is as much informed by my working-class, African
American, Chicago-based experiences as they are by my training and professional affiliations. While it may be true that the leaderships and the
rank and file of our professional music societies have remained committed
to the ideals of cultural diversity, true diversity will mean a change in what
counts as valuable knowledge in our professional discourses. New criticisms demand new attitudes.

The other thrust of this chapter discussed a more contentious topic: the
role of white scholars in the new black music criticism. Because I do not
argue for a colorblind approach in identity politics, my views may be at
odds with many of the leftist and progressive sensibilities driving the new
cultural criticism. While it is highly improbable that the writerly stance I
have called the invisible white critical "I" will become obsolete, I believe I
have suggested a promising alternative. I want to make clear that I am not
advocating a confessional mode among white scholars that smacks of the "I
once was blind but now I see you" type of reflexivity so brilliantly critiqued
by Ann duCille.[131] I argue, rather, for accounts that, while acknowledging
white privilege, move into theorizing other areas of white lived experience
that will shed light on the complex reception histories of black music.

The nuts and bolts of this theoretical strategy must be done by white
scholars themselves. I, for one, feel inadequate to this particular task
because it is not my lived experience. And while I understand that this
vacuum created by my white colleagues might, in fact, be a strategic
silence, a political move to counter past wrongs, I still argue that we need
this perspective in the discourse. But it should be forwarded in tandem
with the theorized experiences of a critical mass of black scholars. Only
then can we achieve a true and balanced dialogic fulfilling the goals of
equality we all surely share.

All of this means facing not only the music but also some difficult questions. Will we police the number of black scholars working with the polite
nervousness that whips through a white suburban neighborhood when a

black family moves in, fearful of lowered property values and scholarly standards? Will the few black scholars in the field be able to concede some of the authoritative voice that the inevitable condition of our tokenism grants us? Will theorizing black scholars make the turn from the "family romance" paradigm to a more diverse idea of blackness than the historical and practical work that our pioneer scholars advanced out of necessity? Will nonblack scholars greet black scholars' assertion of identity politics with the same enthusiasm they celebrate from the black musicians they study? Will such an assertion be considered white-bashing "Crow Jim"-ism or a reverse racism in the same way that black feminism is often critiqued as anti–black male? Will the feel-good rhetoric of cultural diversity and multiculturalism be allowed to stand in for a thorough desegregation of our field's professional ranks? Will we achieve signifying difference without significant blackness? Will this new body of scholarship be "in the pocket"—heterogeneous yet composite? As we face this music, whose ears will hear?

3 The Pot Liquor Principle

DEVELOPING A BLACK MUSIC CRITICISM IN
AMERICAN MUSIC STUDIES

This chapter reflects on black musical culture in the United States and its criticism with an eye toward how these ideas implicate new directions and areas of potential growth in the burgeoning field of American music studies writ large. We cannot fully understand American music and its study without intensely engaging the parts that comprise its sum. The relationship of African American musical studies to American music studies remains a symbiotic and dynamic one and, therefore, we must keep in mind that any discussion of either should recognize that they simply would not exist in their present forms without each other.

Yet one of the first orders of business in this exercise is a difficult and, to some, potentially divisive task: facing and coming to terms with some uncomfortable truths about the black experience both in historical America and its oft-proclaimed, enlightened present.[1] Specifically, the study of African American culture inevitably leads us to a consideration of

"The Pot Liquor Principle: Developing a Black Music Criticism in American Music Studies," *American Music* 22, no. 2 (Summer 2004): 284–95. This essay grew from a conference paper for the International Association of Music Libraries, Archives and Documentation Centres at Berkeley, California, in 2002. The session was entitled "Disciplining American Music: Issues Affecting Scholars, Teachers, and Librarians."

the idea of race and its trusty companion, racism. As Wahneema Lubiano has argued, the structures and operations of these two have acted as "a distorting prism" through which the United States citizenry could "imagine itself functioning as a moral and just people while ignoring the widespread devastation directed at black Americans particularly, but at a much larger number of people generally."[2]

As an African American scholar of American music, discussing and sometimes even thinking about such issues in the professional realm can be an agonizing experience. In addition to the fact that race and racism constantly impact my life in particular ways, there are other reasons for my anxiousness. First, music scholarship has traditionally shied away from directly confronting or even acknowledging some of the uglier aspects of human nature, opting instead to concentrate on the beautiful. Indeed, the world of music seems to provide a convenient shelter, a vagary from the struggles of everyday existence. In fact, until quite recently music had been studied by music scholars as an artistic endeavor that, in the words of Richard Leppert and Susan McClary, "shapes itself in accordance with self-contained, abstract principles that are unrelated to the outside social world."[3]

But after the "cultural revolution" (of sorts) that occurred in my home discipline of musicology during the 1980s and 1990s, something changed. The outside world rushed in, bringing with it a critique of artistic autonomy and new and penetrating methodologies applied to repertoires that were at one time deemed unworthy of serious study. These developments rumbled through the "Americanist" wing of music scholarship with a particular force. Topics of all stripes in American music, especially jazz, gradually became popular choices among graduate students. As early as 1975 the field saw the establishment of the Sonneck Society for American Music (now called the Society for American Music, or SAM). In 1983 SAM established a scholarly journal named *American Music*. Three years prior, the Institute for Research in Black American Music at Fisk University (now called the Center for Black Music Research at Columbia College, Chicago) began publishing *Black Music Research Journal*, which established a new scholarly outlet for work on all musical styles from the diaspora.

Yet, for all of this important activity, neither American nor African American music studies (separated here for the sake of argument) has fully established a level of criticism that does justice to the complexity of these respective topics, notwithstanding some impressive, isolated efforts.[4] As I have written elsewhere, I suspect that the critiques of black culture that already exist in other disciplines will appear with greater frequency in American music studies when a critical mass of black scholars becomes part of the mix and participates as a full partner in its development.[5] Why? Because I believe that the theorized social experiences of black critics (and audiences, too, for that matter) need to form an integral component of the emerging profile of black music criticism. And because of the close, interdependent relationship existing between American and African American topics, such a criticism would necessarily transform American music studies.

Fortunately, models for this kind of criticism already exist. The appearance and growth of feminist and gay and lesbian critiques of culture in musicology have demonstrated that voices from "the margins" can invigorate a discipline. And we have witnessed over the last decade or so the appearance of several essay collections that chart new theoretical directions for music criticism. For the most part, the focus of this body of work is the Western art music tradition.[6] There are several reasons for this limitation, in my view. First, scholars interested in deconstructing the canons and ideologies that have gotten us in our present-day pickle of musical hegemony can have a field day on the discourses surrounding Western art music. Centuries of documentation have left us a long paper trail of theories, facts, and figures showing how certain social orders have been established, maintained, and exported through the years. We can rest assured that any music scholar working today has been thoroughly indoctrinated in these preciously held discourses. Their ubiquitous state has made them important targets for the "brush clearing" that usually accompanies dramatic paradigm shifts such as the one we have experienced recently. With the structures of domination so obvious, so carefully archived, and so well known, feminist and gay and lesbian scholars could make visible the ideologies that have subjugated or erased them and then erect new ways to write themselves into history and interpret their own cultural expressions.

Thus, what we find in these developments is new emphases on "idiotheory," that is, on critical thinking that was established within and emanated from communities considered "different" or subaltern. These theories have been made possible by the new visibility of these minorities (and I certainly use this term advisedly) in academia, groups that have shown the importance of everyday living—or social experience—to the study of so-called art. Furthermore, these developments have been made possible and have taken flight primarily, but not solely, because of the efforts of a critical mass of scholars who claim membership in these respective communities.

One of the more dramatic aspects of these new methods of inquiry has been the self-conscious acknowledgment of the critical "Self" in contemporary theories. This development has opened up new ways to explain musical difference. It also has helped us to see how music can work as an important mode of representation, community building, and identification among all groups of people. While these interventions have not been institutionalized thoroughly—there are still naysayers (or "haters" in African American colloquial terms)—the order of things has changed in many regards. These critiques have greatly enhanced our knowledge and, indeed, the power and relevance of canonical repertoires and other kinds of musical practices. Taking my lead from these new methods and some of their accompanying politics, I'd like now to explore some issues raised by the establishment of a black music criticism within the context of American music studies. What are some of the specific intellectual and methodological questions that need vetting before a black music criticism will succeed as others have?

An important issue at hand here concerns the maligned notion of essentialism in black critical discourse. In today's academic climate it has become fashionable—in fact, downright honorable and politically correct—to identify and then denounce essentialism as part of a cluster of racist ideologies that have aided in the subjugation of scores of groups throughout history and all over the world. But, in my view, not all notions of essentialism need to be considered racist per se; some exist as powerful displays of human agency, intention, and culture building.

Certainly, to claim that one group or another possesses qualities or traits that are essential to that group's "nature" forwards dangerous stereotypes about its behaviors, worldviews, collective intellectual potential, and so on. Such ideologies have had staggering and adverse effects for all involved, and cultural critics have spilled much ink identifying them. But, on the flip side, all communities have well-formed ideas about who they are in the world and what behaviors, worldviews, and cultural practices define them best. Furthermore, as the late Philip Brett argued in an article titled "Musicality, Essentialism, and the Closet," dominant culture has a tendency "to project itself onto everything it encounters and to assimilate everything to its own idea of itself . . . instead [of] valuing, exploring, and trying to understand different things, people, and ideas, in terms that are closer to the way in which they perceive themselves."[7]

Without question, critiques of essentialism (or anti-essentialism) have achieved a lot of moral good. But I wonder if the dismissal of ethnic (or, better, social) particularity in cultural criticism leaves us with an undesirable, universalistic blandness that refuses true cultural difference. Allow me to expand on my views here by way of a creative analogy. Pot liquor, for those who are not familiar with it, is the liquid base of many southern dishes. It provides the juice in the variety of beans and greens dishes that my southern-born and -raised mother cooked almost daily. As pot liquor is appreciated by connoisseurs of this style of cuisine as a rich source of flavor or essence, so, too, has the black muse functioned in American society. In my view, there is a fundamental problem with some of the theories of anti-essentialism circulating in today's cultural studies of minority groups. Our efforts to "de-essentialize" our thinking about culture sometimes results in our draining in-group sensibility of what makes it a good thing. If we take away the "essence" or flavor, what remains is a pot of sustenance with some nutritional value but nothing you can sop up with your cornbread. Nobody asks for pot liquor specifically, but it's understood as necessary and desirable.

Despite the influence and importance of queer and feminist musicology, black music research has seemed to move along another track. As I have already stated, the lack of a critical mass of black scholars in the music disciplines has influenced the trajectory of black music studies. The foundation of black music research's modern profile dates back to the same moment of radicalism in American history that inspired the feminist and queer movements, namely the late 1960s. The methods within the resulting bodies of academic criticism have moved beyond what some have called the compensatory history work, activities that unearthed knowledge about people, viewpoints, and musical works that had previously been silenced. With the initial spadework done, feminist musicology began to theorize gender as a unit of analysis in its research in order to understand how it shaped musical discourse and, in turn, how music shapes our experience of it. Likewise, we can only move closer toward institutionalizing a contemporary black music criticism by first getting beyond the compensatory model of research. We can then push off into the challenging, choppier waters of theorizing blackness but with the well-seasoned substance of rich pot liquor that makes overcooked legumes and vegetables such a satisfying meal.

A criticism of black music explains the cultural work that music performs in the social world. It seeks to understand what various styles and gestures mean and how they generate and achieve a signifying effect. It identifies a work's most important musical gestures and then positions them within a broader field of musical conventions. These conventions can then be theorized into broader systems of cultural knowledge (e.g., the historical contexts in which a musical style appeared and the lived experiences of audiences and musicians).[8] But black music research has been generally a somewhat conservative enterprise through the years, drawing any "radical" profile from the subaltern status of blackness in American society at large, and not from dramatic shifts in theoretical or methodological intervention. The unspoken mantra seemed to be "let's work within the paradigms of the discipline in order to establish our place in academic discourse. Get in the boat, but don't rock it." Moreover, identity politics have been practically nonexistent in this research. By comparison, forceful currents of theoretical activity have marked black literary studies. Passionate debates filled scholarly journals with interesting, heartfelt arguments about what tools of analysis might be best applied to this body of literature. And these efforts were nothing if not self-reflexive. What keeps black music research from moving full throttle into this mode?

Fortunately, in the last few years we have seen the appearance of work that provides some direction for these kinds of interventions, most notably Samuel Floyd's *The Power of Black Music* and Ronald Radano's recent series of essays that will soon culminate in a much-anticipated book-length study. Floyd's work uses methodology from black literary theory and African American history. Radano's work fits more squarely in cultural studies.[9] These works are representative of two ways of thinking about "theory" in black music studies. In the future I plan a more extensive comparison of the intellectual camps from which these works proceed. For now, it suffices to say that the black Subject in Floyd's work seems to grow out of the ideologies of the 1960s and 1970s black power movement. Radano's appears to grow out of the post–black power movement and poststructuralist critiques of black subjectivity and other forms of identity.

We might characterize this subtle difference with the help of the term "social construction." Briefly, the intellectual thrust of this term has worked to (1) destabilize hegemonic ideologies by making various forms of domination less "natural"; (2) emphasize the contingency of knowledge and value; and (3) explain the "imagined" nature of what populist thought has passed off as "ancient" and permanent. Even identity is considered one of the by-products of systems and structures beyond the control of historical actors. If Radano's work, like other poststructuralist research, privileges the "construction" component of the social construction equation, Floyd's is more focused on the "social," or on who groups of people agree that they are in the world. Again, this difference is subtle. We'll need public, printed debate that explores the tension between these two before we can achieve a better understanding of blackness as a unit of analysis in American music scholarship.

A criticism that centers the social experiences of race and racism in America will necessarily take the field of American music studies in directions that many may simply not want to go, because it will be grounded in some of the struggles of the everyday. Indeed, some of these experiences will shatter what Wahneema Lubiano, in the quotation cited at the beginning of this chapter, called the "distorting prism" of the American public imaginary. As a case in point, allow me to recount an experience that I find relevant to the present discussion of the social experience of race, especially as it relates to the rather intense refashioning of American identity due to recent horrific events.

On December 29, 2001, almost four months following the infamous 9/11 attacks on the United States, I experienced something that will forever shape my reactions to that horrible act of terrorism and my academic reflections on race and cultural analysis in America. At approximately 6:45 in the morning, while I was driving my teenage son and his teammate to a track meet, I avoided a head-on collision with a small sedan with tinted windows by turning abruptly into a one-way street and stopping suddenly. A Philadelphia policeman, who confused his original prey with my passengers and me, was, it turns out, chasing the sedan. Before I could process what was taking place, we were all looking down the barrel of the policeman's cocked weapon and being ordered to hold our hands outside the car windows. I heard the words "three black male suspects" among the officer's insistent request for backup and his almost out-of-control commands for us to maintain our submissive positions. Within seconds we were surrounded by other squad cars, more cops, more guns, and a swirl of other sights and sounds that overwhelmed my senses, causing my heart to pound through my chest with enough force to cause my breathing to be labored.

As I lay facedown on the cement seven blocks from home, one block from my children's Catholic school, and eight blocks from the Ivy League campus that employs me, my wrists were tightly secured behind me with handcuffs. A large officer's knee pressed the small of my back as another one interrogated me, claiming that he had chased me at high speeds down another street a few minutes prior. My young passengers, both standout athletes in football and track and routinely touted by local sports journalists as among the area's best, endured similar treatment. The more that I insisted that this was a mistake, that they had the wrong men in the wrong car, the louder and angrier the young—and, by the way, black—male officer became, threatening that if I didn't come clean with a confession my troubles had only begun. My denials expressed in the most articulate, measured tones that I could muster seemed to be making this unthinkable nightmare worse. Then I uttered four magical words that turned the tables and ended the state-sponsored terrorism we were experiencing.

"I'm a Penn professor," I stated. This, it turns out, was the big joker in my sorry deck of cards. What my BMW, fresh-faced, clean-cut passengers, and larger-than-what- is-necessary-for-everyday-existence "can't you tell I'm pedigreed" vocabulary couldn't accomplish, a red, white, and blue piece of plastic achieved. When they took my Penn ID out of my wallet and determined its validity, my sense of terror began to subside. For the first time in our verbal exchange the officers began to treat me like a citizen in the land of my birth, on the street where I had purchased a larger-than-what-is-necessary-for-everyday-existence home. As their blunder became more apparent, the officers called my house and asked my wife—

an accessory that I had unfortunately left home without—what time I had departed. (Black men in America with middle-class aspirations learn early to accessorize carefully—kids, wife, tie, attaché, glasses, and so on—if they don't want to be confused with the criminal element.) My wife's brief explanation confirmed my account, and an uneasy tension wiped across the faces of all the officers present. We were soon set free.

I am determined to reject the conventional wisdom of academia that would encourage me to purge such experiences from my thinking when it comes to doing my "real work." This unspoken mantra is especially problematic as I consider what it means to use race as a unit of analysis in my work on African American music. The post-9/11 world has seen many of the world's unsettled issues pushed to the forefront of the popular sphere and public culture. We now understand (or should) that we ignore the world's so-called hotspots at our own peril. They are not just somewhere over there. We know now that angry chickens will surely come home to roost. What we still fail to realize, however, is that some of these problems exist in our own backyards, city streets, spacious skies, purple mountain majesties, and amber waves of grain.

It may seem at first consideration that events like those of 9/11 and my personal experience with Philadelphia's finest are unlikely to inform in a useful manner the way in which I go about the daily work of musical analysis. I beg to differ. Such social matters are always mediating one's intellectual life, whether these connections are explicitly stated or not. It is my contention that the social experiences of critics and audiences do matter and should be considered an important component of the profile of cultural analysis. But how does this help us theoretically?

Presently, I think about the myriad ideas concerning race as clustering around three primary streams, which I divide into social race, cultural race, and discursive race. Social race constitutes the lived experience of race in the everyday realm. As work such as Radano's and Bohlman's *Music and the Racial Imagination* shows us, this experience is contingent on many factors, including geographic location and historical moment, among others. And this social experience of race exerts great influence over how and where we educate our children, worship, recreate, and so on. I should point out that I believe I am thinking differently about "social race" than what is captured by the term "social construction," the latter of which is very familiar to many academics. Cutting to the chase, I believe that there has been much more emphasis on the "construction" or "invention" component of this equation than on the social. While I recognize the inventive nature of the practice of identity and community building, I also insist that it is important to keep central the socially agreed-upon ideas about who individuals and groups believe they are in the world. And these ideas are, in fact, more real in the social sense than their "constructed-ness."

Cultural race concerns, in my view, the explicitly performative and expressive realm of the social experience. These compelling performed gestures (be they acted out in speech, music, and dance) allow our social identities a kind of materiality. Of course, the thorny issues of ownership, borrowing, and even stealing abound in the cultural realm, especially when our stubborn ideals about how social identity and cultural performance should somehow "match up" are contradicted or compromised.

My third category, discursive race, is of recent vintage and comprises the densely theoretical, postmodern exegesis of race. I consider these explorations to be as constructed and invented as any other cultural expression. Thus, we can ask the same kinds of questions of this particular academic practice as we can of any other performative gesture. We can ask, for example, what cultural work are these theories doing for their audiences and practitioners? An overt concern embedded in discursive race has been the dismantling of the notion of essentialism, the idea that groups of people are biologically endowed with specific attributes. I want to argue, however, that some of what has been dismissed as essentialism has been part of the very practices that provide groups with their deepest sense of pleasure, accomplishment, and psychic and social well-being, not to mention counter-hegemonic relief. The effort to dismantle essentialist thinking is laudable and politically noble for the most part. Essentialism, of course, has a long history in Western thought. It has operated as an important component of what Radano and Bohlman call the "racial imagination," a concept that they define "as the shifting matrix of ideological construction of difference associated with body type and color that have emerged as part of the discourse network of modernity."[10]

But not all definitions of essentialism so clearly differentiate between the social and the biological. In fact, most collapse social ideas with the biological and, as a result, do great harm to the cause of cultural equity that many cultural critics claim to champion. And it is here that I see the greatest danger in any theory that does not keep central the social experiences of race like the kind that I recounted above. If a theory of any cultural practice doesn't grow out of a specific context of domination and resistance; if it doesn't center the social realities of real historical actors; if it promotes master narratives that attempt to explain all difference, what humanistic or even political good is it? If discursive race eclipses and flattens out social race, if it seeks to make cultural race practices homogenous, I wonder if it might not become a discourse about itself and not about real people's actions in the world.

So where does all this leave us in our exploration of the role of black music criticism in American music studies? One legitimate concern among more socially conscious scholars is that the development of one more microtheory in the field will only divide Americanists into fiefdoms that are uninterested in the kinds of dialogue that will enrich the discipline. On the contrary, I believe that such a development (and the dialogue that it will certainly encourage) can only enhance our understanding of American music generally. The key is that we need to have true dialogue, which is to say that voices that are generally not heard must be afforded a space to speak. We will collectively, however, have to confront what I believe is a fear of the "black Other" within the scholarly musical community. (How else can we explain the voluminous contributions of African Americans to this country's musical profile and the embarrassingly small number of black music scholars in the ranks of our profession?) Why is it that the words "black musicology" (indeed a strange collision of terms and signs even to my ears) will probably never be employed in the field in the same way that "feminist musicology" or "gay and lesbian musicology" is today?

To those who believe that the kind of attention to the specifics of African American musical culture and its criticism that I am proposing here will estrange rather than unify us, I beg to differ. It can only increase exponentially the unfinished cultural conversations that have characterized the growth of American society since its inception. As Marcia Citron has argued, "Instead of limiting interpretive possibilities, specificity yields multiplicity, multiplicity in the number of theoretical models and in the kinds of responses that follow those models."[11]

I return to my pot liquor analogy one more time. When I announced the title of my talk, "The Pot Liquor Principle: Theory, Method, and Essence in Black Music Studies," to fellow panelists at a recent conference, Dale Cockrell, my steady-handed, white, and southern-raised comrade in the Americanist foxhole wrote in a personal correspondence:

Hey Guy,

For me, pot liquor was specific to the juice off the turnip greens, always to be consumed with cornbread (which turned a sickly, washed-out green when dunked in the pot liquor). Ah, how far we come (or go): I now prefer my turnip greens parboiled quickly (to retain texture and color), then sautéed in olive oil, garlic and seasoned. Cornbread is still de rigueur, though. (And then, sometimes, I'll cook it for hours with saltback, and it's still good . . .) And you?

What I believed was a specific gesture toward African American culture turned into an exchange that demonstrated a shared culture across region, race, and recipe. My vernacular revelation and Cockrell's response and query open dialogue rather than shutting it down. This serendipitous model—albeit unpretentious—can serve as one (of many) road maps toward a future in which an emergent black musical criticism might help this country square in a small way its lofty, pluralistic ideals with its day-to-day realities.

4 Secrets, Lies, and Transcriptions

NEW REVISIONS ON RACE, BLACK MUSIC, AND CULTURE

Here is what race means. Race is a socially constructed process that produces subordinate and superordinate groups. Racial stratification is the key social process behind racial classifications. The meaning of race depends on the social conditions in which it exists.

Tukufu Zuberi, *Thicker Than Blood: How Racial Statistics Lie*

Searching for the historical essence of black music leads not to a primordial nature but to the second nature of the public sphere, as myths of presence give way to modern representations of blackness as swing, soul, funk, and groove. It is this instability of difference that grants to African-America its special, seemingly miraculous musical power. And it is this same difference that continues to baffle and confuse an American populace still convinced that the blackness and whiteness of sound is fundamentally, essentially, real. The whole, authentic truth of black music becomes but a lie, a social narrative that ascribes difference in order to repress subtexts fundamentally resonant in black and white.

Ronald Radano, *Lying up a Nation: Race and Black Music*

"Secrets, Lies, and Transcriptions: New Revisions on Race, Black Music, and Culture," in *Western Music and Racial Discourses (1883–1933)*, ed. Julie Brown (Cambridge: Cambridge University Press, 2007), 24–36. This essay grew from a paper delivered at the conference "Western Music and Racial Discourses, 1883–1933," which took place at the Institute of Romance Studies, University of London, in 2002.

In his study of the black spiritual, *Culture on the Margins: The Black Spiritual and the Rise of American Cultural Interpretation,* Jon Cruz notes that as early as 1845, the year that Frederick Douglass's autobiography was published, the latter had admonished his readers to listen to the spirituals because within these "songs of sorrow" existed a strong indictment against the institution of chattel slavery. Cruz argues that as abolitionists and other proponents of human rights began to value black music as expressed in the genre of the spirituals, they also began to identify with the slaves as modern subjects. This heightened interest in the slaves and their music was part of a larger, powerful cultural current that he calls "ethnosympathy," his term to describe "the new humanitarian pursuit of the inner world of distinctive and collectively classifiable subjects."[1]

This new interest in black subjectivity was linked to other developments in the human sciences. In a groundbreaking study provocatively titled *Thicker Than Blood: How Racial Statistics Lie,* Tukufu Zuberi, a sociologist and demographer, reveals how the quite biased cultural work of "objective" statistical data became particularly important in both the world of science and the ambitious chore of sociopolitical domination. Rooted in the fifteenth-century expansion of European nations, race's association with biological differences was cemented in the late nineteenth century. Linked to the economics of imperialism and the racialization of colonialism and slavery, the supposed biological basis of race was a relatively new idea that profoundly shaped America's socioeconomic history.[2] It was soon keenly felt in cultural production, especially in the area of music.

If European imperialism was made possible by Europe's superior ships and cannons, then riff, rhythm, and repetition became both gifts and curses in the cultural politics of liberation and subjugation of the African American descendants of enslaved Africans. Along the historical trajectory between early European scientific classifications of human populations and the "naturalized" notion of white supremacy there existed many debates and paradigm shifts.[3] And surely we see the traces of these conversations every time we read a music trade journal such as *Billboard, Variety, DownBeat,* or *Metronome,* in which broad musical categories, genres, and substyles often reflect, and in fact inform, racial logic in the social world.[4]

This chapter considers recent strides in research on black musical culture from the mid- to late nineteenth century up to the 1930s, focusing on how different ideas about "race" are treated in each. As the twentieth century drew to a close, the 1990s witnessed the questioning and complication of our "common sense" attitudes about race, especially among academics. Scholars created new ways to discuss the dialogic nature of racial identity and forever changed how we talk about race in the contemporary moment.[5] These new approaches to race and African American culture and its interpretation have begun to reorder our view of key historical events, movements, figures, and cultural practices.

Collectively, the research under discussion here pushes race discourse in exciting new directions through interventions on several fronts. It explains, among other issues, the strained relationship between late nineteenth-century notions of black uplift and the so-called vernacular musical arts. This work also underscores the importance of the appearance in American culture of the Negro spiritual specifically, reflecting on the processes that it underwent to become an index of the cultural and social consciousness of African American culture and that of the larger communities into which it was disseminated, and how they came to be both celebrated and disparaged. Furthermore, it brings into high relief how the "objective" thrust of scientific investigation has affected the study of African American music historically, from the spirituals to jazz. In fact, attitudes about the nineteenth-century spirituals carried over to that of later musical forms of early twentieth-century black music such as jazz. As we will learn, the philosopher Alain Locke has emerged as a key transitional figure in contemporary cultural criticism because of the new light being shed on his views of black culture in the early twentieth century. As a bridge scholar between the spirituals and jazz, one who discussed both genres, Locke cleared space for the latter's new pedigree as America's classical music on the one hand, and the notion that black music provided a window into the souls of black folk on the other. Moreover, the acts of notating and recording the spirituals were mediations of black culture that played important roles in the rise of African American music in the American social consciousness.

Robin D. G. Kelley has written about the 1960s as a time when social scientists converged en masse in urban ghettos in search of a real and authentic black culture that could be explained in measurable terms. What cultural practices these ethnographers "discovered," however, were more often than not reduced and described as coping mechanisms and survival strategies.[6] Indeed, as I stated above, this search for authentic blackness had begun almost a century before, at a time that also marked major shifts in American intellectualism. Cultural practices such as music—particularly the slave song—invited new sites for scientific, objective inquiries into the souls of black folk. "Their songs," Cruz writes, "were to be grasped as testimonies to their lives, as indices of their sense of social fate."[7] Importantly, this view of black song would eclipse the political potency of the literary protest embedded in the slave narratives. The freshly discovered, newly aestheticized, and selected-out black spirituals emerged as a powerful vehicle in the Negro liberation struggle. It became a singing testament that would be celebrated as a passage into the secrets of blackness, a blackness that, at the same time, began to inform America's emerging sense of its own national identity beyond that of a cultural colony of Europe.

One of the most dramatic, transformative gestures during this dynamic process comprised the act of transcribing the spirituals. The spiritual's move from oral expression to literary representation constituted a large symbolic leap and held many consequences beyond the spiritual's accessibility and mass mediation within the larger public sphere. In written form, the spiritual became "increasingly considered as a modern scientific artifact, a specimen fit for capture by the spreading nets of an emergent ethnoscience."[8] Through this new modality, the spirituals' cultural work in American society musically affirmed black humanity on the margins of society. At the same time, this body of song also served the interests of a modernist scientific impulse to classify and objectify racialized people and their attendant cultural artifacts.

As I have written elsewhere, James Monroe Trotter's 1878 study of nineteenth-century black music, *Music and Some Highly Musical People*—the first of its kind by an African American writer—demonstrates this desire to write blackness into the consciousness of both the nation and modernity through the discourse of science. He writes in the book's unnumbered opening page, "The collection is given in order to complete the author's purpose, which is not only to show the proficiency of the subjects of the foregoing sketches as interpreters of the music of others, but, further, to illustrate the ability of quite a number of them (and relatively, that of their race) to originate and scientifically arrange good music."[9] One certainly gets the message in all of this that (oral) songs did not become "music" until they were presented in written form. Although Trotter recognized as important "orally transmitted racial music," he clearly prioritizes the written Western art-music tradition, as many of his fellow black intellectuals did.

The space between musical orality and musical literacy is a powerful one and has analogies in other domains of knowledge. Music historian Gary Tomlinson has recently summarized the historical development of the twin quasi-disciplines of ethnography and historiography, and this work can help us understand the spiritual's journey from musical orality to literacy. Tomlinson has argued, for example, that musical practice itself can help us understand the differences and similarities between anthropology and history as disciplines. He opens with a summary of Michel de Certeau's ideas on orality and literacy:

> Where ethnography has taken as its object *orality*, historiography scrutinizes *written* traces; where the one has wanted to describe an atemporal *space* of culture, the other follows change through *time;* the one starts from a gesture of radical estrangement and *alterity*, the other from an assumption of transparent *identity;* the first analyzes collective phenomena of a cultural *unconscious*, the second the *consciousness* of historical self-knowledge.[10]

These distinctions and oppositions cut a number of ways and have major implications for music study. Tomlinson insists, for example, that we rethink the commonplace view of musicology's "birth" dating to the mid-nineteenth century. Rather, he extends it back a century, when the presence of *singing* stood "at the heart of eighteenth-century accounts of the history of European society, of Europe's relation to other societies, and indeed of the origins of all societies."[11] Singing or song existed as a category of music making that linked Europe to its unlettered Others. Gradually, however, between 1750 and 1850, a modern conception of music emerged in Europe, one that was considered aesthetically superior to song. "Music", Tomlinson argues, "lodged itself at the heart of a discourse that pried

Europe and its histories apart from non-European lives and cultures." He continues, "Perched at the apex of the new aesthetics, it came to function as a kind of limit-case of European uniqueness in world history and an affirmation of the gap, with the cultural formation of modernity, between history and anthropology. Music, in this sense, silenced many non-European activities that it might instead have attended to."[12]

The new conception of music included two important and related developments: the rise and privileging of virtuoso instrumentalism and the advancement of the written musical representation thereof. The perceived power of instrumental music peaked over the course of the nineteenth century, and this development was coupled with new views about music's ability to transcend its social setting, instrumental music's nonmimetic expressive capacities, the musical work's perceived fixity and discreteness in notation, and "even a revising of the human subject that perceived all these things."[13] For my present purposes, these observations have enormous import for the Negro spiritual and subsequent black music making in America.

As it did for the new conception of music in European history, the act of notating the Negro spiritual carried out some important cultural work. If notation served to detach or abstract music from its original contexts, then it could be argued that the spirituals' notated form divorced them from black culture. While this may be too severe a view, this move from orality to literacy did impact how observers perceived their access into black culture, albeit an idea of black culture that conformed to the goals of the protoethnographers fascinated by them. According to Tomlinson:

> The notated work took on almost magical characteristics, projecting spirit outward in legible form, and traversing the distance between musical exegete and composer. The search for the secrets of this written work could in large degree ignore and thus conceal the social interactions of performers and audience at the scene itself of music making.[14]

This "black music without the black folk" magic was a complicated matter, indeed. In fact, the search for the secrets of blackness in the spirituals whispered through a notated score seemed to encourage the transcribers to "overcode" them with meanings that were, in Cruz's view, embedded in the ethnographers' religious frameworks and political agendas if not always in those of the performers themselves. (We have certainly witnessed this development in subsequent genres and historical moments.) Despite the costs of such an abstraction, the act helped to move African Americans from objects of history to bona fide subjects in the American consciousness. Indeed, the desire to "advance" African Americans through the creation of authoritative texts and artifacts that could be unperformed yet comprehended solely from their notation situated their new modernity in strictly Eurocentric terms, and in some of the same terms that had earlier separated Europeans from their "simply" singing non-European global neighbors. With one gesture of the pen, untutored orality becomes lettered culture, space becomes disciplined identity, cultural unconsciousness becomes historical consciousness. Black music would continue this crucial role in African American cultural politics throughout the next century and beyond.

If Cruz explains how the "discovery" of the Negro spiritual shaped the course of American intellectual history, and Zuberi has documented the crucial role of racial stratification in the development of social "objective" science, then Ronald Radano in his exhaustive study *Lying up a Nation: Race and Black Music* adds yet another dimension to this historical moment. Radano argues that the very idea of black music is constitutive of the broader idea of race itself in American history. In fact, his discussion of black music's emergence challenges—with more than a hint of revisionist zeal—the idea that modern black music extends solely from the traditional impulses of a singular black mainstream. Radano's work defies "those strategies of containment that uphold the racial binaries informing the interpretation of black music. It goes against the grain of a pervasive, yet remarkably underanalyzed, assumption that correlates an enduring black music presence with the myth of a consistent and stable socio-racial position of 'blackness.'"[15]

In Radano's view, African American music is a modern construction of many racialist discourses that clustered together, gathered steam, and culminated in its contemporary form around 1900. Black music has been inextricably linked to our understanding of "blackness" writ large—as a knowable, learnable, and teachable fact of social reality and identity. He believes that this identity has been largely dependent on the aforementioned musical developments. With these arguments, Radano calls for a reinterpretation of contemporary black musical forms, indeed, a radical rehearing acquired from a new set of subversive listening skills. These are tall orders.

How does he begin to convince us? He begins with a lie. Drawing on the ethnographic work of Zora Neale Hurston as set out in her *Mules and Men*, Radano relates a story, one that inspired both the title and intellectual license for his study. Hurston wrote in her 1935 study that as she moved about her native Eatonville, Florida, rural community collecting stories and other data, the citizens told what they called "lies."

They were not literal lies but, rather, creative expressions of poetic license—allegories that celebrated the ironic twists of fate giving substance and texture to the art of southern black living. The better the story, the better the lie; the better the lie, the closer one gets to the ironic pleasures and terror of America's racial sublime. In an opening sequence Hurston, standing back uncharacteristically from the text, requests a story from her friend, George Thomas. Thomas replies matter-of-factly, "Zora, you come to de right place if lies is what you want. Ah'm gointer lie up a nation."[16]

Radano's account, an epic act of signifyin(g) and speculation on the very idea of black music in the white, public consciousness, argues for a mulatto understanding of African American culture in much the same spirit that Albert Murray did in his classic *The Omni-Americans* in 1970. American racial consciousness by its very nature, however, has produced a conflicted affect for black music (or Negro music, as it was known earlier). It developed together with American notions of racial difference—as a way to subjugate black humanity and as a way for black Americans themselves to express a musical identity. Thus, nineteenth-century black music represented much more than just sound—or noise, for that matter. It became an audible index of many ideas about race, cultural politics, and national identity. Indeed, we have learned that black music has comprised the soundtrack for the dance of an emerging American cultural identity, signifying "both the integrationist completion of a nation as well as a racial threat to the integrity of whiteness."[17] In the acts of notating the spirituals, in the contemporaneous statistical verification of racial differences, and in the very idea of black music itself, we see several important issues surfacing. They were embedded in nineteenth-century cultural politics, religious ideologies, and racialist discourses, all of which carried many implications for the subsequent development and reception history of African American music throughout the next century and beyond.

The first thirty years of the twentieth century saw a hurricane of creative and scholarly activities that moved African Americans from behind the Du Boisian veil and into modern life. These publishing, musical, and entrepreneurial activities were anything but uniform and monotone; they embodied myriad angles, positions, and propositions. As a period witnessing the inauguration of the African American literary criticism tradition, writers defined the moment with pointed debates about the use of black literature as cultural propaganda and argued publicly not only about the nature of black creativity but also about its relationship to African American subjectivity. Music also figured prominently during this time, and all manner of music making and related activities characterized these pivotal years: from Western art music to the blues, from the collection and transcription of folk music to the development of nonpatronizing stances in criticism and cultural interpretation.

All of this work sought to discipline the black muse even as it documented various moments in Afro-Americana's rise from the outhouse of presumed primitive origins to the big house of modernity. The hands, hearts, and pens of the "talented tenth" members of "the Race" held the belief that intersections with mainstream culture could transform black vernacular music into something worthy of the skeptical white (and black) aristocratic gaze. Or so they hoped.

Of the musical styles that grew from the cultures of Afro-Americana, jazz has inspired the most extensive scholarly attention to date. Beginning with early twentieth-century record-collecting enthusiasts seeking to impose order on an exploding and eclectic discography, the field of jazz studies (as it is now called) is today in the vanguard of academic enquiries into American culture.[18] This new field attracts scholars from many disciplines, including the "musicologies" (ethnomusicology, musicology, and music theory), American studies, history, cultural studies, and sociology, among others. The energy created by this interdisciplinary activity has inspired the feeling among many observers that jazz represents the quintessential American expression, America's classical music, indeed, the country's only true art form.

The historical grounding of this new pedigree of jazz and its study can be traced back to the 1920s and 1930s, when a confluence of discourses converged in heated debates about the future of African Americans and their culture. As the historian and cultural critic Eric Porter has recently argued, writers and musicians such as James Weldon Johnson were faced in this moment with a conundrum. The debates surrounding the supposed biological or cultural racial distinctiveness of black Americans created something of a crisis. Indeed, settling the thorny question of nature versus nurture in African American culture has become an important concern throughout the history of jazz studies. It is useful to revisit this historical moment in light of recent developments in scholarship because it highlights a shift concerning the cultural work of "race."

In his intellectual history of jazz titled *What Is This Thing Called Jazz?*, Porter provides a virtuoso portrait of the 1920s jazz world, a bustling scene in which he depicts African American musicians as self-consciously participating in the struggles over black representation and social advancement.[19] He charts, for example, an emerging sense of modernity among African Americans themselves, not simply as historical actors unwillingly swept up in a tide of social events but as astute social agents with specific ideas about where they and their creations fit into the larger scheme of things. Musicians such as Duke Ellington, W. C. Handy, James Reese Europe, James Weldon Johnson, and Louis Armstrong together with the writers W. E. B. Du Bois, Zora Neale Hurston, Joel A. Rodgers, Dave Peyton, and Alain Locke, among others, struggled over some of the pressing issues of the day: most prominent among them, racial uplift on the one hand and the shaking of black (and white) bottoms on the other.[20]

The contested space between "uplift" and "get down" existed as a continuum between two poles. At one end rested the idea that African American achievements within the forms and techniques of Western European music culture would somehow vindicate black citizens within American society and the world. At the other end stood the belief that black music could serve to distinguish black culture from the rest of the nation. While it may be an exaggeration to assert that every musician composed and performed in a heightened state of politicized and racialized identity awareness, Porter convincingly paints a portrait of musicians aware that they were involved in deliberate negotiations of their social world through their creative work. They wanted to make a difference. As Porter argues, "Making sense of jazz often involved a struggle, for various political and ideological reasons, to elevate the music as a black expression in spite of, or in response to, its precarious place in American life. These debates about music were also a pointed commentary about the liberating and constraining aspects of racial thinking in a segregated, racist society."[21] Indeed, black music in general, and jazz in particular, represented key figures in racialist discussions throughout the twentieth century with little sign of abating.

Modernism—or, better, "Afro-modernism," as I have called it elsewhere—was a central issue of the Harlem Renaissance, a moment in African American history self-consciously entrenched in the "culture as capital" debates of the early twentieth century.[22] Key writers emerged as leaders in this eclectic movement. In *Deep River: Music and Memory in Harlem Renaissance Thought,* Paul Anderson portrays the person who is considered its leading architect, Alain Locke, a writer best known for his editorship of *The New Negro* (1925).[23] As a black intellectual embodying a complex and shifting set of values throughout his career, Locke cuts a fascinating figure. In my earlier work, I, along with many others, believed that Locke's views on culture were simply Eurocentric. Anderson, however, clears the way for other interpretations of Locke's work. This repositioning of Locke and other writers of the period through the lens of black music and social memory allows us to see Locke's vision in all of its nuance and as an important precursor to contemporary black cultural criticism.

Locke emerges as a transitional black intellectual. As a direct heir of the ethno-sympathy strain of the spirituals' transcribers, he took the idea that one could understand the people through their music but coupled it with very strict views about the relative value of oral music and the written, arranged spirituals. Thus he, like his earlier counterparts, privileged the written, more "modern" renditions of these songs. Furthermore, while he did believe that jazz was a valuable, though raw, musical form, the vernacular music ironically achieved what Locke wanted for black classical music: prestige and currency in America's cultural profile.

Jazz's pedigree grew from several conflicting, though sometimes related, discourses. In addition to the view held by Locke, Anderson describes how many white intellectuals of the period invested in jazz with what he calls "a countercultural aura of erotic liberation."[24] And a younger generation of black intellectuals represented by the writers Langston Hughes and Zora Neale Hurston, who eschewed both of these views, argued instead for the self-sufficient relevance of popular music such as blues, jazz, and the core-culture Negro spirituals. Thus, three views prevailed. One belief—that black folk music was best expressed in the trappings of modernist concert music—has been most typically linked to Locke. Another view privileged the white gaze of primitivism from the outside in. And the third dispelled both the cultural evolutionary model of the first and the romanticized "noble savage" ideal of the second, opting instead for a self-satisfied celebration of the everyday blackness of the proletariat. In practice, however, none of these views stood in complete opposition to one another, as Anderson's detailed and compelling intellectual portraits of major figures of this period show us.

Locke's racial and artistic philosophies reveal a complex bundle of ideas, some of which prefigured those of contemporary black cultural criticism. While Locke believed in racial specificity, for example, he also championed the idea of the hybridity of African American culture—a "cultural racialism" that would transcend the class boundaries that were an inevitable consequence of the upward mobility of the black middle class. Anderson shows us, however, that Locke's educational experiences, friendships, intellectual attachments and legacies, and the ebb and flow of the contemporaneous debates surrounding his ideas portray a thinker free of simplistic binaries and whose ideas are rich with complexity.

One of these complexities is embodied in Locke's views about jazz and other forms of popular music. Locke believed, for example, that black vernacular forms and American art music would be mutually transformative, and "that the elaboration of African American cultural difference would *not* exclude a mutually transforming integration; integration would be fulfilled only when white racism and its pervasive institutional and ideological effects had been decisively eviscerated."[25] While Locke's cultural relativism guided some of his writings, one could question whether he truly understood the formal and creative processes of popular forms or even that of the "universal" formal concert music that he adored. Nevertheless, Locke's notion of cultural racialism has been remarkably influential, and even if it is not directly referenced, it certainly prefigures some of the contemporary ideas about jazz and culture that I discuss below.

As I wrote earlier, in Tomlinson's configuration, a complex notational system served to make Western art music more autonomous and prestigious. But black music's journey to this pedigree has been a more contentious and certainly less direct route—if it has reached that pinnacle at all. In fact, it would not be until much later that instrumental jazz would be able even to approach such a distinction, when the genre would be separated from the others marketed under the "race music" rubric. Even in the nineteenth-century quest for scientific representations of the spirituals, the function of African American music would always be perceived as serving a specific role in America's race industry. It would always perform specific kinds of functional, cultural work for its performers, transcribers, and audiences, though not always the same kind. In other words, African American music would always be tied inextricably to a specific social function.

Ironically, however, recording technology and not notation technology would point black music toward this ideal of autonomy, albeit autonomy with a difference. As Mark Katz argues in *Capturing Sound: How Technology Has Changed Music*, sound recordings carried specific consequences for jazz and its study. Like the transcriptions achieved for the spirituals, recordings disseminated jazz widely, allowing a repeatability that privileged sound over the printed score. "In jazz," Katz writes, "the values of the classical world are inverted: the performance is the primary text, while the score is merely an interpretation."[26]

Another distinction about recordings can be made here, one that inverts some cultural work that Tomlinson addressed earlier in this essay. Katz makes this point clear when he argues that "a recorded improvisation ... is music of the moment made timeless, the one-of-a-kind rendered reproducible, the spontaneous turned inevitable."[27] On the one hand, science in the form of recording technology served similar functions as notation did for instrumental Western European music and for the spirituals: it allowed a musical experience to be engaged outside the circumstances of its original social and historical contexts. On the other hand, the orality of sound recordings, indeed their decidedly nonliterary quality, undermines many modernist ideals that privilege the written as the sole signs of progress, history, and consciousness.

Through mass-produced recordings, black music and subjectivity in the public sphere sprouted wings and took flight. Eventually recordings would inspire future kinds of scientific study, first, in the activities of the discophiles that in typical modernist fashion collected and cataloged them, and ultimately in the modern practices of musical analysis and historicist cultural criticism. Mass-mediated, recorded music became an important reservoir of memory, culture building, and pleasure that opened both material possibilities in the marketplace and new dimensions for expression. Katz highlights this cultural work concisely: "True, mass-reproduced art does lack temporal and physical uniqueness, yet reproductions, no longer bound to the circumstances of their creation, may encourage new experiences and generate new traditions, wherever they happen to be."[28]

The new repeatable, portable blackness that appeared in the early twentieth century and the score-bound blackness of the nineteenth century beg us to rethink race, particularly when it is used as a unit of analysis in music studies. Music presented both a challenge and rich potential to black intellectuals devising ways to argue for black social equity in the 1910s and 1920s. These musical arguments comprised competing, though not mutually exclusive, "modernisms" represented in two developing genres: jazz and the spirituals.

In the spirituals, we see the more common modernist idea of cultural evolution: the spirituals could serve best as the raw material for a cosmopolitan art manifested in art song, opera, chamber music, and symphonies. Composers such as James Weldon Johnson set the spiritual in modernist dress, canonizing these new settings in the concert literature, especially among black musicians. But the unruly muse of recorded jazz presented a challenge to the cultural evolution model. While "symphonic jazz" experienced a period of popularity during the 1920s and 1930s, jazz has, in many ways, developed along its own trajectory. Jazz has certainly responded stylistically to other genres, but it did so without shedding core elements of its distinctive character. Thus, jazz represented what might be thought of as a different kind of modernism, one reflecting the sensibilities of the black masses—an Afro-modernism so to speak. Interestingly, neither the spirituals nor jazz monopolized black musical modernism. The appearance of gospel music, for example, could also be considered an important modernist form, one cloaked in the "folksy" galloping refrains and rejuvenating cries and groans of the storefront, urban black church.

I conclude by offering a way to discuss how this new historical work can help us talk about race in the contemporary moment without falling into patterns of essentialism and in ways that lend to African American culture the distinctiveness that historical and contemporaneous actors seem to grant it—the quality that allows it to circulate compelling ethnocentric social energies throughout its many worlds. These energies were disseminated through the historical notations and recordings during the late nineteenth and early twentieth centuries, encountering other cultures and taking on new meanings as they moved along. One must take this movement into account as we discuss race as a unit of analysis in musical discourse.

I have begun to think about race as a tripartite concept with porous boundaries separating each stream.[29] Social race embodies the social experience of being a racialized subject. It constitutes the realm of the everyday and is always bound to such variables as geographic location, historical moment, and agency through self-fashioning. Cultural race constitutes the performative dimensions of the social experience. It includes the expressive gestures of speech, music, dance, and so on that provide us with a way to communicate to others how we situate ourselves socially in the world. Theoretical race comprises the dense academic (and deliciously speculative) treatments of race in contemporary cultural theory; many of these have sought to deconstruct and de-essentialize racial thinking.

Several points are important within this paradigm. It is useful to keep in mind that as we scholars live race, perform race, and theorize race, we participate in the same discursive networks that recordings and transcriptions do. Thus, our scholarship is embedded in the same system of social, historical, and cultural contingencies as our objects of study, and our subjectivities are indeed a large part of our "objective" work. It is not, in other words, autonomous. The new reorientation of blackness in American musical history represented in the research discussed here is a significant step forward in African American studies. Perhaps the next step in our recontextualization of the past will involve revealing some of our own secrets and lies and how they have shaped the music and work to which we are undeniably devoted. In this way, the lesson of "blackness," theorized or Otherwise, may become not a lie but one of America's undisputed truths.

5 Muzing New Hoods, Making New Identities

FILM, HIP-HOP CULTURE, AND JAZZ MUSIC

We make our lives in identifications with the texts around
us every day.

Anahid Kassabian, *Hearing Film Music*

The medium of film has communicated, shaped, reproduced, and challenged various notions of black subjectivity in twentieth-century America
since D. W. Griffith's *Birth of a Nation* appeared in 1915. Writing in 1949,
Ralph Ellison argued that *Birth of a Nation* "forged the twin screen image
of the Negro as bestial rapist and grinning, eye-rolling clown—stereotypes
that are still with us today."[1] Such depictions in cinema had already existed
in print media; and they have persisted in all mass-mediated contexts in
varying degrees throughout the century. Film, however, has provided a
most salient medium for the visual representation of African American
subjects. If, as Manthia Diawara has argued, the camera is "the most
important invention of modern time," then it becomes an even more powerful tool when its technology is combined with the powers of music.
Indeed, when filmmakers combine cinematic images and musical gestures
they unite two of our most compelling modes of perception: the visual and
the aural.

"Muzing New Hoods, Making New Identities: Film, Hip-Hop Culture, and Jazz Music,"
Callaloo 25 no. 1 (Winter 2002): 309–20. This essay was written for a special issue of the
journal *Callaloo* that was focused on new interpretations of jazz and on interdisciplinary
approaches to Black music.

Below I consider two films produced during the Age of Hip-Hop: Spike Lee's *Do the Right Thing* (1989) and Theodore Witcher's *Love Jones* (1997).[2] On an immediate level, I am interested how music shapes the way we perceive these cinematic narratives individually; how music informs the way audiences experience their characters, locations, and plots. But I am also making a larger argument for how the musical scores of these films are sites for the negotiation of personal identity and self-fashioning on the one hand, and the making and negotiation of group identity on the other. Both of these activities inform "meaning" in important ways. Jazz music in these films generally serves as a foil to hip-hop music, which the directors use as the primary musical index for the black "authentic" subject. While the use of jazz in these three films may be comparatively minor, a discussion of it is instructive about the developing meanings of various black musical styles.

Below, I address several questions with regard to this cinematic function of music in hip-hop film. What role does musical discourse play in cinematic representation? If one of the primary thrusts of black cultural production has been the resistance to and countering of negative black stereotypes forwarded since *Birth of a Nation,* how does the musical score of the film participate in this agenda? How does the score, in fact, score or artistically (re) invent a black cinematic nation? The musical scores of *Do the Right Thing* and *Love Jones* provide excellent examples of the fluidity and contestation embedded in the notion "black identity," a topic that had become such a compelling one for theoretical, political, and artistic reflection in the late twentieth century. Before moving to the music in these films, I need to address an important topic raised in most discussions of them: the degree to which they accurately portray an "authentic" black cultural experience.

KEEPING IT REEL: DIVERSITY, AUTHENTICITY, AND THE HIP-HOP MUZE

Hip-hop culture has taken on the profile of a cottage industry because of aggressive corporate commodification. The postindustrial decline of United States urban centers, a downward turn that ironically spawned the development of hip-hop, has been co-opted by corporate America and represented as a glossy yet gritty complex of music idioms, sports imagery, fashion statements, racial themes, danger, and pleasure. While history shows us the persistence of the exploitation of African American culture in the United States, hip-hop represents an exemplary case in this regard. As the historian Robin D. G. Kelley writes, because of "few employment opportunities for African-Americans and a white consumer market eager to be entertained by the Other, blacks have historically occupied a central place in the popular culture industry."[3] Kelley argues further that

> Nike, Reebok, L. A. Gear, and other athletic shoe conglomerates have prof-ited enormously from postindustrial decline. TV commercials and print ads romanticize the crumbling urban spaces in which African American youth must play, and in so doing they have created a vast market for overpriced sneakers. These televisual representations of "street ball" are quite remark-able; marked by chain-link fences, concrete playgrounds, bent and rusted netless hoops, graffiti-scrawled walls, and empty buildings, they have cre-ated a world where young black males do nothing *but* play.[4]

The omnipresence of such imagery in the media has made a strong impact on notions of "authenticity" in African American culture. And, moreover, music and musical practices continue to play a crucial role in the creation, renegotiation, and critique of the authenticity trope.

The intersection of hip-hop musical practices and film serves as a cogent example. Hollywood in the early 1990s presented young fans with films like *New Jack City, Boyz N the Hood, Strictly Business,* and *Juice,* among others. Taken together, these films have helped to create a highly recognizable hip-hop mode of representing a one-dimensional black youth culture. As filmmaker Spike Lee notes, these "inner-city homeboy revues" created a world in which "all black people lived in ghettos, did crack and rapped."[5] As thematic heirs of the 1970s blaxploitation genre of film, the 1990s versions have been dubbed "rapsploitation" or, as Henry Louis Gates Jr. has labeled it, "guiltsploitation." Gates uses the latter term to characterize what he sees as a key message underlying many of these films: ambiguity about upward mobility. His observations about class sta-tus and black mobility are worth noting:

The politics of black identity, and the determined quest to reconcile upward mobility with cultural "authenticity," is a central preoccupation of these films. If genuine black culture is the culture of the streets, a point on which the blaxploitation films were clear, how can you climb the corporate ladder without being a traitor to your race? What happens when homeboy leaves home? A new genre—guiltsploitation—is born.[6]

Gates sees this trend as directly linked to the attitudes and backgrounds of the filmmakers. Rapsploitation of the early 1990s occurred, in part, because of an emergence of young, black, college-educated, and middle-class directors. Gates argues that these auteurs did not choose to close "the gulf between the real black people behind the camera and the characters they've assembled in front of it."[7]

Beyond this underlying class status tension, critics have also raised questions with respect to gender issues in these films. Feminist critics such as Valerie Smith, Michele Wallace, bell hooks, Wahneema Lubiano, and Jacquie Jones, among others, have noted that the perceived "realness" of the rapsploitation film genre is also real hostile to black women. But the class-based and feminist critiques of these films are sometimes difficult to articulate because of the compelling nature of the film experience itself and what Smith has identified as a documentary impulse. Michele Wallace, for example, admitted, "The first time I saw John Singleton's *Boyz N the Hood* [1991], I was completely swept away by the drama and the tragedy. It was like watching the last act of *Hamlet* or *Titus Andronicus* for the first time. When I left the theater, I was crying for all the dead black men in my family."[8] Upon subsequent viewings, however, Wallace noticed the strain of misogyny running throughout much of the film. She perceived that *Boyz* and other films like it seemed to be saying that the dismal social conditions depicted in these films were due to character flaws in the women.

Valerie Smith has argued that a documentary impulse authenticates these films with claims that they represent the "real." They achieve this documentary aura through an uncritical use of various aural and visual markers of "real" black living conditions, reproducing stereotypical ideas about African Americans. The boundaries separating fact and fiction, truth and artistic invention become blurred. Smith notes that critics, reviewers, and press kits assure audiences that these black male directors were "endangered species" themselves and are thus "in positions of authority relative to their material."[9]

While the importance of film cannot be dismissed, we should be careful to recognize the difference between cinematic entertainment and the "truth" of lived experience. There does not exist a one-to-one homology between lived experience and representations of such in film. At the same time, we should keep in mind that the same social energy that sustains ideologies like misogyny and other forms of discrimination also circulates in the narratives of these films. In other words, these directors didn't invent the misogyny, but they help to reproduce it. In this sense, they—perhaps unconsciously—kept it real, as the saying goes.

Writer Lisa Kennedy has argued that the complex of money, narrative, and pleasure bound up in film experiences makes them "extraordinarily powerful." Film, she writes, "is how America looks at itself." Nonetheless, she warns us against confusing the "individual vision" of an artist like a filmmaker with "the" collective reality of a group of people. Despite this warning, the dialogic interplay among "real" lived experience and film narratives (and, for that matter, television shows news programs, independent documentaries, print media, and music) remains an important fact of late twentieth-century life. In the case of film, "the real lives of people are substantiated by their reel lives."[10]

And, as I will argue over the next few pages, the nexus of "reel life" and musical practices has import on the topic of black music and meaning. What interests me here is not so much the critique of monolithic representations of black class status and life expectations represented in these films. (As we shall see, the film Love Jones does this more than adequately.) Nor do I want to question Hollywood's capital-driven fixation on exploiting this topic. Rather, I want to explore film as one way to enter into an analysis of the intersection of black identity and musical practice. As writers, directors, producers, and composers work together to create convincing characters and story worlds for audiences, they do so with the help of musical codes that circulate and in some ways create cultural knowledge, in the present case, about how "blackness" is experienced in the social world at that historical moment in question.

WHAT'S THE SCORE? FUNCTIONS OF MUSIC IN FILM

Before turning to the specific films in question, it is necessary to provide a brief overview of how music in cinema works generally. Broadly speaking, music works to enhance the story world of the film; it deepens the audience's experience of the narrative and adds continuity to the film's scene-by-scene progression, providing what Claudia Gorbman calls the "bath of affect."[11] Anahid Kassabian argues that the study of music in film should not be an afterthought to what might be considered the more important areas of plot and characterization: "Music draws filmgoers into a film's world, measure by measure. It is ... at least as significant as the visual and narrative components that have dominated film studies. It conditions identification processes, the encounters between film texts and filmgoers' psyches."[12]

The music in contemporary Hollywood films can be divided into two broad categories. The first is the composed score, which consists of music written specifically for the film. The second type is the compiled score: songs collected from sources that often antedate the film. According to Kassabian, these two modes of musical address are designed to generate different responses from the perceiver. The composed score, she argues, is usually associated with the classical Hollywood score and encourages "assimilating identifications," that is, it helps to "draw perceivers into socially and historically unfamiliar positions, as do larger scale processes of assimilation."[13]

The scoring techniques of the classical Hollywood cinema can achieve this end because of their unconscious familiarity to filmgoers: they have become naturalized through constant repetition. With few exceptions, the musical language of nineteenth-century Romanticism forms the core musical lexicon of American films. Music's cultural and cinematic work depends on its ability to signify an emotion, a location, a personality type, a frightening situation, and so on. The specific musical language of nineteenth-century Romanticism works well in this function because it has been used in this way repeatedly since the 1930s. This repetition has produced a desired result in film scores, since, as Gorbman notes, "a music cue's signification must be instantly recognized as such in order to work."[14]

We can experience the hallmarks of these scoring techniques in the classic Hollywood film *In This Our Life*.[15] As the opening credits roll in this black-and-white film, we hear Max Steiner's familiar orchestral strains typical of films during this era. The string section bathes the soundscape with sweeping melodies and a Wagnerian orchestral lushness that signals to the audience intense emotion and melodrama. Throughout the film, orchestral codes sharpen our perception of characters' interior motivations, propel the narrative forward, and help to provide smooth transitions between edits. During the plot exposition of the film, for example, we meet the vixen Stanley, played by the inimitable queen of melodrama, Bette Davis.

Although the dialogue of the other characters has revealed some of her less than desirable personal qualities, the orchestral strains of the score reveal to the audience much more than mere plot exposition could ever suggest. In her first appearance, Stanley drives up to the house with a male passenger. Viewers hear an ominous-sounding minor chord that is scored in the lower registers of the sounding instruments. As it turns out, the passenger is her sister's husband, a man with whom Stanley is having a torrid affair. After a brief dialogue between the two reveals Stanley's manipulative personality—underscored, of course, with melodramatic orchestral passages—the score transitions into animated rhythmic gestures that dissolve into an ascending pizzicato string passage as Stanley leaves the car and bounds up the steps into the family's spacious Victorian home. The music has helped to situate us in the plot and to identify with its characters despite our own subject positions, which may or may not be quite different from those depicted in the film.

The compiled score, a staple feature of many Hollywood films since the 1980s, brings with it "the immediate threat of history."[16] It encourages perceivers to make external associations with the song in question, and these reactions become part of the cultural transaction occurring between the film and its audience. Compiled scores produce what Kassabian calls "affiliating identifications." The connections that perceivers make depend on the relationship they have developed with the songs outside the context of the film experience. "If offers of assimilating identifications try to narrow the psychic field," Kassabian argues, "then offers of affiliating identifications open it wide."[17] The discussion that follows will explore how such distinctions bear on the interpretation of music in hip-hop film, a body of cinema with obvious and strong associations with a genre of music with a discreet history unto itself.

Both the classic and compiled scores' relationship to the story world of the film can be divided into two primary modes of presentation: diegetic and nondiegetic music. Diegetic (or source music) is produced from within the perceived narrative world of the film. By contrast, nondiegetic music, that is, music produced from outside the story world of the film, serves the narration by signaling emotional states, propelling dramatic action, or depicting a geographical location or time period, among other factors. Most of the music in a film fits into this category.

Another kind of musical address in film blends the diegetic and nondiegetic. Earle Hagen calls this type of film music source scoring. In source scoring the musical cue can start out as diegetic but then change over to nondiegetic. This kind of shift usually occurs concurrently with a change in the cue's relationship to onscreen events, most likely with the narrative world and the musical score demonstrating a much closer fit.[18] With these ideas about music in film in mind, I turn to Spike Lee's now-classic film *Do the Right Thing*.

DO THE RIGHT THING

As I stated above, Griffith's *Birth of a Nation* stands as the symbolic beginning of American cinema, providing a grammar book for Hollywood's historic (and unquestionably negative) depiction of black subjects. Likewise, Spike Lee's *Do the Right Thing* (hereafter *DTRT*) may be viewed as a kind of urtext for black representation in the so-called ghetto-centric, New Jack flicks of the Hip-Hop Era. This film is important for a number of reasons. Lee succeeded in showing powerful Hollywood studios that this new genre of comparatively low-budget films could be profitable for the major studios. *DTRT*'s popular and critical reception (it earned millions and an Academy Award nomination) caused Lee's star to rise to such a degree that he became the most visible black filmmaker of the past decade. Hollywood studios tried to duplicate the success of *DTRT*, allowing other black directors access to the Hollywood production system, albeit within predictably prescribed limits.[19]

Lee's use of rap music (and some of the musical practices associated with it) demonstrated how it could be used to depict a range of associations. Some of these include black male and female subjectivity, ethnic identity, a sense of location, emotional and mental states, a specific historical moment, and the perspectives of age groups. In these realms, *DTRT* cast a long shadow over the repertoire of acceptable character types, plots, and themes in subsequent ghetto-centric films during the Age of Hip-Hop.

SCORING THE RIGHT THING

DTRT conforms to some of the conventions of classical Hollywood cinema discussed above but with marked differences. Victoria E. Johnson has recognized the importance of music in *DTRT*, calling it Lee's most musical film. She identifies two primary modes of musical rhetoric in the score. What she calls the "historic-nostalgic" strain encompasses, for the most part, orchestral music written by Lee's father, Bill Lee. The sound is reminiscent of some of the chamber music by African American composer William Grant Still—quaint, genteel, and staid. Interestingly, Branford Marsalis's jazz-inflected saxophone and Terence Blanchard's trumpet perform the melodies.[20] This music is always nondiegetic and, in Johnson's view, serves to convey a romanticized vision of community in the ethnically mixed neighborhood in which the story takes place. This use of music corresponds to the classical approach.

Rap music rests at the other end of the aesthetic continuum in this film. The group Public Enemy's rap anthem "Fight the Power" (1989) is heard diegetically at various points in the film as it pours out of the character Radio Raheem's boom box. Johnson argues that the other musical styles heard in the film, which include jazz, soul, and R & B, mediate the two extremes represented by rap and Bill Lee's original score. There is one exception to this observation, however. Jazz is also used nondiegetically to help depict emotional exchanges between characters.

While I generally agree with Johnson's reading, I depart from it on several points. Johnson stresses that Lee is conversant with classical scoring conventions and that he "manipulates convention in a traditional manner to orient spectators within the film story."[21] I experience *DTRT* somewhat differently here. The unconventional approach of the score "disorients" the audience in my view. This musical strategy is joined to unusual cinematic techniques such as "unrealistic" visual angles that call attention to the camera, and a use of music that moves back and forth between "bath of affect" and "listen to me" narrative positions.

The three modes of musical language in the film—the orchestral music of the Natural Spiritual Orchestra (nondiegetic), the popular music played by the WLOV radio station (diegetic), and the rap music from Radio Raheem's boom box (diegetic) create a rather hectic and conflicted semiotic field. Consider, for example, the first five scenes in which we hear the orchestral music that Johnson believes signals a romanticized community. During a monologue in front of the Yes, Jesus Last Baptist Church, the speech-impaired character Smiley talks about the futility of hate in society while holding up a small placard of Malcolm X and Martin Luther King Jr. Smiley's stammering seems somewhat at odds with the placid musical gestures heard in conjunction with it.

The next time we hear this mode of music, the Italian pizzeria owner Sal and his sons Vito and Pino drive up to their shop, which sits on a garbage-strewn corner of a primarily black neighborhood. (Ironically, other scenes in the film portray the neighborhood as whistle clean.) In this scene we learn of the deep hatred Vito harbors for this neighborhood and for the people who live there. Although Sal admits with glib resolution that the air conditioner repairman had refused to come around without an escort, he can barely contain his anger over Vito's attitude about working in the neighborhood. This scene does not, in my view, conjure a romanticized community. Again, the placid strains of the score seem strangely at odds with the narrative world on screen.

When the character Mookie (played by Spike Lee) exits his brownstone into the morning sun, the neighborhood is stirring with Saturday morning activity. The orchestral strains do portray a cozy, communal feeling in this third instance of hearing this mode of music. But in the very next scene in which music of this type is heard, the characters Mother Sister and Da Mayor, the neighborhood's matriarch and patriarch, respectively, trade insults with one another. The fifth time the orchestra is heard, Jade, Mookie's sister, is lovingly combing Mother Sister's hair on the sunbaked front stoop of a brownstone. The communal feeling created by the music and the scene quickly dissipates, however, as Mother Sister deflects a compliment from Da Mayor, responding to his polite advance by hurling more insults. Thus, I see the score not so much signaling community. It functions, rather, to highlight conflict and tension in the narrative world of the film. This strategy sets the viewer on edge and frustrates any "settled-ness" that might be forwarded in the scene.

But the music that Mister Señor Love Daddy plays on the radio station WLOV *does* seem to signal community. It marks the geographic space of the neighborhood and underscores his references to love and the importance of community togetherness. In the early scenes of the film, the radio music, which consists of various styles of R& B—replete with gospel singing and funk beats—is heard in sundry settings. We hear it in Da Mayor's bedroom as he rises, in Mookie's and Jade's apartment, in a Puerto Rican home, and in a Korean-owned grocery store—in every cultural space except Sal's Pizzeria. This compiled score music inspires the idea of a "community," one created by the spatial boundaries of the radio station's broadcast span.

Nonetheless, WLOV's programming inspires one instance of community conflict. When Mookie, an African American, dedicates a song (Rubén Blades's "Tu y Yo") to his Puerto Rican girlfriend, Tina, a group of Puerto Rican young men enjoy the tune on a front stoop. As Radio Raheem passes by playing "Fight the Power," a battle of decibels ensues. "Fight the Power" wins the bout as Radio Raheem's boom box overpowers the scene with one turn of the volume knob. This confrontation contrasts with the first meeting of Radio Raheem's music and that of WLOV. Community alliances, like Lee's cinematic uses of various musical styles, are fluid and situational. Why, one might ask, didn't the Puerto Ricans identify with the "Fight the Power" message?

Gorbman writes that "music is codified in the filmic context itself, and assumes meaning by virtue of its placement in the film."[22] Because of the audience's familiarity with rap music and the dynamic formal qualities of the music, Lee is able to highlight its "difference" from other musical styles in *DTRT*'s score. As the film progresses, however, the audience experiences a level of familiarity with "Fight the Power" because of its persistent use. Lee is able to re-encode rap music's signifying affect during the film's narrative.

Lee can achieve this because he capitalizes on the history of Public Enemy's reputation outside the use of "Fight the Power" in this film.

Clearly, this use fits into the affiliating identifications category. At the same time, the repetitive hearings of the piece also allow us to spill over into the assimilating identifications arena. The repetitive use of "Fight the Power" allows Lee to manipulate audience members of different subject positions to relate to the musical conventions and political message of the piece because they understand what it means cinematically. Viewers have been assimilated into a particular reaction or identification with the music and, perhaps, the story world and its characters as well. If the typical classic Hollywood film score renders the audience "less awake," as Gorbman contends, then Lee's use of rap music breaks that pattern. He positions it as an intrusive, embodied presence in the film.

Among all the music rooted in the black vernacular, jazz plays a minimal role in the movie. When jazz is heard, it functions much like the music of classical Hollywood scoring. Its signifying affect narrows the psychic field, assimilating a diverse audience of perceivers into identifications with an emotional state, for instance. This observation cuts two ways. For one, it shows where jazz is situated in hip-hop discourse of the late 1980s. It had a somewhat marginal status, one that would certainly change, however, in subsequent years. Second, jazz had achieved a level of familiarity that approached that of nineteenth-century orchestral music and could therefore be used to situate a listener's identifications in the story world of a film. As we shall see below, jazz-related and jazz-inspired practices would soon become a more important factor in hip-hop's aesthetic profile.

CONSTRUCTING THE NEW BLACK BOHEMIA IN *LOVE JONES*

The film *Love Jones* expands the hip-hop lexicon of acceptable black subjects and their corresponding musical associations. The film, an urban Afro-romantic comedy written and directed by Theodore Witcher, is set in contemporary Chicago. Darryl Jones, a bassist and native Chicagoan, scored the original music. *Love Jones*'s eclectic soundtrack and the "musicking" practices associated with the music distinguishes the film from run-of-the mill romantic comedies.

Consider the first few minutes of the film, in which Witcher (like Lee and Singleton before him) sets the tone for the story that follows. During the opening, Witcher strings together a jumble of short urban scenes, including the Chicago skyline, the El train, a run-down neighborhood, a modest storefront, trash-lined railroad tracks, a Baptist church, the hands of a shoeshine man, and the faces of black people—old, young, some posing, others showing no awareness of the camera at all. Filmed in black and white, Witcher's stylish montage forecasts an approach to the presentation of inner-city blackness that departs from and is, in my view, more expansive than the two films I have discussed previously.

The music underscoring the opening features the genteel song "Hopeless," performed by singer Dionne Farris. The tune borders on soft rock and has virtually none of the hip-hop conventions heard in *DTRT* and *Boyz N the Hood.* The lyrics of "Hopeless" play a slight trick on the viewer because we hear the lyric "hopeless" against the first few scenes in the montage, which at first appear to paint a somewhat bleak depiction of inner-city life. But, as the visual sequences progress, smiles begin to appear on the subjects' faces. And as the musical narrative spins out, we learn that Farris is singing about romantic love and not social commentary: she's as "hopeless as a penny with a hole in it."

Love Jones features an attractive posse of educated, widely read, comfortably middle-class twentysomething Generation X–styled characters. Their hairdos (always a political statement with regard to African American culture) cover the spectrum: close cropped, dreadlocks, braids, chemically straightened. They live in tastefully appointed homes, lofts, and apartments that are lined with books and stylishly decorated with modern and African art. They are dressed for success and "wearing the right thing," if I might borrow Lee's title for the moment. Intrablack diversity is the feeling. The characters listen to jazz, the Isley Brothers, and urban contemporary music. Their calculated and robust funkiness translates into frank talk about sensuality. They read Amiri Baraka, smoke, drink, swear, play cards, and talk a boatload of shit in grand style. Like carefree adolescents, they delight in playing the dozens with each other. And with fluency they pepper their musings on poetry, sexuality, Charlie Parker, gender relations, religion, and art with spicy, up-to-the-minute "black-speak" rhetoric. Witcher apparently wants us to recognize these verbal exchanges and their accompanying body attitudes with a contemporary performance-oriented African American culture.

Love Jones's characters portray a hip "big shoulders" black ethnicity that insiders recognize as realistic in cultural spaces like contemporary black Chicago. In this setting, the film's narrative winds through various venues and situations wherein acts of ethnic performance can take place. One such space is a nightclub called the Sanctuary. Modeled after a jazz club, the Sanctuary features spoken-word poetry and live music. The Sanctuary appears to cater to black Generation Xers. Its audience respects the performers, paying rapt attention to the time, timbre, lyric, and substance of each poet's offering. Quiet diegetic music from the bandstand and jukebox envelopes the Sanctuary with the soundtrack of hip, polite society.

The film tells a love story between Darius Lovehall, an aspiring novelist and spoken-word poet, and Nina Mosley, an ambitious freelance photographer. Darius is a regular performer at the Monday night open mic session; Nina, who is on the rebound from a bad relationship, is there relaxing with a female friend. Nina and Darius meet. Nina initiates a conversation, following their exchange of curious glances. Shortly thereafter, an MC invites Darius to the stage and he performs a sexually explicit poem, which he titles at the last moment (in true "Mack Daddy" fashion) "A Blues for Nina."

The performance itself is, in fact, not blues or jazz performance but what might be described as easy listening funk: an ostinato bass pattern in D minor splashed with subdued colors from a saxophone's soulful riffing. References from black music history inform the poetry; in one line Darius says that he's "the blues in your left thigh, trying to become the funk in your right." The audience, which is depicted in a series of very flattering close-ups that are reminiscent of the opening montage, responds with sporadic declamatory affirmations. These vocables provide an obligatory bow to the southern past, even if these verbal exclamations may no longer signify that history solely.

Music in *Love Jones* works overtime. Its characters are, in my view, more fully constructed, engaging in more musical practices and cultural spaces than in *Do the Right Thing*. Music in the pool hall, the nightclub, the house party, the WVON "stepper's set," the reggae club, and the residences expands the representations of Hip-Hop Era blackness on screen. While this depiction of black bohemia may be a caricature itself, when compared to contemporaneous visions of black life in America like *DTRT, Love Jones* can only be viewed as a counterweight to those characterizations.

Although contemporary R & B forms the core musical lexicon of *Love Jones,* jazz references surface in the Sanctuary's performance space and as a way to show how "enlightened" the characters are. In one case, the jazz/blues piece "Jelly, Jelly, Jelly" becomes the soundtrack of sexual frustration as Darius and Nina try to suppress their lust for one another. Importantly, rap music is heard only one time in the film: during a car scene in which one of Darius's friends is courting Nina behind his back. In this very brief scene, rap music becomes associated with a questionable character trait.

Interestingly, in both these films (and in John Singleton's *Boyz N the Hood*), music is linked to other black cultural practices like the dozens, dance, card playing, and so on. Music is central to constructing black characters within these films' narratives. Rap music, for example, helps to create specific kinds of character traits in (male) subjects: politicized, nihilistic, or underhanded. Various styles of jazz are used for their identifications with middle-class culture or to enhance the audience's experience of emotional states. R & B styles, for the most part, are used to depict communal associations. The quasi-orchestral music linked most closely to the sound of classic Hollywood scoring—when it does appear in these films—is used in traditional ways: to assimilate audiences into a particular mode of identification with characters and plot situations.

During the Age of Hip-Hop filmmakers like Spike Lee and Theodore Witcher, among others, worked to portray what they thought were realistic portraits of urban life. While their portrayals were popular, many critics believed that they helped to erect harmful stereotypes. Witcher, director of *Love Jones,* for example, was challenged to convince film executives that his kind of story could find a niche in the market or was even plausible because of the ghetto-centric focus of so many black films of the early 1990s.[23] Thus, despite the way in which directors might have positioned their work as countering hegemony in Hollywood, their approaches and the repetition of them became conventions against which those interested in other kinds of representations would have to struggle.

The juxtaposition of different black musical styles in these films demands that audiences grapple with the ways in which numerous musical developments have appeared under the cultural umbrella of hip-hop. How these styles relate to one another cinematically represents only one arena of interest. These expressions have enlarged the boundaries of hip-hop, and this expansion has inspired celebration, dissent, and, of course, debate of exactly where these boundaries should be. Because of the persistence of older styles of black music and their continual evolution of meanings during the Age of Hip-Hop, filmmakers were able to use these external associations as part of the way in which audiences would experience these scores, and thus their cinematic representations.

Do the Right Thing's and *Love Jones*'s characters are meditations on how modern blackness is experienced in cities that in the 1940s represented the promised land—the cultural spaces to which black humanity flocked in order to participate fully in modern America. The urban conditions recently called the postindustrial and the artistic responses to these conditions reflect the changing social configuration of the late twentieth-century American city. Just as Dizzy Gillespie's Afro-Cuban experiments participated in a new demographic shift in the 1940s (that is, Cubans migrating to the United States), today's musicians mix hip-hop conventions with other expressions to reflect the configuration and constant refigurations of their social worlds and the statements they want to make in them.

If it is indeed true, as the epigraph to this chapter proposes, that contemporary people fashion their lives with the texts around them, then the study of hip-hop film provides a fruitful site of inquiry in this regard. In *Love Jones* and *DTRT*, directors and composers worked together to create narratives in which audience members could engage and with which they could form identifications. These texts became ways through which some understood themselves and others in their social world. Music formed an important component in these narratives, serving to order the social world in both the cinematic and real-life domains.

6 Afro-Modernism and Music

ON SCIENCE, COMMUNITY, AND MAGIC IN
THE BLACK AVANT-GARDE

The Negro music that developed in the forties had more
than an accidental implication of social upheaval associated
with it. To a certain extent, this music resulted from conscious attempts to remove it from the danger of mainstream dilution or even understanding.

Amiri Baraka (LeRoi Jones), *Blues People*

This chapter first explores that critical period between the flowerings of
the Negro Renaissance and the burgeoning fight for civil rights in the
United States (roughly the 1940s through the 1960s), referred to here as
the era of Afro-modernism. The musicians of this time refused to limit
themselves in any way, and the musical creativity that emerged during
Afro-modernism responded variously to the original calls set forth in previous generations. The resultant musical contributions represent a shared
commitment to breaking rules and tearing down restrictions imposed by
mainstream society on black expressive artists. Both composers and performers were energized by the kind of freedom originally espoused by
Toussaint Louverture, as, over the course of the twentieth century, these
musicians could explore new tonalities, invent new styles, and take advantage of new opportunities—including those afforded by international

Samuel A. Floyd Jr. with Melanie Zeck and Guthrie P. Ramsey Jr., "Afro-Modernism and
Music: On Science, Community, and Magic in the Black Avant-Garde," in *The Transformation
of Black Music: The Rhythms, the Songs, and the Ships of the African Diaspora* (New York:
Oxford University Press, 2017). I contributed this chapter to my mentor Samuel Floyd's
book at his request to help complete his magnum opus.

travel, higher education, and the rising field of black music research. This chapter draws on historical accounts of music making, reviews of groundbreaking sound recordings, and commentary written by the musicians themselves, all of which shed light on how black musicians perceived themselves and were perceived as agents of change during this era.

As the civil rights movement progressed, a need for new platforms of expression arose, and we note that as people moved into new circumstances and had access to new resources, they also needed new tools to help navigate their new situation. The field of black music answered this need, providing a space to chronicle black music making from a more academic perspective. Thus, an extension of the time frame above is necessary here because during the 1970s, 1980s, and 1990s black composers, musicians, educators, and historians accomplished a series of noteworthy "firsts." New professional organizations such as the Society of Black Composers (1968), the Black Music Caucus for music educators (1972), and the Center for Black Music Research (1983) were founded to provide like-minded individuals with institutionalized support for their endeavors. Academic journals, including the *Black Perspective in Music* (1973–1990) and the *Black Music Research Journal* (1980–), fostered both positivistic research (based on discovery and description) and critical discourse (positioning these discoveries and descriptions against the backdrop of changes in colonial rule, improvements in human and civil rights, and shifts in academic trends, for example). Thus, this chapter also introduces the longitudinal implications of Afro-modernism for the ability of black musicians to succeed in mainstream educational and performance venues.

For black politics and culture in America and internationally, the period between the 1940s and the 1960s was a watershed moment. The term "Afro-modernism" is useful to express many of the political, social, economic, and artistic changes that occurred, capturing all of the activities and social energies that made these times so dynamic and relevant. "Afro-modernism" identifies how blacks throughout the world responded to the experience of modernity, globalism, and anticolonialism as well as to the expanded sense of artistic experimentation and visibility of black expressive culture. Indeed, the years between the so-called Renaissance era of the 1920s and the civil rights and black consciousness periods of the

1960s and 1970s were ripe with dreams of freedom, acts of activism, and boundless creativity.

These political and creative waves took on many forms. In the United States, black soldiers fighting fascism in World War II returned to a changing sociopolitical environment charged with a new attitude that demanded abolition of inequality at home. The status quo was no longer an option. The Double V campaign (victory at home and abroad) fueled the fight for fair access to jobs, education, and the right to vote without strictures or harassment. Through their participation in defending America's military and political positions on the global stage, black Americans were clearly now poised to press claims for full participation in national life on all levels. It was yet another battle to be fought, but this time it was on domestic soil.

A massive black migration to northern cities continued throughout the 1940s and into the 1970s. The desire for greater job opportunities and lifestyles unconnected to the stifling, and sometimes deadly, social arrangements under the South's Jim Crow inspired waves of humanity to bring all of their hopes, dreams, fears, and talents to northern cities. Aspirations for black freedom were not limited to the United States. Abroad, the collapse of colonialism stirred across the African continent. These political movements became important conduits that linked Africans around the world politically and creatively with unprecedented fervor. Intellectuals, journalists, artists—poets, visual artists, musicians, and more—used their work to move the black liberation struggle forward with purpose and commitment.

An array of dramatic social changes of this era include the fall of colonialism in Africa, which served to unite black people around the globe; the gradual desegregation of the music industry; the civil rights movement; the radical and sometimes militant black consciousness movement, inspiring new approaches to art and its interpretation; and the emergence of a post-soul moment, which was caused, in part, by the corporate takeover of black cultural production, particularly music. The role of black music as a primary conduit circulating energy, inspiration, and information throughout various movements of resistance such as pan-Africanism, negritude, black consciousness, and hip-hop culture politics cannot be overestimated. This chapter illuminates how music participated in this wave of black sociopolitical resistance.

Jazz, the music that named "an age" in the 1920s, continued to represent a space for forward-thinking ideas about culture. It was in bebop, for example, that scores of artists from poets to painters found inspiration and a model for experimentation. Bebop (also known as modern jazz) emerged in the early to mid-1940s as an instrumental approach to the swing dance aesthetic, an innovation that abstracted some of swing's core conventions. Drummers disrupted the steady dance beat by dropping dramatic offbeat accents called "bombs." In order to sidestep paying copyright fees, musicians wrote compositions by creating new, more challenging melodies on the harmonic structures of existing popular songs. The harmonic structures themselves featured a sophisticated approach that exploited the upper partials—ninths, elevenths, and thirteenths—and a strong emphasis on the tritone relationships and flatted fifths, about which I will go into detail later. The virtuosic improvisations of instrumentalists Charlie Parker, Dizzy Gillespie, Bud Powell, and Max Roach set jazz on a new and demanding artistic course. Vocalists Sarah Vaughan and Betty Carter influenced legions of singers with their command of bebop techniques. Pianist Thelonious Monk's idiosyncratic compositional approach and acerbic solo approach emerged as the quintessential voice of a new era in jazz. And, as we shall see, the bebop movement became the starting point for a musician who took jazz into new realms of experimentation.

As for its relationship to the larger cultural and theoretical model of Call-Response, the 1940s should be seen as somewhat of a departure from earlier practices. If Call-Response details a dynamic historical "conversation" with and among black musical tropes, then what we see in the 1940s and beyond is a dramatic transformation of these practices. With the opening up of educational opportunities for black citizens across the board, musicians experienced more unprecedented "movement" in spaces previously denied them, and with this they adopted and reworked musical techniques that originated outside of black culture, as will be explored shortly. These devices were mixed with black musical tropes, demonstrating in musical terms the aspirations of social progress and freedom that "Toussaint's Beat" represented. Women musicians, who were for many years denied full acknowledgment of their abilities, thrived in the historical arc between the 1940s and 1960s and fully participated in this new shift of musical priorities. As Farah Jasmine Griffin has argued, the idea of "movement" perfectly characterizes the imperatives of black and Latino artistic circles and particularly that of black women in New York of the 1940s:

> Literally, it means a change in position or place, as in the movement of those black and Latino people who were migrating to New York in record numbers. "Movement" is also an important concept in the arts, one that applies to diverse art forms. In dance it may simply mean a change of position of posture, a step or a figure. In music it signifies the transition from note to note or passage to passage, or it may refer to a division of a longer work. In literature, "movement" signals the progression or development of a plot or a storyline. Finally, there is the "political movement," defined as a series of actions on the part of a group of people working toward a common goal. Black people were on the move in the 1940s, migrating, marching, protesting, walking, dancing. These artists sought to imbue their work with this sense of mobility as well.[1]

This sense of Afro-modernist urgency, begun in the 1940s and continuing to the years of the black power movement, demanded new music for new times.

In a letter to the editor of *Black Perspective in Music*, George Russell (1923–2009) expressed his displeasure with the title of an interview that was published in the *BPIM*'s Spring 1974 issue, in which his ideas about the Concept were interrogated by Olive Jones.

> The only thing about the forthcoming article . . . that I take issue with is the title "A New Theory for Jazz." It places a limit on the "Concept" [that] it does not have. . . . In fact, the purpose of the study is to close the cultural and intellectual gap between so called Jazz and European Music.[2]

In the letter he also lays out his future projects, which include a book analysis of the music of Johann Sebastian Bach, Igor Stravinsky, Anton Webern, and Alban Berg, among others, with respect to his by-then-famous Lydian Chromatic Concept, otherwise known as the Concept. Twenty-one years earlier (in 1953), he had published his book aptly titled *Lydian Chromatic Concept of Tonal Organization: The Art and Science of Tonal Gravity*. At the time, Russell seemed to have been targeting jazz musicians and their quest for ideas to improve their improvisations when he wrote:

The Lydian Chromatic Concept is an organization of tonal resources from which the jazz musician may draw to create his improvised lines. It is like an artist's palette: the paints and colors, in the form of scales and/or intervallic motives, are waiting to be blended by the improviser. Like the artist, the jazz musician must learn the techniques of blending his materials. The Lydian Chromatic Concept of Tonal Organization is a chromatic concept providing the musician with an awareness of the full spectrum of tonal colors available in the equal temperament tuning.[3]

Between the time his book was published (1953, revised 1959) and the appearance of the *BPIM* article and letter, Russell came to believe that his work had developed a more universal potential beyond the American jazz world. Indeed, his musical ideas were of interest to and accepted by Europeans, as Russell had made his home there from 1964 to 1969.

The bebop movement had certainly inspired Russell as a theorist and a composer, as it did many African American male artists, and some of his earliest compositions date from the late 1940s, coinciding with the emergence of bebop. The flatted fifth's ubiquity in bebop's harmonic language led him to explore and develop a theory based on the Lydian scale.

After achieving a certain degree of success composing, Russell said that he began to think about the United States as "a closed door for what I wanted to do." He believed that there were only two viable musical routes for him to pursue at that time: the "freedom" direction and the "commercial" direction. On the one hand, the freedom direction included some of the free jazz players, who in Russell's estimation presented "a kind of stream-of-consciousness playing, very angry music and very intense—you know, shouting and screaming—with free use of all kinds of musical resources." On the other hand, the commercial route represented, to Russell, "the Hollywood scene." Neither route was of interest to him. Only Europe provided the outlet he desired.[4]

While he was abroad, he toured with his own band and made connections with the Western art music world of experimental music. Moreover, as Russell mentioned in the letter to the *BPIM* editor, Danish Radio produced in 1965 two performances of Karlheinz Stockhausen's *Piece for Three Orchestras* with a strategic performance of his own sextet between them. He and Stockhausen developed a friendship and discussed on Danish television the mutual influence between contemporary jazz styles and what he called "New European Music." Europe, in Russell's estimation, gave him the appreciation and attention for his experimentalism that the United States did not: "I had to leave because my inner self didn't feel that that [i.e., the existing state of jazz] was a very comfortable position for me to be in."[5]

There is much evidence that affirms why Russell was a singular avant-garde, both musically and socially. He believed that, unlike other music theories, the Concept was both a pedagogical tool and a prescriptive theory for creating music and not an explanation of the syntax and grammar of compositional practices already in existence. Like Charles Ives, he composed primarily outside the typical political economies of the art world, a fact that allowed him greater freedom. He did not consider himself to be a regular participant of the music business and could, thereby, freely create from his inner impulse. He believed in a hierarchy of creativity in art. From top to bottom, this meant artist-philosophers, the artist, the popularizer, and the incompetent. No conscientious artist, Russell believed, should think about staying in the status quo to please audiences; artists should continue to grow. This view, of course, goes against the grain of a huge part of the logic of the music industry, which is based on regulation and predictability.

Russell believed in breaking with received notions or "laws" in music, particularly in the case of the Concept, which eschewed jazz's reliance on the major-minor modes. There was a parallel to this for black people in the social world outside of music. Russell thought that his work in tearing down systems in the music world could serve as a model for blacks generally. He appeared to live by a number of mantras: do not accept your social position as the ironclad rule, break the law, resist the powers that be, and think outside the box. Russell said, "So it's OK to talk about black liberation and black this-and-that, but nothing is going to change fundamentally in this society which is ruled by laws that are so precious to their makers. One has to question laws."[6]

The saxophonist and composer John Coltrane was another example of a jazz musician who questioned laws. The musical recordings he made in the years preceding his death in 1967 are considered his "late works," and they brought to the jazz world an idiosyncratic view of spirituality—a view also sated with an experimental, intellectualized approach. As Salim

Washington writes in an essay discussion of Coltrane's 1965 recording "Joy," the saxophonist was searching for a way to make his spiritual investigations of various world religions and the "science," or, rather, the formal execution, of his music answerable to one another. And he searched far and wide with regard to these two spheres. Although some of these techniques put him at odds with jazz critics of his moment, he remained undeterred in his insistence on expanding jazz's sonic language. As Washington puts it:

> It was precisely the musical elements outside the strictures of Western music practice that confounded music critics. . . . His use of long vamps over modal passages, and extended soloing; of non-tempered tuning including shrieks, honks, and screams; of glissandi like smears; and of melismatic melodic gestures were features that earned Coltrane respect and praise from some quarters and opprobrium from others.[7]

Much of Coltrane's work near the end of his life exuded these techniques as well as his concern with the spiritual. As a former addict who had successfully kicked his habit, Coltrane made music that was testimony, in Washington's eyes, of a man determined to live a life beyond the harsh strictures of race and of the typical working jazz musicians by experimenting. Like many other black musicians of his moment, including Rosetta Tharpe—who will be discussed shortly—his early orientation was in the Protestant church. Yet he absorbed those techniques and ultimately transcended them, shaping his music into something that would transport his listeners as well. In this way, Coltrane inserted into Afro-modernism an expansive and heady sense of aesthetics, politics, spirituality, and—as it was interpreted by some—protest.

Another musician in what Salim Washington refers to as "the holy quadrumvirate of free jazz," Ornette Coleman, epitomizes for many the face and sound of avant-gardism in jazz.[8] Washington has argued persuasively that free jazz should not be considered any more revolutionary than jazz's previous stylistic fissure, namely, bebop. The revolutionary qualities on the formal level of the music allowed many to imbue it with an overtly political registration, although some of the musicians associated with it were simply attracted to aesthetic experimentation. It is difficult to pin down exactly why, but Coleman's music seemed to threaten the jazz traditionalists more than Coltrane did, although the latter did draw his share of detractors. Perhaps it was because Coltrane had a longer history in the more mainstream groups like that of Miles Davis. At any rate, Coleman can certainly be considered one of the most polarizing figures in avant-garde jazz.

As Robert Walser points out in a collection of readings in jazz history, when Coleman's groundbreaking recording *Free Jazz* (1960) was released, *DownBeat* published two reviews of the work, one mostly positive and one negative. Showing an apparent disgust and a sense of betrayal, John A. Tynan described the record as "an eight-man emotional regurgitation." To his ears there were no aesthetic rules, and he described the music in mental health terms as nihilistic: "Where does neurosis end and psychosis begin? The answer must lie somewhere within this maelstrom."[9] Tynan accused the group of trying to destroy jazz. Pete Welding recognized the "danger" of collective improvisation in his review, but he was sympathetic to the enterprise for the most part. He writes that repeated listenings allowed him to hear the connection of Coleman's music to early Dixieland jazz. In other words, he entreats listeners to discipline themselves and the music in order to hear logic and history emerge from the cacophony.[10] Add to this critical discourse the idea that free jazz was a direct affront to Western imperialism, as some writers purported, and it is clear how Coleman's Afro-modernism became a most controversial expression. And Coleman's now-famous extended engagement at the Five Spot added a necessary piece to this puzzle—live musical presentation—to the fresh, challenging-sounding recordings and the critical discourse in order to launch his revolution.

When John Coltrane began courting his future wife, Alice, he admitted to being amazed when learning about her many musical talents and interests. She responded, "You never knew a lot of things about me." The same could be said of many women in jazz with respect to their participation in and mastery of the idiom. Born in Detroit in 1937, Alice McLeod, like many black women musicians, began her early musical training in the church, where she was part of a devoted family that strictly adhered to the repertoires and conservative doctrinal teachings of the church. As Tammy Kernodle notes, Coltrane moved back and forth between Baptist and Pentecostal settings as a child, playing a variety of repertoires and crafting a dynamic view of what it meant to be "spiritual." These early experiences make a strong case that the focused spirituality she was known for later in life (particularly after she met and married John) could also be attributed to her childhood. In other words, as Kernodle states, she was more than simply a disciple of her husband's evolving worldviews. And she was more than a church musician who dabbled in other genres. After a teenage life immersed in various kinds of music, she broadened her palette to jazz, particularly bebop, when she became a bebop musician in the likeness of the virtuoso Bud Powell. Powell favored a pianistic style based on fast, angular melodic lines played in the right hand against staccato, scaled-down voicing in the left hand, as opposed to the barrel house "jig" piano style of the church. Alice McLeod met and studied with Powell when she visited and toured Paris in the early 1960s. The arc of her musicianship was, indeed, impressive, stretching from her early beginnings in gospel to her young professional life in bebop. And she would push into yet another realm of experimentations in more free-form jazz styles.

John and Alice's personal and mutually beneficial relationship seems to be the context through which each journeyed further into non-Western forms of spirituality as well as into the soundscape of free jazz. As Kernodle points out, Alice denied that it was she who was leading John in that direction, but some fans blamed her for the transition. Although Alice credits John with teaching her to explore, there were signs that Alice was moving away from standard bebop conventions before she joined John's band. Dennis Maupin, a musician who played with Alice during her bebop years in Detroit, maintains that she experimented with open harmonic structures that invited experimental approaches to improvisation before her marriage to John.[11] "While the marriage of spirituality and jazz was nothing new in the late 1960s, Alice's musical approaches were unparalleled as she combined the nuanced practices of the traditional Black church with religious and musical traditions of the East."[12]

The Afro-modernist practices of Alice Coltrane would come to full fruition after John Coltrane's passing. Between the years 1968 and 1978 she produced what Kernodle calls

the most highly experimental and spiritual music the labels [Impulse Records and Warner Brothers] ever produced. The aesthetic ideals of freedom in the music and faith, that were associated with the avant-garde, were revealed in the level of experimentation that Alice undertook in her record- ings, and her spiritual life and her recordings serve as a record of her self-actualization.[13]

Yet even with this celebration of Coltrane's achievements it is important to keep in mind what she was up against with regard to her being under- stood as an artist. Her journey through gospel, bebop, and free jazz aes- thetics was marked by a stark and formidable challenge, one that did not mark the new "freedom" in jazz as a space for new freedoms for women participants and listeners: "The notion of freedom in jazz became an aes- thetic value that was defined in a more male-centered construct. Freedom of the black male body, his sexuality and identity from centuries of racial and sexual ideologies, became the standard through which the race would be uplifted."[14] Despite these obstacles, Alice maintained her focus on per- sonal spiritual growth and how it could be sustained and experienced through experimental music. This journey led to her exploring South Asian faith traditions under the tutelage of the guru Swami Satchidananda, and she eventually changed her name to Turiya Aparna and formed a reli- gious community in Southern California. Withdrawing from her former public life, Alice wrote compositions that, as Kernodle notes, blended her "gospel and jazz sensibilities and sacred Hindu text, and these adaptions of sacred texts and melodies, much like the religious compositions of Mary Lou Williams, have created a distinct African American tradition within the larger worship life of the religion."[15] As alternative approaches to Afro-modernism, they created what Alma Jean Billingslea Brown calls "alternative epistemologies," new possibilities beyond the male-dominated cultures in which they had worked their entire careers. Alice Coltrane, and indeed Mary Lou Williams, juxtaposed the "science" of technically demanding music with the "magic" of spirituality with a goal of healing and building community.

By the mid-1940s, Mary Lou Williams (1910–81) was perhaps the most prominent woman instrumentalist of jazz. She was introduced to the piano by her pianist mother and was known in her early life as a prodi- gious child who could duplicate what she heard effortlessly. She built a substantial career on the road during the swing era and toured with and wrote for big bands led by men such as Andy Kirk, Benny Goodman, and Duke Ellington. When she moved to Harlem in 1943, she began a quest for greater artistic freedom, for a community of artists that would support her creative impulses, and for a spiritual journey that would help balance her higher purposes and the political economy of the music business. At a time in which leftist politics and black freedom struggles conjoined, Williams was fortuitously booked in New York's Café Society, a nightclub centered in the progressive politics of its day. The circle of artists who performed there represented a community that became linked to black freedom and labor struggles. The Café Society engagement was a turning point for Williams, as she had gigged on the road consistently since she was in her early teens. This, together with the New York apartment into which she moved during this time, provided Williams with a domestic and professional stability that had eluded her during the many years she spent on the road.

As Farah Jasmine Griffin has detailed, Williams had been interested in mysticism since her childhood, and during this fertile and creative period of her life it influenced her music. Her extended composition *Zodiac Suite* began to ferment during her tenure at Café Society Uptown. She wanted this piece to be an amalgam, played by "a group that would bring together black and white, male and female, European classical music and jazz—a truly democratic ensemble."[16] It debuted at Town Hall in December 1945 to critical reviews that labeled it "ambitious" and "innovative."[17] As an extremely gifted and skilled pianist, composer, and arranger, Williams knew she had nothing to prove to the professional music world she had participated in since she was a child. But for all of her accolades, she sought more than fame and fortune: she wanted (as Alice Coltrane did) to make a difference in the lives of her people. "Jazz," Williams once wrote, "is a spiritual music. It's the suffering that gives jazz its spiritual dimension."[18] Williams would later be drawn to mystical practices such as fortune-telling as well as to charitable work that targeted Harlem youths who were suffering the most from Harlem's post–World War II socioeconomic decline. Because of shifts in American musical tastes and her remarkable insistence on musical experimentation, Williams fled to Europe in the early 1950s. After experiencing an emotional crisis there, she temporarily stopped writing and performing, only to eventually return to her pedagogical practices and spiritual works via Catholicism. As Griffin argues, the modernist Williams saw these two life projects—music and spirituality—as one entity.[19]

When the Second Vatican Council issued the *Declaration on Religious Freedom* and the *Constitution on the Sacred Liturgy* between 1962 and 1965, these documents signaled sweeping changes in the Catholic Church's liturgy. In turn, these changes gave Williams an opportunity to creatively contribute to "a progressive musical movement that integrated various musical styles with liturgical forms and altered the performance and composition of music within the Catholic Church."[20] At the request and encouragement of her friend Brother Mario Hancock, Williams composed a piece titled "A Hymn in Honor of St. Martin de Porres" to commemorate the canonization of the black sixteenth-century Peruvian known for his care of the poor. She set music to Father Anthony Wood's original poetry, and the piece debuted in November 1963. Tammy Kernodle has described the piece in her study of Williams:

> A cappella with the exception of an eleven-measure piano solo, [it] consisted of complex harmonies that at times coupled the voices antiphonally against one another. The melancholy, repentant mood of the piece was broken up only by Williams's piano solo, which, with its Latin-tinged rhythms, provided the only cultural link with de Porres's Latin American heritage.[21]

Although the piece received mixed reviews at the time, Williams continued to write music that would unite her passions for social justice and creativity, which she characterized as "jazz for the disturbed soul" and as music for emotional healing. Her "Anima Christi" composition, written in collaboration with the exceptional trombonist and arranger Melba Liston, united gospel, blues, and jazz with this purpose in mind: to reach the average listener. Williams's Afro-modernist period was clearly defined by her search for spiritual meaning and guidance. And, as Griffin argues, Williams's music served as a "spiritual medium, a conduit to something outside of herself as well as a vehicle for expressing a sense of the spiritual, if not the divine."[22]

At the same time George Russell was outlining the Concept and the Coltranes (together with composers such as Dorothy Rudd Moore) were stretching the boundaries of what would be called "black music," the music being produced right in the pocket of the blues aesthetic was undergoing changes that would cast a long shadow into the future. If bebop abstracted swing and popular song, then early rhythm and blues—an umbrella label for a constellation of black vernacular styles that appeared somewhat contemporaneously—took the swing aesthetic and intensified its dance feeling with a heavier backbeat, a proclivity for twelve-bar blues form, repetitious and riff-based melodies, and lyrics whose subject matter comprised all of the earthiness and humor of traditional blues, though with an urbane twist. Perhaps best exemplified by Ruth Brown and Louis Jordan, the rhythm and blues style was sonically related to rock and roll, which emerged in the 1950s as a way to market the new dance music to white teenagers during the beginning years of the civil rights movement and fears of desegregation. Although black performers such as Little Richard, Chuck Berry, and Fats Domino certainly counted among early rock and roll stars—many believed the new genre to be another strain of rhythm and blues—as the style became codified as a genre with its own race-specific social contract, it became understood as primarily "white." The mainstream of rhythm and blues styles featured elements from gospel, blues, and jazz, an imaginative repertoire of lyrics employing vivid imagery from black life, together with qualities derived from specific locations such as the "urban blues" sound from Chicago and Los Angeles. Independent record labels were primarily responsible for recording and disseminating early rhythm and blues.

One of the most dramatic disruptions in the blues aesthetic—the music thought to be most emblematic of an imagined, mythic, and ancient past—occurred in its instrumentation when musicians began literally to electrify it. These sounds were heard as avant-garde even as they also asserted elements of the style's past. When coupled with the sonic elements of the blues and the historical social connotations associated with black musicians in American society, the relatively new sounds of the electric guitar became a charged cultural symbol that reverberated for decades thereafter. Electrified blues established an entirely different trajectory for black music during the same years that jazz was moving from its cultural position as America's sound of pop in the 1930s and 1940s and beginning its "arts" pedigree in the late 1940s and 1950s, a move buoyed by written criticism and theoretical treatises such as George Russell's *Lydian Chromatic Concept of Tonal Organization*.

Steve Waksman's brilliant account of the electric guitar's cultural journey takes the Afro-modernism topic in quite another direction. The invention of the instrument was the result of a small number of experimenting inventors and business-minded people. He lists several notable changes that took place in African American popular music between 1941 and 1955:

> the changing concentration of blues performers in rural and urban areas, as well as between north and south; the displacement of field recording practices in favor of studio recording; the growing African-American acquaintance with technologies of sound production and reproduction like the tape recorder and the electric guitar; and the increased potential of African-American music, and of black performers to "cross over" into success with white audiences. Thus Waters and Berry can be considered as examples, at once representative and exceptional, of the complex range of processes that shaped African-American popular music and were shaped by black performers in the years surrounding and following World War II.[23]

In 1930 the Dobro company made the first electric guitar, and other companies followed quickly thereafter with their own models. What began as motivation to have the instrument heard above the rest of the band became a decades-long obsession exploring the outer limits of technology. Through the materialism of the electric guitar, then, technology became an important platform for establishing an individualized, highly personal voice in the music field. And it did much more than that. Waksman argues that the guitar's role in shaping sound design through manipulation of volume, distortion, feedback, and pitch bends was particularly prominent in how Chicago blues countered the perceived New York–centrism of Afro-modernist sonic experimentation. The great aesthetic-sonic divide between acoustic and electric guitars became a charged ideological field of play, one that pop audiences invested with strong feelings and meanings. If music was able to create, embody, and circulate information that conforms to or disrupts social orders, then electrified blues may be read as a dramatic and important index of change.

Audiences were conditioned to hear the sound of the electric guitar in terms of macho excess—as a sonic shot of power and sexual politics. During the war years there was another twist making the electric guitar's emergence a game changer. In Chicago the specificities of the racial lines reinforcing segregation created an atmosphere in which musicians catered sonic organization to the requirements of their audience and not the larger market forces. In this case, the audience was an Up-South mix of urbanite and newly arrived southerners, the kind of people who would delight in hearing music that resembled their social experience: hardcore, hybrid, and full of elements of a southern "past" and northern possibilities. If during the 1940s and 1950s Alfred Lion's East Coast–based Blue Note label represented for jazz an institutional model for building an "art" world sensibility for the music, then a Chicago record label became an important catalyst for the electric guitar's role in changing the trajectory of American popular music. Waksman shows that beyond the efforts of folk music collector Alan Lomax (who was on his own mission to preserve and protect styles from Afro-modernist experimentation), the Chess label provided a space for new blues territories and musical personalities to emerge.

Just as small New York–based record labels gave Thelonious Monk, Dizzy Gillespie, Bud Powell, Charlie Parker, and other beboppers opportunities to develop their own modernisms, the Chess label helped to cultivate a musical culture that formed another version of Afro-modernism that attracted a popular audience. One modernism was acoustic, this one electrified and electrifying. Guitarists and singers Muddy Waters and Chuck Berry stood at the center of this movement. Although they represented different types of musicians—Waters being an ensemble-focused instrumentalist, while Berry was more of a soloist—together they presented a new type of "performed masculinity" that became a signature of rock, R&B, funk, and rap. The Chess phenomenon also brought into focus the producer as a cultural icon central to making recordings because the Chess brothers inserted themselves into the creative processes of their products. This was markedly different from the live performances of the electrified blues. In live spaces the musicians were freer to experiment and satisfy their own muses and craft highly individual styles in the competitive environment of Chicago nightclubs.

Guitarist Rosetta Tharpe, in many ways, was just as much a pioneer in this world of electrified blues, although the style she played was labeled "gospel." Yet, as her biographer Gayle Wald states, she should be considered as much a progenitor of rock and roll as someone like Chuck Berry.

Testimonies abound about the power of her playing and singing, her charismatic musical personality, and the influence she had on her generation of musicians. For many, she made the guitar "talk." As Wald explains:

> When Rosetta's fans said she could make that guitar talk, they meant she could play the instrument with abandon while still exercising exquisite control. When she made the guitar talk, she gave her audience an opportunity to feel excitement, pleasure, power, and emotional release in the sounds she generated. She loved nothing more than the cacophony of a few hundred—or several thousand—fans yelling out: "Go on, girl! Make it talk, Rosetta!"[24]

Tharpe learned the connection between music and the ecstatic from her upbringing and training in the black Pentecostal sect of the Church of God in Christ (COGIC), a denomination known for its combustible, evocative, and sensational worship styles. Dynamic music plays a key role in connecting congregants with the divine, and as this approach "jumped the track" into popular music styles like rock and roll, Tharpe and others created a standard for American music that would define it as a singular style throughout the world. Indeed, as a woman, Tharpe had an influence that clears room for our need to consider the advancement of Afro-modernist praxis to be as much a female endeavor as it was a male one. Thus, Wald argues, "Well before the guitar gods of more recent decades made a fetish of the guitar solo as an orgiastic expression of male sexual libido, Rosetta perfected something both more subtle and more radical: the art of the guitar as an instrument of ineffable speech, of rapture beyond words."[25]

Although well acquainted with the excesses of black church worship styles and the pleasures of pop music, an important generation of black composers would move in other musical directions, benefiting from opportunities that opened in education as a result of the long civil rights movement. As a result of this shifting tide, many would secure professorships at American universities in addition to earning major prizes and commissions. Their works exemplified several styles, ranging from neoclassical to the avant-garde, and featured equally diverse performing bodies, including chamber groups and symphony orchestras as well as solo singers and entire opera companies, among others. Undine Smith Moore, Ulysses Kay, George Walker, and T. J. Anderson were among those who led the way, establishing reputations within the academy and the larger art music world.

Undine Smith Moore (1904–89) served as a music supervisor in the public schools of North Carolina for one year (1926–27) before commencing her illustrious career at Virginia State University in 1927, from which she did not retire until 1972. A graduate of Fisk University and Columbia University Teachers College, Moore received musical training in piano, organ, theory, and composition. Although many of her instrumental pieces employ standard forms such as the fugue, theme and variations, prelude, and waltz, her extensive list of vocal solos and choral works shows her inclination to compose pieces of a sacred nature and to portray concepts relevant to the black experience. She is often called the "Dean of Black Women Composers" in honor of her myriad accomplishments in an era typically considered closed to black women, and for her dedication to ushering in the next generations of black musicians through her teaching and mentoring. Her commitment to furthering black music in education can best be seen in the essay "Black Music in the Undergraduate Curriculum," which was published in 1973. Her coauthors were Portia K. Maultsby, John A. Taylor, and Johnnie V. Lee. In addition to having an impressive career as a university professor, Moore produced some powerful compositions during her retirement years. She is perhaps most famous for her 1980 oratorio *Scenes from the Life of a Martyr: To the Memory of Martin Luther King*, for which she received a nomination for the Pulitzer Prize. But her final work, *Soweto* (1987), a trio for violin, cello, and piano, attests to Moore's personal awareness of the civil unrest in South Africa during apartheid, and especially during the Soweto uprising of 1976.

Ulysses Kay (1917–95), nephew of the jazz cornetist Joe "King" Oliver, composed approximately 140 pieces over the course of his career. He spent most of his life in the United States, but he was presented with unique opportunities to travel and live abroad. As a result of winning the Prix de Rome twice and a Fulbright Scholarship, he lived in Rome from 1949 to 1952. As part of the U.S. State Department Cultural Exchange Program, he joined the American composers Roy Harris, Peter Mennin, and Roger Sessions on a trip to the USSR in 1958. On his return, Kay wrote of his experiences in the *National Music Council Bulletin* and the *American Composers Alliance Bulletin*, offering his readers insights about the musical and cultural activities taking place in Russia and the Soviet Union, which were not widely accessible to or understood in the West at the time. A 1940 graduate of the Eastman School of Music (University of Rochester) with a master's degree in composition, Kay ultimately pursued an academic career as a professor of music in theory and composition, most notably at Lehman College of the City University of New York from 1968 to 1988. He counted among his many awards the 1972 University of Rochester Alumni Award, as well as several honorary doctorates. At the time of his death he was working on a piece that had been commissioned by the New York Philharmonic.[26]

Also a graduate of the Eastman School of Music (DMA, piano performance), George Theophilus Walker (1922–2018) soloed with some of the world's best orchestras during the early stages of his musical career and went on to capture audiences and win awards with his compositions. Like Kay, he was able to hone his skills abroad; as a pianist, he studied at the American Conservatory in Fontainebleau, France, in 1947, and he returned to Paris a decade later for composition lessons with Nadia Boulanger. During the 1950s and 1960s, Walker taught at a number of colleges and universities, and he served as a professor at Rutgers University from 1969 to 1992. After retiring from the university Walker continued to compose; indeed, his *Lilacs for Soprano or Tenor and Orchestra* garnered the 1996 Pulitzer Prize, making Walker the first black composer to win the prize.

T. J. Anderson (1928–) pursued opportunities in jazz during his formative years but turned to music education (M. Mus. Ed., Pennsylvania State University) and composition and music theory (PhD, University of Iowa) during the course of his graduate studies. Anderson taught at a number of institutions, including the public schools of North Carolina, but he eventually secured a professorial position at Tufts University, which he held from 1972 to 1990. During this time he contributed mightily to the currents in musicological literature and to the burgeoning field of black music research. His essays and articles can be found in publications such as the *College Music Society Report* (1982), *Images of Blacks in American Culture* (1988), and the *Black Music Research Journal* (1990), among others. Moreover, he conducted the premiere performance of the Black Music Repertory Ensemble (the resident ensemble of the Center for Black Music Research) in 1988. In 1972 he was also a founding member and the first national chairman of the Black Music Caucus of the Music

Educators National Conference (MENC).[27] Anderson continues to advocate for music education and music appreciation within the United States.

Moore, Kay, Walker, and Anderson were involved in academic circles as composers, but not all Afro-modern composers pursued university positions. Howard Swanson (1907–78), for example, was employed by the Internal Revenue Service, but he managed to compose prolifically at night. After his formal training from the Cleveland Institute of Music (BM) and additional studies with Nadia Boulanger (1938–40), he saw his *Short Symphony* premiered by the New York Philharmonic (1950–51) and received commissions from the Juilliard School of Music and the Louisville Symphony Orchestra, among others. His works have been the subject of much analysis published in *Black Perspective in Music*, the *Black Music Research Journal*, and the *Negro History Bulletin*.

Although Dorothy Rudd Moore (1940–) did not hold a position at a university, her compositions represent an important musical approach in the era of Afro-modernism. As Alice Coltrane and Mary Lou Williams did before her, Moore confronted preconceived parameters and made her musical mark on her own terms. Beginning her career in the early 1960s, Moore did not mind being labeled an African American woman composer, although she refused to label her output as "black music," a term she believed segregated or "ghettoized" her music from the larger art world. She understood the African American experience to be broad and all-encompassing, and African Americans were "vast and various in their musical tastes and appreciation."[28] Indeed, as author Helen Walker-Hill points out, Moore rarely deployed musical materials from the traditional African American culture in her compositions, choosing rather to work with more abstract gestures and forms and earning a reputation for writing music with "communicative power, integrity, intelligence, and impeccable craft."[29]

Moore spent her childhood in a small black community in an integrated suburban enclave outside of Wilmington, Delaware, one that was invested in concert music and in which her mother was a respected soprano. After rigorous compositional training at Howard University and a summer of lessons with Nadia Boulanger, Moore went on to cofound the Society of Black Composers in 1968, which was formed as a forum to promote and disseminate information about black composers.[30] In one of the organization's newsletters, the group's members argued for the freedom to express themselves as black composers in as many musical languages as possible:

> And while a common vocabulary or grammar is not even desirable among black composers, a new and highly desirable consensus of positive and assertive attitudes is clearly emerging. The questions of a year ago—most often concerning which specific musical sounds and materials would be necessary to make black music—are no longer necessary. We know that because we are black, we are making black music. And we hear it, too![31]

Their optimism and creative works were well received, as many of these composers' pursuits led to international ventures.

Like many women musicians, Moore continued in the tradition of family music making and collective building: she married cellist, conductor, and composer Kermit Moore and wrote music for him, among other commissions. Dorothy Rudd Moore could be considered a feminist in her own right, as she set the poetry of black women in some of her song cycles. Some of her other vocal works focused on the inner emotional lives of women, and her well-known song cycle *Flowers of Darkness* focused on black women, although all of the songs are based on poems by black men. According to Helen Walker-Hill, Moore's music contained experimental elements marked by complex structures, dissonant counterpoint, and tritones that challenged musicians.[32] Certainly, her musical output makes her work as important to black concert music traditions in the 1960s as Alice Coltrane's was to the free jazz movement.

As we can see, in both realms—jazz and concert music—black musicians exercised their right to move beyond traditional materials to express themselves. Talented musicians were operating during the era of Afro-modernism, but their contributions were often ignored by the critical press of their time and by the historical record. If there are threads connecting the work of Afro-modernist women across genres, it would be that they usually were musically nurtured by their mothers, they believed in acquiring technical brilliance and experimental sonic materials, and they felt that one of music's higher powers was its ability to forge strong bonds in a community.

From the mid-twentieth century on, stimulated in part by another south-to-north mass migration during and after World War II, black music with roots in the popular sphere—jazz, gospel, rhythm and blues, and all their multifarious sonic iterations—defined for many the aesthetic core of what was singular about American music culture. Despite their divergent social functions in the public sphere, they shared sonic and conceptual characteristics. As major labels initially ignored these styles, independent record labels were the key in disseminating the music as their owners sought to maximize profits. Ultimately, major labels would seek out, record, and distribute the music, and by doing so facilitate their dominant national and international impact. Black music—and this should certainly include the art music of the black composers discussed above— came to be seen as an important expressive force representing the richness of African American culture. It was a metaphor for the processes of creativity in such fields as literature, visual arts, and dance, and as a symbol for the structural integration of black people into the mainstream of American society. As African American citizens confronted modernity—many would say they were critical in defining it—music was a reservoir of social energies, a fount of and even a mouthpiece for the palpable aspirations of freedom that define the age.

7 Bebop, Jazz Manhood, and "Piano Shame"

In sixth or seventh grade, a time of life when most guys my age were trying on their swagger, I was walking back home from a practice session at a buddy's house that was furnished with a piano. Along the way, my instruction book clutched under my arm like any average nerd, I passed some classmates who asked with simple curiosity and no malice, what was up, where I had been. "Practicing my music," I said, probably looking serious, deep in my thoughts, and studiously absent-minded, as some people say they remember me. "Cool. What do you play?" somebody asked. Before I knew it, the word "sax" fell out my mouth.

I don't know exactly where I had gotten this information, but it was clear to my adolescent, late-blooming ass that claiming the saxophone would make me look more swagger-full than the truth—that I was thoroughly enthralled with the piano. And that my family couldn't afford one at the time so I practiced however I could, mapping out homes in my black, working-class neighborhood with an instrument. It was, indeed,

The Feminist Wire, March 13, 2013, https://thefeministwire.com/2013/03/bebop-jazz-manhood-and-piano-shame/. This essay was based on research for my book on jazz pianist Bud Powell and was aimed at an audience beyond the academy.

another time when a kid with ambitions larger than his immediate circumstances could get a boost from the "Village." I passed what I apparently perceived as the "coolness test," relieved that nobody in the group pointed out that I was not actually carrying a saxophone. The heroic performance of self-assured, cool manhood would finally settle in by late adolescence, as admiring women would quietly pass their phone numbers after a stage show, other musicians would seek me out for gigs, and academic opportunities unavailable to those with picture-perfect crossover moves and jump shots began to open up. Although I've lost the need to lie about music for the sake of traditional manhood, the historical and social grounding of my childhood "piano shame" is a complex matter about masculinities worthy of discussion.

In a mediascape saturated with electronic beats, auto-tuned voices, and urban contemporary styles grounded in hip-hop production sensibilities, contemporary popular music commands the attention of many commenters concerned with gender analysis. Jazz, for the most part, is not seen as a site worthy of such investigations, particularly in social media. Yet it's fascinating to consider bebop (or modern jazz) and what people heard in it as a gendered sonic field doing extraordinary cultural work in the quest for masculinity. Artists such as Amiri Baraka and Quincy Jones have confessed their intense identification with bebop's experimental language as young men, describing it, much like hip-hop devotees, as more of a lifestyle than a musical choice. It may surprise some readers that, like the lyrics of rap, nonrepresentational instrumental music such as jazz can be analyzed with respect to its registration of historically contingent social energies like masculinity in potent and pleasurable ways.

Much of this energy occurs at the borders of a perceived musical style or genre. And here is where the case for gender study gets compelling with regard to jazz and bebop. Feminist musicologist Susan McClary argues that "genres and conventions crystallize because they are embraced as natural by a certain community: they define the limits of what counts as proper musical behavior." Thus, the occasions of stylistic disruption—those times when jazz musicians seemed to push the limit of acceptable generic expectations like they did in bebop—are important sites in which to tease out gendered meanings: in the space between convention and innovation exists the stories of power struggle through experimentation.

In other words, as musicians push against a listening community's acceptable codes of musical behavior, they are usually articulating who they believe they are in the world through displays of musical prowess, stylistic challenge, and experimentation. All of this has circulated, by the way, within a network of ideologies in which popular and "Other" cultures were historically rendered as "feminine" or nonprestigious when compared to an intentionally "butched-up" Western art music discourse, illustrating yet another example of how musicality and gender are diligently policed performance fields.

What are some of the historical politics of " jazz manhood"?

Writing in 2001, in the context of a wave of scholarship named the New Jazz Studies, Sherrie Tucker argued persuasively for the inclusion of gender in jazz studies in many publications. Rather than seeing her project as aimed solely at recovering the history of women participating in jazz, Tucker suggested a more radical strategy. She pushed for the placement of jazz studies over the field of gender as a way to understand how the latter structures all aspects of the jazz field. While the compensatory histories of women in jazz are useful and long overdue, the critical study of gender in jazz studies should involve more than the "women were there, too" framework. All this work demands that we see jazz*men* as possessing gendered identities, too: the music was an activity in which they negotiated their sense of manhood in American society. Although we've come a long way since the days when women's bodies were used as a sign of music being "not real jazz" in publications such as *DownBeat*, the time is ripe for critical expansion. As Tucker argued, we "need to conceive of gender not as a synonym for women, and not just as a critical description of sex and gender roles, but as one of the primary fields 'within which or by means of which power is articulated.'"

An intense, aggressive virtuosity within and on top of the structures of American popular song constituted the heart of the bebop aesthetic. One scholar called this aesthetic a "politics of style," a concept describing the specific mode of cultural work the music achieved in its time. The young black men in the bebop movement found in its sounds and politics a patriarchal, heroic performance space, one that became the new musical language of "jazz manhood." One such musician was pianist Bud Powell (1924–66). The subject of my book *The Amazing Bud Powell: Black*

Genius, Jazz History, and the Challenge of Bebop, he was certainly "the man" of bebop piano. He was a talented but introverted boy whose musical skills and seriousness about his craft paved the way for his meteoric rise in the New York jazz world. According to various people who knew Powell in his younger years, he had become enamored with the modernist sound elements in bebop before he was twenty years old. Former acquaintances shared stories of an increasingly impatient young man who sought out competitive situations in which he could show off his technical command in the new style in the tradition of the stride piano contests of previous generations. Otherwise soft-spoken and withdrawn, Powell was known to want his own way in purely musical settings—never with violence, but often with the seething insistence of someone with little regard for the feelings of others. Whether he was refusing to play a bandleader's desired number or brusquely removing another pianist (or competitor) from the instrument to brandish his own "weapons," Powell's single-minded, almost myopic focus on showcasing his own gifts was often excused by others as harmless, youthful unruliness. But his exposure to alcohol and drugs, a nocturnal lifestyle that had interrupted his education, and the overall phallocentric vibe of the scene no doubt caused the sheltered prodigy to grow up and man up fast—both artistically and otherwise—although one can surmise from various accounts that Powell was still very much an adolescent emotionally.

What were the technical specifics of this language of jazz manhood in which Powell would immerse himself? And in which historical and material notions of the gender/music relationship were this language and its social environment grounded? What were the terms of Powell's social contract as a black virtuoso in the bebop scene?

Although historians may still debate whether bebop was a revolutionary or an evolutionary style development, agreement exists on its core qualities. Most prominently, bebop consists of an enriched melodic, harmonic, and rhythmic vocabulary that required astute musicianship and a virtuosic bravado. Bebop's most significant contribution to the jazz tradition was in the area of improvisation, both in soloing and accompanying. Improvised bebop solos shared the melodic and rhythmic character of many bebop themes, including a frequent use of asymmetrical phrase structures; a harmonic vocabulary that employed ninths, elevenths, and thirteenths; and chromatic melodic lines that often stressed the weak beats of the measure. Swing, bebop's immediate stylistic predecessor, used more uniform phrases, structures, and accents and had less varied rhythmic patterns and less emphasis on harmonic dissonance.

Frontline virtuosos such as Charlie Parker and Dizzy Gillespie attracted the lion's share of public attention as they wove intricate solos before awestruck listeners. Yet much of the musical enchantment of bebop emanated from its new conception of accompaniment in the rhythm sections, which created brilliant sonic tapestries supporting the dramatic solos. Pianists, drummers, guitarists, and bassists supported bebop's themes and solos with a rich and sometimes cacophonous mix of timbres, harmonic substitutions, and polyrhythmic accents that complemented and at the same time challenged the soloists. All the while, they maintained the fixed rhythmic pulse that linked the music to traditional black dance music forms. Bebop innovations brought about a heightened tension in melody, harmony, and rhythm that was, on some levels, a break with earlier styles of jazz. Thus, bebop musicians struck a balance that both satisfied modernist ideals of musical "complexity" and situated their music conceptually under the umbrella of black Atlantic musical traditions. The dynamic grooves struck by modern jazz musicians such as Powell were as central to the music's influence as the work of frontline soloists. It was there—in the midst of the give-and-go of rhythms, subtle timbral shifts, and cagey harmonic embellishments—that audiences were able to discern that a new day had dawned in popular music, and that new communities and identities were being formed as well.

These new musical conceptions, together with a new social contract with the listening public, signaled that jazz had experienced a generic shift; that it had, in other words, become something new. Because social identities are "made" and often communicated to others within the context of expressive culture, one can look to concepts such as gender and genius to interpret modern jazz's generic development.

In his discussion of gender and jazz in the 1930s, Patrick Burke argues that white masculinity in this context was constituted at "the tangled intersection of ideas about race, gender, labor, and musical practice." In the after-hours cultural space of 52nd Street's Onyx Club, a popular speakeasy, white male musicians negotiated their own sense of identity through several means, including their emulation of stereotypes about black musical spontaneity and "hotness," the marginalization of women, and their antagonistic views about a supposed antithetical relationship between their lucrative gigs and "authentic expression." These musicians were not exceptions in this regard: many throughout the history of the music have negotiated their identities in the jazz world. In this particular social setting, racial ventriloquism and anticommercial sentiments were rehearsed within a culture of urban bachelorhood. This was a powerful cocktail indeed.

How might the setting of the Onyx Club help us understand the world of black male musicians who, like Powell, played bebop at a later historical moment? As they operated within somewhat different social standings, white and black masculinities in the musical world of the 1940s shared little save the marginalization of female musicians, especially instrumentalists. Black musicians negotiated their immediate social worlds to procure for themselves some of the traditional advantages of male power—earning wages, spectacle, and hegemony over women—in the context of a growing black, urban, and artistic proletariat. Significant work in gender and music has, of course, been developed in studies of Western art music and popular music studies. When we work with those insights into jazz and black music specifically, we must account for their similarities to and differences from both of those realms.

As noted by Gavin James Campbell, by the early 1900s, a "classical sphere" network based on European traditions of composition was clearly in place in America, and it included "performing groups, concert halls, conservatories, and enough public interest in these institutions to support them financially." Involvement with classical music became at this time a set of activities—performance, promotion, and audience participation—in which "men and women articulated their anxieties about changing gender roles." As women pushed for fulfilling lives outside the home and the domestic realm, careers in music provided new alternatives: professional women musicians became emblematic of women's desires for more satisfying public lives. Many formed civic clubs in which they exercised control over the community's musical life and other realms of the public sphere. For their part, men tempered their muses by emphasizing their enthusiasm for "boxing, wrestling, or other similar activities, or by expressing their interests [in music] solely as a civic and husbandly duty." Gender distinctions were a pressing concern, and America's classical music world was a potent place in which to struggle with them, indeed, to "arbitrate anew the meanings of masculinity and femininity" in modern industrialized society.

During these same years, jazz emerged as a musical form distinct from "classical sphere" music and its concerns, replete with varying ideas about gender, class, and, of course, race. Jazz became part of the popular sphere, and, as Richard Crawford has noted, "popular entertainment was well on its way to becoming modern 'show business.' And the workings of this new entertainment industry depended on a new approach to creating and marketing popular song." The elements of this emerging structure created a space for a wide range of social formations. For example, it provided opportunities to work out gender roles in the public sphere, and African Americans were crucial in these new formations because the industry offered one of the precious few opportunities for them to be considered something more than servants and menial workers with the lowest pay.

The great jazz composer and pianist Jelly Roll Morton's discussion of his childhood musical attitudes and aspirations in early twentieth-century New Orleans gives us a snapshot of how race, gender, and class shaped his thinking. As Creoles, his class-conscious parents wanted him to play the "proper music heard at the French Opera House" and not popular music. As a child, he heard a man play a classical recital, and he was attracted to the music. But there was a problem. The gentleman had "long bushy hair, and, because the piano was known in our circle as an instrument for a lady, this confirmed for me my idea that if I played the piano I would be misunderstood." In his own words, Morton "didn't want to be called a sissy." Because of this aversion to one of the prevalent social meanings of the piano in his world, he decided to study other instruments, "such as violin, drums, and guitar, until one day at a party I saw a gentleman sit down at the piano and play a very good piece of ragtime. This particular gentleman had short hair and I decided then that the instrument was good for a gentleman same as it was for a lady."

Fletcher Henderson's educated parents stressed piano lessons in the home as a crucial part of a thorough, well-rounded education in the Deep South at a time (the early twentieth century) when the instrument was a symbol of uplift and middle-class respectability. Everyone in the Henderson household read music and played the piano, although the repertoire was circumscribed to "classical and church music." Because of this background, the pull of financial gain and masculinist success was strong and inevitable. Henderson would eventually forgo his plans to earn a master's degree in chemistry at Columbia University to pursue a successful career in dance music. The music industry at this time, together with a heightened African American cultural presence in American consciousness, provided what Jeffrey Magee has called "unprecedented opportunities for African Americans with ambition and talent." Henderson clearly possessed both, and by 1923, three years after he arrived in New York, he was thoroughly ensconced in the city's popular musical world.

One of his activities involved the new blues craze of the 1920s. Although he was not a blues or jazz musician per se when he came to New York, Henderson accepted the professional challenges of this environment, one far removed from his sheltered upbringing in the upper crust of the new black South. He enjoyed the money, notoriety, and popularity with the ladies. Indeed, the music industry became a promising alternative realm for black men—even well-educated, prepared men such as Henderson—to make new meanings in masculinity.

Here it is important to remember that the popular sphere also gave women a platform to attain the empowering visibility and wage-earning potential that defined traditional masculinities. The blues industry in particular provided women with their own stage on which to publicly negotiate gender roles. The rise of black popular culture was part of a larger shift in the 1920s that wrested the sole responsibility for black progress and representation away from the educated, literate men of the "Talented Tenth." In her study of 1920s blueswomen, Hazel Carby argues that black power and representation were up for grabs across the board—not just in the realm of music—as various constituencies jockeyed to publicly claim that their own group best represented "the experience of the race." Thus black musical masculinity was performed in a larger cultural frame of diverse intra-African American struggles for social power, including but not limited to both men and women actively stepping out of traditional subservient roles.

We see multiple shifts occurring here. Popular music became an important province for African Americans, and classical music solidified their own idea of authenticity. Each realm was an important cultural territory for negotiating power through gendered meanings, and they would collide in the bebop movement. For black men, popular culture provided an arena of accomplishment that was thoroughly rooted in wage earning, visibility, and creative expression. Since the public aspect of popular culture remained, for the most part, segregated, it provided little threat to the "separate but equal" doctrine that policed race relations. In other words, there existed—on the surface, at least—few risks of direct sexual, financial, or social competition with white men.

The ascendancy of popular culture tended to flatten out class distinctions within the black community as well, as black middle-class musicians flocked to the unprecedented opportunities and prestige that it offered. Apparently, what the cultural arbiters of good taste considered "lowbrow" was a shot at upward mobility for these "Others." What was perceived as a threat to virile masculinity and good class standing by Jelly Roll Morton's generation—particularly seen in his apparent view that "classical" music posed a threat to perceptions of his masculinity—was a springboard to becoming a sex symbol and iconic success for Duke Ellington, Willie "The Lion" Smith, and other, later musicians. It is within this historical, social, and material grounding that bebop and the new idea of "jazz manhood" emerged.

With all of these histories swirling around music, gender, and sexuality, it's easy to understand why I bailed on my beloved piano and claimed an instrument in which I had little interest. Ideas about manhood and musicality have always been fraught, fickle, and powerful.

8 Blues and the Ethnographic Truth

Because art is invention, "truth" is generally held to be a false standard by which to evaluate a writer's work. This should be the case whether the issue is Alice Walker's representation of black men or Spike Lee's treatment of black women. Yet . . . this is precisely the leap of faith that critics of African American literature continue to make. Texts are transparent documents that must tell the truth as I know it. Failure to tell my truth not only invalidates the text, it also discredits, de-authorizes, and on occasion deracializes the writer. Truth, however, like beauty, is in the eye and perhaps the experience of the beholder.[1]

In a 1993 essay, Black feminist literary critic Ann duCille argued for critics to spare artistic works such as novels of the burden to tell the truth. Although she believes that art performs important cultural work in the world, duCille calls for critics of literature—and her argument extends easily to other forms of artistic expression—to understand that an essential and "absolute historical truth" about the African American experience

"Blues and the Ethnographic Truth," *Journal of Popular Music Studies* 13, no. 1 (Spring 2001): 41–58. An early form of this essay was presented at the "Around the Sound" conference in 2000 at the University of Washington. It forecast some of the methodologies I'd use in my book *Race Music: Black Cultures from Bebop to Hip-Hop* (2003).

does not exist. This diversity of experiences among African Americans shapes, in duCille's view, how critics engage the works they explicate and interpret. She writes, "Readings are never neutral. All criticisms are local, situational."[2]

At first glance the title of this chapter may suggest something otherwise, but I am arguing that the idea of ethnographic truth captures the spirit of the local and situational quality of knowledge and experience—be it in an artistic work or in the criticism that tries to interpret it. Even the idea of an existing ethnographic truth about the blues seems to suggest a "common-sense," casual relationship between a cultural practice and a group of people. But again, this relationship is always local, situational, and specific. The truth and meanings of such can be better understood if the critic positions them within the experiences of specific historical actors.

"The blues" in the title of this article refers to the family of idioms connected to the blues genre and to the conceptual framework of music making known popularly as the African American musical tradition.[3] Both these conceptions of the blues have been understood in many quarters as the quintessential musical expression of Black culture. This particular view has been widely critiqued from various standpoints, all with the goal of opening up the cultural possibilities, the representations, and the critical approaches of and to African Americans.[4] Critiques of the blues as a key symbol of African American culture have grown out of larger concerns about the limiting notions of "authenticity" and "essentialism." As duCille argues, criticism that treats the blues as a "metonym for authentic blackness" or as the "grand signifier of *the* black experience" fails to take into account other important cultural expressions that have been just as significant.[5]

It is certainly beneficial to heed the warnings of this line of thinking. Yet, at the same time, we must also recognize the importance of the blues modality to African American culture. Although we should work against the sense of romantic folk authenticity that does not account for diversity, we must also acknowledge the importance of this musical modality to African Americans and to audiences around the globe.

In this chapter I will explore some of the possible meanings of blues modality in a specific faction of African American culture at a particular historical moment. One of my central arguments is that meaning in music is generated, in part, in what I call community theaters. Among other cultural spaces, these public and private arenas comprise film, churches, family and ethnic histories, nightclubs, and even the "theater of the literary"—written music criticism and scholarship. In the larger study from which this chapter is drawn, I have highlighted the impact of these community theaters on the making of musical meaning through several modes of inquiry, including history, cultural and social memory, and contemporary theory.[6] Here I will discuss one of the ways in which I have tried to consider the relationship among cultural and social memories, historical moments, and musical discourses.

HOW DOES IT MEAN? MEMORY AND HISTORY

Memory

Like all expressive culture, music possesses the capacity to "mean" for audiences and critics alike. Music scholars over the last few years have developed various strategies for exploring music's ability to communicate for musicians and to communities of listeners. Many of these strategies have taken into account the contingency of value and taste, especially when dealing with the artistic expressions of groups that are considered subaltern or marginal. Meaning, in other words, like truth and beauty, is in the eyes of the beholder.

I try to get at meaning or an ethnographic truth of the blues through a set of methods that cluster around three areas: memory, history, and theory. In this model, memory is best exemplified by the ethnographic element in this essay. James Clifford has written that ethnography comprises "diverse ways of thinking and writing about culture from the standpoint of participant observation."[7] Since the 1980s, the human sciences have questioned ethnographic method from all angles, opening up new ways to think and write about culture.[8] This self-reflexive moment has left its mark on the music disciplines (especially ethnomusicology), and one development has been that more and more scholars have begun to consider the role of their own subjectivities in their critical approaches.[9]

My approach to (cultural) memory and to what might be called an ethnographic stance is illustrated by one of my writerly strategies: the way I have transformed into a narrative some of the data collected in oral history interviews from the larger project from which this chapter is drawn. I have attempted to capture the spirit, and the ethnographic "truth," "situational-ness," and thrust of the stories told to me. In his 1995 study *The Power of Black Music*, Samuel A. Floyd wrote that cultural memory refers "to the nonfactual and nonreferential motivations, actions, and beliefs that members of a culture seem, without direct knowledge or deliberate training, to 'know'—that feel unequivocally 'true' or 'right' when encountered, experienced, and executed." Furthermore, Floyd argued that cultural memory is "obviously a subjective concept" and that it is "connected to cultural *forms*—in the present case, music, where the 'memory' drives the music and the music drives memory."[10] Life experience, of course, shapes these cultural memories and our responses to them.

The male protagonist in the 1939 recording "Goin' to Chicago Blues" expresses a sentiment found in many blues songs: a male fleeing an unfulfilling heterosexual relationship and escaping to another location, presumably to reestablish himself in a new living environment and, perhaps, with a new love interest. Cast in the familiar twelve-bar blues pattern, the song features the great blues vocalist Jimmy Rushing supported by a small jazz combo led by Count Basie.

Black urban centers like Chicago, Harlem, and Philadelphia began a steady decline during the Depression that continued throughout the latter half of the twentieth century. But these centers continued to attract scores of Black southerners and the years surrounding World War II saw an accelerated flow of Black bodies, hopes, and fears to northern cities. Much has been written in the historical and social science literature about the economic and political reasons for these citizens leaving the South. Clearly, job opportunities, racial oppression, and the promise of economic security influenced many to "go to Chicago." Yet, as we will see, other, more deeply personal reasons account for some of the demographic shift that is represented in "Goin' to Chicago Blues."

During 1996, I conducted interviews with some of my older relatives, African Americans living in Chicago, Illinois. Some were migrants who had moved from Georgia to Chicago in the years immediately following World War II. Others were second-generation migrants whose parents had come to Chicago in the late 1910s. One reason I elected to conduct these interviews—usually lively sessions of conversations and storytelling—was to understand and to question the historical and material grounding of my own critical biases and assumptions as a musicologist. I sought, in other words, to reveal to my readers something that is usually cloaked in much of the cultural criticism and music scholarship appearing in the contemporary moment.

This strategy positions my work in the experimental ethnographic work that has appeared in the last twenty years. I engage something that anthropologist Jose Limón observed: that scholarship itself should be considered expressive culture about expressive culture.[11] For me, the interviews, together with other methods of inquiry, provided a way to connect an audience's real-life experiences (or ethnographic truth) to the themes, tropes, and practices of African American music at specific historical moments. I believe this strategy provides readers access into some of the ways in which musical meaning is generated among audiences and insights into the manner in which critics and scholars attempt to articulate that social and cultural transaction.

On the microlevel of culture, we find that during the 1940s African American domestic spaces experienced profound changes, of which the story related herein represents a specific yet typical example. When I began these interviews and asked why each of my interviewees had left the South and moved to Chicago, I fully expected to hear horrific stories about white racism and the North being a "better place." Instead, their stories, like many of the rhythm and blues songs recorded in this era, focused on love and family relationships.

History

I read the historical moment under consideration through the prism of "Afro-modernism," which, in my view, accounts for the social, economic, cultural, and political factors that emerged in African American culture during the 1940s. Indeed, the 1940s saw a number of remarkable shifts within the nation's intellectual, political, cultural, economic, and artistic life. As American intellectuals began to rethink how they perceived American culture and heritage, a new sense of nationalism emerged, a "baby boom" and a new prosperity shaped American family life, a modernist sensibility swept through the arts, and a new efficacy among working-class citizens transformed economic relationships and popular culture. As historian George Lipsitz noted, mobilizing for World War II and the reconversion process after the war shook American culture to its core, sending waves of change through almost every realm of the American experience. Music of this period cannot be divorced from these developments. Dizzy Gillespie, for example, reminded us in his autobiography that even the performance rhetoric of modern jazz was linked to the specific tenor of the postwar moment: "My music emerged from the war years . . . and it reflected those times in the music. Fast and furious, with the chord changes going this way and that way, it might've looked and sounded like bedlam, but it really wasn't."[12]

For many African Americans, however, these times were bedlam. In the interlocking realms of politics, economics, and culture, the 1940s saw many developments that touched the lives of all Americans but held specific consequences for African Americans, especially within their expressive cultural practices. Chief among these developments, and in many ways causing them, was the dramatic demographic shift created by thousands of Black citizens leaving southern states for urban communities such as New York, Chicago, and Los Angeles.

The force of this migration would carry long-term effects for the country's social policies, and especially for its artistic and cultural profile. The 1940s were marked by contradiction. On one hand, the Jim Crow system that appeared after Reconstruction seemed to be drawing its last breath because of political, legal, and economic pressures mounted by African Americans in grassroots protests. On the other hand, the shifting maze of discriminatory practices constantly undermined these various struggles for equality. These cultural dynamics played themselves out in postwar African American expressive culture such as literature, the visual arts, and music.[13] One notable shift occurred in the "race" division of popular music, where fragmentation took place, separating genres into different marketing categories.[14]

A booming wartime economy, a huge migration of rural citizens to urban centers, and technological advances in the recording industry also promoted change. The postwar period's strong economy had a profound impact on the American entertainment industry, most notably in the area of record sales. In 1945, for example, the recording industry anticipated a sales boom of six hundred million records because of postwar consumers' appetite for new artists; few in the business predicted the doubling of sales that occurred. New technology emerging from military efforts during World War II improved sound reproduction, further encouraging American interest in purchasing recordings. Among the new advances were wire and tape recording and reproducing machines and a Russian-captured German Magnetophone, which gave superior fidelity to American commercial recordings. In 1948, Columbia Records introduced long-playing discs (LPs), allowing about twenty-five minutes of uninterrupted music on each side. This technological advance was well suited for the inspired freedom of modern jazz solos.[15]

The atmosphere was ripe with new possibilities, experimentation, and innovation. Musicians and entrepreneurs alike exploited the situation, seizing the moment. Fledgling record companies such as Mercury sought out new artists and attempted to find a niche in the market for themselves by satisfying the public's growing appetite for new talent. As a result, the postwar years spawned hybrid styles that proliferated in the popular music industry. An impressive array of new artists appeared, many of them recent migrants to northern cities. The shifting profile of urban America throughout this decade changed American musical life. George Lipsitz has noted the importance of Black *and* white migration to America's cities, contending that "the new urban realities of the 1940s . . . allowed for new cultural exchanges that would have been impossible in prewar America." Industrial labor created by defense production for World War II, for example, provided unprecedented interaction among diverse ethnic groups and their musical sensibilities.[16] These new cultural exchanges produced a variety of musics that were popular among urban Blacks and whites. Accelerated by advances in communications and transportation technologies that were "making the world an ever-shrinking globe," these musical developments encouraged changes within the popular music industry.[17]

For my purposes, Afro-modernism is closely linked to the new urbanity of African American communities, the heady sociopolitical progress and the changing sense of what constituted African American culture (and even American culture in general). This idea helps us to interpret the various "race musics" that appeared as historically specific social discourses. This social energy shaped the formal procedures of race music and helped give it meaning and coherence for audiences. The music, in turn, influenced the social setting of the Afro-modernist moment. Moreover, we see at this time the development of a continuum with two rhetorical performance modalities at each end, represented by the North and the South, a notion that brings into sharper relief the import of migration and urbanity on African American musical culture during the 1940s and thereafter.[18]

If the previous section fixes the idea of Afro-modernism within large sociocultural processes, the following passages situate it within the politics of the personal. In a recent critique of resistance studies, anthropologist Sherry B. Ortner argued that insufficient focus on ethnography within them limits these studies' usefulness. She called this blind spot "ethnographic refusal."[19]

Ethnographic refusal manifests itself, first, by limiting study of the "political" to the relationship between subordinate groups and those who hold power over them and not recognizing power conflicts and struggles *among* subalterns. Another form of ethnographic refusal fails to grant subalterns an "authentic" culture that is created out of their own systems of meaning and order and not merely as a response to the situation of social and cultural domination. As Ortner argued persuasively:

> If we are to recognize that resistors are doing more than simply opposing domination, more than simply producing a virtually mechanical reaction, then we must go the whole way. They have their own politics—not just between chiefs and commoners or landlords and peasants but within all the local categories of friction and tension: men and women, parents and children, seniors and juniors; inheritance conflicts among brothers; struggles of succession and wars of conquest between chiefs; struggles for primacy between religious sects; and on and on.[20]

Much of the research on African American music discusses "the black masses" or working-class folks, without forwarding the specificity of the ethnographic stance of which Ortner wrote. More attention, for example, should be paid to the more "private" spaces of Blackness—the "drylongso" ways in which Black ethnicity is "performed" outside of the public discourses upon which scholarship usually relies to access and represent it. Interrogation of this arena of cultural memory and historical concerns enables us to perceive more accurately connections among community theaters, collective memory, and musical practice. For example, for some African Americans, leaving the South during the migration was about more than racism and power relationships between Blacks and whites. My relatives told stories that concentrated more on power relationships *among* family members. And the storytellers spoke of things other than "struggles": they told tales of the celebratory rituals of their southern and northern lives and of the social and material circumstances in which these activities were played out.

"GOIN' TO CHICAGO": MIGRATION AND THE DOMESTIC SPACE

The Rosses of Valdosta, Georgia, were one of many southern Black families who migrated to the North in the years following World War II. One by one, each left Georgia's red clay for Chicago's paved streets to build a new life, shedding various aspects of their southern, rural past. Peter Mallie Ross (1895–1975) and Martha Bynum Ross (1907–91) married and had five children: Celia, Marjorie, Peter Mallie, Dorothy, and Bobby Lester. The elder Peter was born in a tiny hamlet called Wacissa, Florida, which lies outside the city of Tallahassee. The lifestyle in Wacissa was rural and possessed few of a larger city's amenities. Celia and Marjorie both recalled that, during their visits in the 1930s and 1940s, the extended Ross family comprised a fairly large number of the town's population. Peter's adult children explain that "in this particular area, there wasn't anybody around that wasn't a Ross. It was sort of like the Kennedy compound," they recalled with sarcastic and signifying delight, "only southern-style—in the woods, without streetlights and stuff." As the Ross children came of age and married, some of them experienced domestic difficulties, including Marjorie, whose partial migration story is presented here.

> Marjorie packed her belongings with a defiant conviction. She and her infant daughter would have to execute this escape with a calculated precision. It seems like something was always happening to her. Strong-willed and fun-loving since childhood, her resolve and force of personality deposited her squarely in the middle of many family conflicts and all of its pleasures while growing up. Marjorie's tongue spoke what her mind thought. She always stood her ground, took the dare, danced the best, protected those she loved, kept the atmosphere dense with the joys of living. Now she needed

her family's aid to make the quick transition. Her youngest brother, Bob—a lanky, carefree teenager with a wide, toothy grin and a mischievous twinkle that consumed his slightly slanted eyes, which were a family trait—had to help her perform some sho-nuff magic—the feat as old as love itself: to disappear from Valdosta, Georgia, without a trace.

She was going to Chicago, where her mother and sister—both whom had migrated earlier—awaited her arrival, but she couldn't take the direct route. So she began by making her move at night, packing all her worldly possessions in whatever could contain them and then stowing them under the house, near the chimney, out of her husband's sight. The next day, she would leave this unhappy home, despite the chilling thought that he would almost certainly pursue. He wanted to possess her—just another person controlling her and another good reason to flee. She needed to throw him off the scent of the trail, so she decided to get to Chicago in a roundabout way by Trailways Bus, stopping first in Tallahassee, Florida. Timing would be crucial. So when Bob didn't show up at the designated meeting point to help her with the bags and her infant daughter, her faith began to wane. Where was he? Marjorie eventually made it to Chicago, an entirely different and to her exciting social and cultural environment, although she, like many migrants before and after her, would have to make many adjustments.

The interviewees told many other stories involving difficult relationships and the financial challenges of growing up poor in the South. They spoke knowledgeably about the music in various southern cultural spaces like the jook joints, about their socialization into northern life, including their adapting to new cuisine, house parties, and being introduced to "the jazz" by in-laws who had been raised in Chicago. Throughout these interviews the females situated themselves as the true culture bearers. They told the stories from their perspectives and were often the central characters in the narratives, although, according to one female, the blues relate what "the man" has gone through. Music constituted a central space for historically specific "culture making" in the interviewees' memories.

AFRO-MODERNISM, MUSIC, AND MIGRATION AT MIDCENTURY

During the 1940s, a confluence of social, cultural, and economic conditions shaped Black cultural production in profound ways. Likewise, music helped to shape important aspects of the social reality of many living in America during this time. During World War II, African Americans experienced what has been called the most profound Americanization of their collective consciousness since the Civil War.[21] In reciprocal fashion, during this same period America at-large experienced a definitive "Afro-Americanization" due to an increased Black presence in the nation's mass media.[22]

Against the backdrop of an intensified call for equal rights from all sectors of African American society, the "Newest Negroes" of the 1940s media participated in a number of remarkable developments with respect to African American self-understanding and America's cultural profile broadly conceived. Music bears all the traces of this new cultural figuration. As Tera Hunter has written about earlier blues forms, "the centrality of the singer's individual persona, the highly personalized subject matter of songs, the thematic shifts toward the material world and the pursuit of pleasure were all characteristic of an emergent modern ethos."[23] In other words, African American music culture registered and participated in the cultural shifts occurring at midcentury.

As I have argued above, Afro-modernism is closely linked to a performance continuum with two rhetorical modalities: the North and the South. Attention to the musical rhetoric that was produced by the exchange of the social energies circulating between the North and the South allows us to analyze important aspects of the cultural work being performed by specific pieces of music. Moreover, the North/South cultural dialogue carries larger implications for the significance of the relationship between African and African American music.

While the African past is obviously a historical/anthropological fact, it was continually manipulated with different kinds of signifying affect throughout the twentieth century. A host of historical actors have alternately valued the African past either as a rhetorical tool in African American cultural politics or as proof of Black citizens' cultural inferiority. What is crucial here is how the troping, or repetitive use, of various musical techniques, musicking activities, myths, canonical stories, cuisine, and so on have signified for many not Africa per se but a southern-based cultural system. Thus, as Hans A. Baer and Merrill Singer argued:

The current importance of these African elements derives not from their possible source but in the part they have played and continue to play in the crafting of special mechanisms for social survival, emotional comfort, and transcendent expression under the harshest of physical circumstances.[24]

Throughout the twentieth century—particularly during the World War II years—the flow of Black migrants to urban commercial centers such as Chicago supplied northern cultural spaces with "southernisms" that constantly interacted with urban expressions and with European and American cultural practices. Mass migration; the use and misuse of the Black body; a new urban profile; a swelling sense of Black political, economic, and social efficacy; and conflicting discourses on art's role in social change all set the stage for new cultural expressions in the 1940s. Taken together, these developments and tensions constituted a musical Afro-modernism at midcentury. The recordings and artists discussed below provide examples of how the social energy circulating in the ethnographic truth of specific audience members and the sociocultural developments of the moment could be conveyed, commented on, and troped in specific mass-mediated recordings.

"IT'S JUST THE BLUES": CODES, RHETORIC, AND MIGRATION

When the Four Jumps of Jive recorded "It's Just the Blues" in September 1945, they inaugurated Mercury Records, the first independent record label to appear following World War II.[25] The lyrical and musical content of "It's Just the Blues," its performance rhetoric, the backgrounds of the composers and performers, and its appearance at a specific historical moment and geographic setting have important implications for the criticism of Black music of the 1940s. The Four Jumps of Jive consisted of vocalist and pianist Jimmy "Eugene" Gibson, lead guitarist Bernardo Dennis, and rhythm guitarist Ellis Hunter. The most notable member of this group was its bassist, Willie Dixon (1915–92). A native of Vicksburg, Mississippi, Dixon migrated to Chicago and, after a brief career as a prize-fighter, began a musical career, singing in gospel quartets and playing bass in secular settings. Dixon's compositions and performance techniques—similar to those of Muddy Waters—helped to define in the next decade not only the Chicago urban blues sound but early rock and roll as well. "It's Just the Blues" was composed by Gibson and Richard M. Jones, the A&R (artists and repertoire) man for Mercury records who, like Dixon and many other Black musicians in race musics, had experience in gospel music as well.[26]

The tune is a twelve-bar blues repeated over eleven choruses that alternate between two vocal strains followed by one instrumental. It opens with an entire instrumental chorus of musical codes and gestures drawn from Black vernacular and popular sources. The most prominent of these features is a shuffle-boogie beat, created by Dixon's heavily accented chord outlines and Hunter's steady rhythm-guitar strumming that interlocks with the bass line; they continue this pattern throughout the recording. Bernardo Dennis's sparse melodic figures and Gilmore's vocal declamations ("Well-weeeeeell-well!") round out the introductory chorus. The absence of a drummer in this rhythm section leaves enough of the soundscape free to give the performance the characteristic lightness of many jump blues combos. Since this group was a "cocktail outfit" working in a Chicago nightclub at the time of the recording, it is likely that they opted out of having a drummer for economic, or perhaps even logistic, reasons. If Gilmore's declamatory style during the introduction brings a "country" or rural modality to this decidedly urban-sounding recording, the remainder of his performance highlights the tension between these two ideals.

Gilmore sings in what might be called a "blues-croon" style, which, while capturing some of the immediate emotional impact of the "flat-footed" blues belters of the day, also signified a kind of urbane sophistication. Another affect in Gilmore's blues-croon presentation is a warbling technique that he employs on various words, especially those falling on the lowered third, fifth, and seventh scale degrees. Gilmore securely mixes these rhetorical gestures. The lyrical content of the song continues this code-fusion aesthetic. In the first two vocal choruses of the song, we learn that, like many other blues lyrics, the narrative poetry of "It's Just the Blues" will be cast in the arena of the body, in sexual politics. The protagonist speaks directly to the object of his desire; he is feeling amorous, and his "good whiskey" is obviously helping his "blues," which in this case is not a bad thing because he's "got the blues and feeling mighty *fine*." Gilmore's use of Afro-urban argot—describing his female friend as "fine and mellow," her influence over him as "sending," and his male companions as "cats"—centers his rhetoric within the up-to-date field of contemporaneous African American dialect. Yet the metaphor "high as a Georgia pine" and Gilmore's exclamatory "Heeeeey-ya!" concluding the second chorus highlight the code-fusion between urban and rural (read southern) references.

These code-fusions continue in the third chorus. During the vocal choruses guitarist Bernardo Dennis plays simple riff figures beneath Gilmore's melodic lines, adding to the sense of propulsion derived from Dixon's and Hunter's rhythmic foundation. In the fourth, seventh, and tenth choruses, Dennis plays pentatonic scale–based electric guitar solos, none of which is necessarily highly technical in the Charlie Christian sense, but each of which draws attention to the instrumentalist as the central "voice" in the text. During all of these solo spotlights, Gilmore exclaims stock phrases that might well be heard in everyday conversation, such as, "Rock on," "Well, well," "Knock me out," "Heeey now," "If that's the way you feel, it's a good deal." One might interpret these solos in several ways: as the missing voice of Gilmore's love interest, as a gesture toward jazz solo virtuosity, or perhaps as musical contrasts in the narrative. We never hear what has gone wrong with the relationship portrayed here, but as the song progresses it becomes clear that it is not ideal, as Gilmore exclaims:

> Come back here pretty baby, talk some of that sweet jive to me.
> Come back here pretty baby, talk some of that sweet jive to me.
> And I don't want you to hand me none of that stuff,
> Talking about "things ain't what they used to be."

In fact, by the end of the piece, Gilmore decides to leave his love interest because he doesn't want to get played for a fool. This reference to the song title, "Things Ain't What They Used to Be," indeed, even the name of this group, The Four Jumps of Jive, firmly position the lyrical aspect of this recording within the social web of Black urban culture. But, as we have seen, other features reference the "country" or the South. In order to explore some of the meanings that these code-fusions may have generated, we need to situate this text more firmly in its historical moment.

The subtle crisscrossing of stylistic borders in "It's Just the Blues" signified profoundly. *Billboard* reported in October 1945 that the Chicago-
based Mercury label had only signed Negro artists, including two "cocktail
units" such as The Four Jumps of Jive and Bill Samuels and His Cats 'N'
Jammers; singers June Richmond, Sippie Wallace, and Karl Jones; and
pianist Albert Ammons. Mercury would eventually cast a wide net for
customers—a diverse range of American popular musics filled its catalog.

But the company also deliberately courted a specific clientele: not the
flood of southern Black migrants who streamed into Chicago throughout
the 1940s, but "the established South Side population which already
prided itself in its urban sophistication."[27] Indeed, Mercury's producers
appeared sensitive to the intra-Black cultural dynamics caused in part by
the migration and how elements of musical style could signify into them.
The musicians responded to the diversity of musical tastes among the
Black communities created by geographic segregation. They also recognized Chicago's position as a commercial center; as an important site of
Black cultural production since the 1920s; and as home to a thriving network of churches, theaters, lounges, nightclubs, and dance halls as well as
a vibrant (and for the most part underdocumented) "house party" culture.
Therefore, Mercury executives' simple business decision to carve out a
musical niche in this specific market rested on their understanding some
of the rapid, intense social and cultural shifts occurring in urban centers
such as Chicago, New York, and Los Angeles and in the nation as a whole.

Again, Marjorie's and her family's personal narratives bear the traces of
the intra-Black cultural dialogue between northern and southern sensibilities. Below she recounts some of her experiences in the jook joints of
rural Georgia in the early 1940s and her new life in Chicago, which began
in the post–World War II years. Back in Georgia, she recalls, "music was
just the thing" and "I was the one that really could dance." While living in
the city of Valdosta, Georgia, where her family had once settled, she frequented the jooks that were part of the scene in the outlying rural communities. She remembers:

> Friday, Saturday, and Sunday. That was juke night. That was juke night. And
> I would love to go out in the country because I knew I could dance. And
> I knew everybody was going be standing around looking at the city girl

coming and dancing. And we would be in, just a wood frame, you know. And we would just . . . that was the best time of my life. I really enjoyed those times. It wasn't nothing but the blues. You know. Blues. Juke music and everything. Those times were really, really . . . it just stays with me all of the time.

After moving to Chicago in the late 1940s, however, she believed that culturally "the whole tone changed." Adjusting to the food and music of the North stood out in these migrants' minds as some of the more signifi-cant modifications they had to make. After arriving in the Windy City, Marjorie wondered, "Where's my type music?" The following passage recounts verbatim an exchange among Marjorie and her siblings, Celia and Bob, during an interview. Although these particular memories high-light the differences they perceived in their new northern lifestyle, in other stories they stressed some of the continuities that existed in the cul-tural terrain. They maintained, for example, that adjusting to "the jazz" wasn't that difficult once they started learning who particular performers were.

MARJORIE: When I came here, then the whole tone changed for me. The music. Like the food. Now, chitterlings and all this kind of stuff, okay, we didn't eat that. And when I came here . . .

CELIA: It was a delicacy.

MARJORIE: All you could see is people saying about chitterlings and spaghettis and coleslaws and all this kind of stuff. And we didn't eat that. They threw that away . . . because we could go to [the] . . .

BOB: Slaughterhouse.

CELIA: We cleaned out the chitterling. We cleaned out the chitterling and we stuffed meat in them and that became our sausage.

MARJORIE: But I couldn't understand, when I came here, then that's when I went into the Ella Fitzgerald and the . . .

CELIA: Lady Day.

MARJORIE: Lady Day and all this. And it was a whole changeover for me because I was there with blues and whatever.

CELIA: B. B. King.

MARJORIE: And Muddy Waters and all of them.

CELIA: Muddy Waters and all them. That's all we knew.

MARJORIE: And I came here and they was coming to the houses and stuff.
             Meeting to the houses. And of course you had all of the nightclubs
             and things here. But then the families . . .

CELIA: They called them house rent parties.

MARJORIE: Yeah. House rent parties. You'd pay and come in . . .

CELIA: A quarter. Quarter parties.

MARJORIE: And then you'd see these chitterlings. People talking chitterling din-
             ners and all of this. And I'm wondering "Well, what's so great about
             this?" You know. And then you'd go into this jazz music that . . . And
             I'm looking, "Where's my type music?" But you gotta mellow on
             down to the Lady Day and the Ella Fitzgerald and all this. And the
             finger popping [snaps her fingers] and the spoon popping and
             whatever.

CELIA: When we met the Ramseys, they introduced us to the jazz.

MARJORIE: A whole different thing.

CELIA: It was them. The Ramseys introduced us to jazz.

MARJORIE: I guess maybe they had never . . . you know blues is everywhere, but
             not so much as the way it was back there.

CELIA: Down South.

MARJORIE: That was the thing there.

"It's Just the Blues" was drenched in Afro-modernist sensibilities that
served as a backdrop for these migrants' experiences. The recording codified a specific moment of urbanity for African Americans. Even the "commercialism" of the piece is suggestive of the aggressively new economic
clout of African Americans, particularly those who lived in the urban
North. A specific and quite modern audience base interpreted the narrative codes of "It's Just the Blues."

One of the important points here involves how bodies signified both in
this piece and in others like it. The public celebration (some would say
objectification) of the woman's "fine and mellow" body in the lyrics, the
alcohol-induced "blues" in the protagonist's body, and even the Black (and
very likely white) bodies that without doubt danced to this recording
marked a new beginning—a new cultural politics in African American
history. If one of the legacies of nineteenth-century minstrelsy involved
the public degradation of the Black body in the American entertainment

sphere, then one hundred years after minstrelsy's emergence, African Americans used this same signifier to upset a racist social order and to affirm in public entertainment and in the private sphere their culture and humanity.

Although it has some precedent, the new attitude was so prevalent that it represents a huge departure from earlier modes of "racial uplift," especially the "politics of respectability" championed by Black professionals and upper-class citizens, who sought to discipline Black bodies into bourgeois submission.[28] A reliable measure of this new attitude in the realm of music can be found in the Black newspaper the *Chicago Defender*. Coverage of African American music during the 1940s shifted significantly toward the entertainment/dance music field and away from the activities of the Blacks in classical music who had at one time dominated the society pages of the *Defender*.

·   ·   ·   ·   ·

By combining ethnographic interviews, historical concerns, and musical and cultural analysis, my work uncovers some of the connections among the lives of real people, the musical discourses that were important to them, and the historical moment in which these cultural transactions occurred. History, memory, and contemporary theories of race, gender, and class are brought together in the larger study from which this chapter is drawn to identify the social energies from which meaning in music was generated—meanings that helped to shape the social world, or the "truth," for many listeners.

9 Time Is Illmatic

A SONG FOR MY FATHER, A LETTER TO MY SON

Dedicated to G. P. Ramsey Sr. (1924–94) and R. G. Ramsey (b. 1984)

Nas's recording "Life's a Bitch" is a song of its time, rich in its multiple layers of historical, social, and cultural dialogues. The year it appeared, 1994, was a watershed moment in hip-hop cultural production; many say that it was the genre's shining hour. Although hip-hop was in its "pre-bling" stage, consumerism, commercialism, and critiques of black access to capital—especially as all of these concerned contemporary black masculinity—emerged as thematic tropes in the music. Like the bebop moment in the mid-1940s, hip-hop's mid-1990s aesthetics seemed posed to succeed at the unlikely mix of musical experimentation *and* commercial viability—so much so that today 1994 is remembered nostalgically as "the year hip-hop was reborn," the days when "hip-hop was an art form," or "hip-hop's last great year." Indeed, Nas's *Illmatic* stands as an artistic emblem of that moment: thematically complex, immaculately, eclectically, even delicately

"Time is Illmatic," in *Born to Use Mics: Reading Nas's Illmatic*, ed. Michael Eric Dyson and Sohail Daulatzai (New York: Basic Books, 2009), 61–74. This essay was part of a larger study in which scholars were assigned to write about different tracks on the rapper Nas's critically acclaimed and historically significant 1994 project, *Illmatic*.

produced, and rich in layered textures and colors: a hip-hop version of Miles Davis's signature work *Kind of Blue* of 1959, if there ever was one.

The poet Gwendolyn Brooks once proclaimed during the Black Arts Movement of the 1960s and 1970s that it was no longer a "rhyme time." But rhymes would make a triumphant return and do so with a vengeance in hip-hop culture, an art in which rhyming performed in semi- to nonmelodic declamation, otherwise known as rapping, became a key sign of authenticity for two generations of listeners to date. Around 1994 hip-hop was marked by a growing and self-conscious eclecticism that was regionally oriented across the black, urban archipelago. The group Outkast hailed from the South, Notorious B.I.G. from the East, Snoop Doggy Dogg from the West, and Da Brat from Chicago—smack dab in the middle of the shit, Brooks once proclaimed—forming a dynamic and creative landscape.

In 1994 we also saw the appearance of another emblem of hip-hop culture: the publication of Tricia Rose's landmark study *Black Noise: Rap Music and Culture in Contemporary America*, the first book of its kind, one that thrust hip-hop into the academic world of postmodern ideas. Rose's work helped to initiate another space for experimentation and commercial efficacy in hip-hop. Following her lead, hip-hop scholarship and its cousin "journ-academic-criticism," a rich blend of academic cultural theory and journalism, has blossomed. Hip-hop bibliography, blogography, and other forms of mass-mediated commentary have exploded across libraries, bookstores, and the internet.

More than a decade later, "black noise" is, indeed, a veritable cottage industry, spawning a growing field of pundits, academic specialties, and book deals in and through which blackness is explained to a consuming public fascinated with it. This critical community praised Nas's work as a towering artistic statement. And its status as artistic invention has not prevented it from spilling over into lived experience, into other domains of culture. A telling turn in hip-hop exegesis, for example, occurred at the nexus between hip-hop musical practice and the realm of its study.

This junction has been a rich if sometimes controversial one. When scholar Mark Anthony Neal coined the term "ThugNiggaIntellectual" to describe the social contradictions some black male intellectuals experience, he apparently borrowed from the linguistic flair and penetrating poetics of MCs such as Nas. And scholar-preacher Michael Eric Dyson's penchant for breaking into sing-song rap lyrics to illustrate points during formal lectures and sermons is now legendary. For his part in this dialogic, Nas has been criticized for reading way too many books for an MC. This anti-intellectualism can cut both ways as some scholars, such as Cornel West, Kyra Gaunt, and Cheryl Keyes, have been criticized for even engaging hip-hop culture too seriously in the first place—either as participants or as "objective observers." Many of the nation's most respected hip-hop critics, I should mention, hold PhDs or are otherwise impressively pedigreed or very gainfully employed. Thus, the social energies permeating hip-hop's critical establishment and hip-hop's musical community have mixed, exchanged, and blended. Each of these aspects of the hip-hop enterprise set high benchmarks for both the music and its study. In fact, I am proposing here that these kinds of dialogues—social, musical, emotional, and scholarly ones—can illuminate the impact of the song "Life's a Bitch."

Back in 1994, debates about artistic authenticity and commercialism in popular music, hip-hop culture, and black identity raged—on the recordings, in the trade press, and on the street. It was in that year for, example, that jazz star Branford Marsalis released a recording under the name Buckshot LeFonque. Originally a pseudonym for another genre-busting jazz musician, Julian "Cannonball" Adderley, the project was an eclectic mix of hip-hop, jazz, rock, R&B, and all manner of pop. Marsalis and his collaborator, the producer DJ Premier, defied the generic marketing categories that typically order taste and the cash register in the music industry. As one of America's most familiar faces in entertainment because of his previous stint as the musical director of the *Tonight Show* band, Marsalis thumbed his nose at the industry by forwarding music that experimented and toyed with generic expectations. Definitely an "in-your-face move," the project was highly successful artistically but challenged its own status as a commodity in the conservative, nonprogressive marketplace, and thus did not gain commercial support. "Why was a 'jazz musician' doing this?" the market seemed to ask.

Nineteen ninety-four was also the year of Prince's infamous battle with Warner Bros. over the financial and artistic control of his work. It disintegrated into a full-scale war. Prince's public struggles with the corporation became an important symbolic and subversive act that brought into high relief and subsequently critiqued his artistic output as commodity. Nas's work appeared in the context of the struggle by highly visible black musicians to maintain their artistic freedom, a struggle in which they were willing to sacrifice commercial success in order to win.

As we can see, the combination of art and money shows, among other things, each new generation of artists creating their own styles and investing in them meanings specific to their own needs. Audiences respond in kind, making their own sense of the world, in part by engaging, in the present case, a musical work. These crosscurrents of investments are powerful and show how very complex the rich networks of meanings generated in the listening experience are. And getting at what the music might mean requires taking into account the deeply personal ways in which listeners engage music.

I am fascinated with the changing senses of authenticity in black musical communities across time and place. How one interprets these communities is always a direct function of the subjectivity of the analyst. As a forty-something black American myself, I've lived through and negotiated, on a personal level, a number of them: jazz, Motown, traditional and contemporary gospel, black art music, pop, soul, funk, fusion, and now hip-hop. I have experienced these musical styles as social markers of a constantly moving, forever searching, and always challenging idea of "musical blackness." Misunderstandings can arise between the generations surrounding the ideas about musical tastes, meaning, and identity. And sometimes demonstrating the social and political divisions of a "community" is precisely the cultural work a musical work is intended to do. Yet at other times, music resonates and engages dialogues across generational boundaries. "Life's a Bitch" is one such recording, in my view.

The formal plan of the song features six large structures that are unified by a two-measure gesture loop throughout the recording. Despite this rather simplistic design, the song packs lots of rhetorical and thematic information. The modes of delivery move from spoken dialogue in the introduction, a rapped refrain featuring AZ, and two verses divided between as many rappers, to an ending with a muted, subdued trumpet soloist in the coda. The brief refrain or hook is not sung but rapped, positioning it formally as a dialogue between traditional popular song and rap music conventions. The trumpet solo is an obvious nod to jazz and stretches the envelope of generic expectations in hip-hop.

The song's rhythm track is sampled from the Gap Band's 1981 R&B hit "Yearning for Your Love," a song that lyrically could not be further in tone and tenor from "Life's a Bitch." But, as we will see below, context, history, and memory can radically change what meanings are conveyed to listeners by songs. The formal qualities of these pieces share a basic rhythm track, a point that would encourage the connection between them for someone of my generation. "Life's a Bitch" is an example of sample-based hip-hop, the art of which is the sole focus of Joseph Schloss's book *Making Beats: The Art of Sample-Based Hip-Hop* (2004), an academic study in the intellectual lineage of *Black Noise*. The book is pitched as a statement that explores the relationship of its subject matter to the academy. As much as my ear can discern, Nas's piece ignores the introduction of the earlier recording and employs throughout the entire piece a two-measure loop lifted from the opening bars of the first verse.

The two-measure passage comprising the sample is revealing. It contains all of the timbral components of the original but with major shifts in the sonic field. The ostinato bass line is placed more prominently in the field, not as support but unleashed as foreground, freeing it in same manner that bebop moved drummers from timekeepers to becoming one of the main points of the modern jazz enterprise. While the keyboard and drum parts remain intact, the repetitious rhythm guitar line is dropped in favor of the residue of a single note from the lead guitar, perched together with an even higher-pitched string sounding far above the field. This arrangement clears midrange space for the dense narrative that will be performed by the rappers AZ and Nas, even as it provides an ominous accompaniment to the gripping drama that will unfold.

If the pleas of Charlie Wilson, the Gap Band's lead singer, express in "Yearning" the frustration of unanswered adoration in the kind of virtuoso performance that has made soul vocals the lingua franca of global pop, AZ and Nas achieve a similar result but on hip-hop terms. Again, these respective authenticities are striking when contrasted. Wilson's cultural work takes place in the context of a song with few lyrical complexities, depending largely on his husky yet flexible delivery, spattered with well-placed melismas for its rhetorical power. The form of "Yearning" comprises a looping verse section, a harmonically different chorus, and a bridge providing further harmonic contrast. As I mentioned, Nas's rhythm track is decidedly simpler. It's basically a two-bar loop, yet one cannot imagine a denser narrative packed within its three and a half minutes. Let's turn now to the poetry.

Although "Life's a Bitch" features two rappers with distinct delivery styles, they do not participate in the typical male braggadocio that has marked the performance realm of the genre since its beginning. In the song's introduction, we hear a conversation between two male comrades participating in a seemingly ritualistic division of spoils of presumed illegal activity.

AZ opens the song proper with a powerful missive detailing the life philosophies of a young thug whose understanding of status and manhood are, not surprisingly, tied to the acquisition of money. While he portrays this mantra as a function of his upbringing in the ghetto, we know that to "stack plenty papers," as he puts it, is to participate in the all-American, middle-class dream of upward mobility. Yet he credits his money-oriented mentality to a street ghetto essence that guides him through the challenges of life and the paper chase. Although his young peers are imprisoned or dead, he vows to live the dream for them until his own inevitable death. On the one hand, his game is marred by a stunning fatalism and a lack of hope: "keepin' it real, packin' steel, gettin' high, cuz life's a bitch and then you die." But on the other hand, our protagonist is assured that, at the very least, his thievery will allow him to leave a little something behind for those who survive him.

Musically, AZ demonstrates in his verse the rhetorical dexterity that earned him status as a well-respected MC. The urgency of his delivery is mostly a function of his sixteenth-note drumlike subdivision of the loop. Together with a vocal quality that strains at the top of his range, the rhythmic character of the piece puts the listener on edge, especially because it is staged within a somewhat tame rhythm track. One of the most rhetorically rich moments in this verse occurs on the words "cause yeah," "now some," and "dough so" because they break the verse's hypnotic affect with their stress on weak beats. The irregular placement of these gestures adds to the musicality of the whole. Other similar moments happen on the lyrics "all gotta go" and "keepin' it real, packin' steel, gettin' high" when AZ delivers them in a sing-song manner; the notes he sings create tension with the underlying harmonies of the rhythm track.

After the introduction's dialogue, the verses that Nas and AZ split can be interpreted as the voices of an inner dialogue between different aspects of one protagonist's searching consciousness. He wakes up on his twentieth birthday reflecting on his life up to that important landmark. He is no longer a teenager and is facing the uncertainties of manhood. One side of him accepts the fate of an involuntary "ghetto essence inside us," while the other uses his experiences earlier in life as a stepping-stone to a higher level of consciousness. In Nas's verse the resolve of fatalism morphs into a more mature understanding of life and the consequences of choices. This comparison is perhaps more feasible because Nas's verse lacks the echo effect that surrounds AZ's verse, and thus gives it a more ethereal quality. Nas's rhythmic rhetoric is richer and more nuanced than AZ's here. With its less emphatic delivery, the mood conjured is more contemplative than reactionary. Nonetheless, two gestures on the words "got rhymes" and "once I" hint at a musical connection between the two verses as Nas performs them similarly to AZ by accenting weak beats. Nas's work has been hailed for its lyricism, a depiction surely meant to describe both the weight and inventiveness of his words and the rhythmic and timbral rhetoric moving them through time.

The coda with its jazz inflection brings the piece full circle. In a musical environment that was rich in intragenre dialogue, as I have noted above, this piece does not disappoint. Nas's father Olu Dara plays a plaintive, poignant solo on muted trumpet, providing a sonic link to the late Miles Davis's work in the 1980s. Importantly, this intergenerational dialogue between father and son is but one in the recording—we also hear it between jazz, hip-hop, and R&B, and between two aspects of the protagonist's consciousness. Dialogue is, of course, fundamental to appreciating sample-based hip-hop. Listener competence—based on personal experience—always determines how clearly one will hear the conversation.

For reasons that I will discuss below, when I first heard the recording I connected it to my father's death in 1994. Dad died at the age of sixty-nine, which, unfortunately, represented a ripe old age for black men of his generation. A stroll through the funeral home where his remains lay revealed room after room of deceased black men around his age and some even younger. It is well known to health care officials that African American men have the highest death rate and lowest life expectancy of any other racial or ethnic group, male or female, in the United States. According to the National Center for Health Statistics, homicide tops the list as the leading causes of death for African American men between the ages of eighteen and thirty-four, and it is the fourth leading cause for African American men between eighteen and sixty-four. If they are lucky and survive being "one of the number," African American men also rank higher than other groups for death by AIDS, heart disease, and prostate, lung, and colon cancers. These dismal statistics are linked to the reality that they also lead the way in unemployment, a fact that negatively impacts access to quality health care in this country. These statistics suggest that life, death, and the borrowed time in between should be a central concern to black men in America and is an issue that connects black men of all generations. Nas's work underscored hip-hop's important role as social commentary; it showed how a musical form could be just as engaged and relevant as scholarship.

During the mid-1970s to mid-1980s I considered myself primarily a jazz head, as a musician somewhat narrowly focused on the post–classic bop mainstream jazz world. As I have related elsewhere in my writings, I was raised in a musical environment in which jazz was but one of many tiles in a sonic mosaic that included gospel, rhythm and blues, and soul music. Yet a taste for jazz, as I think back, was an important way in which younger males in the family experienced a spiritual connection to older Ramsey men and to others of their generation. So deep was my Uncle W. J.'s identification with jazz, for example, that his funeral service was filled not with traditional Christian hymns and choral music but with the sounds of hard bop. It was authentically "him." To this day I can't hear some stomp-down blues played by an organ, guitar, and drum trio without thinking of my family's departed patriarchs.

As I have written in my book *Race Music: Black Cultures from Bebop to Hip-Hop*, after Dad's funeral we ate, danced, and played cards at a relative's house. The song that jumped off the party happened to be the Gap Band's "Yearning for Your Love." Obviously, in the private community theaters of black culture and in the more public forum of hip-hop sampling, the recording was still doing important cultural work some thirteen years after its release. The act of interpretation depicted here teaches us a lot about the dynamic nature of the listening experience. In this case, we witness a reworking of the lyrics or the "truth claim" of this torch song/ slow jam: in this theater of mourning this community spontaneously elected to transform the recording into a blues-stomping, cathartic affirmation of life before the unflinching face of death's reality. This recording will always "mean" this to me. And whenever I hear it on the radio or in a club, it transports me back to that bittersweet moment in time. Thus, context can best explain the question of musical meaning, especially in how individuals construct their very strong identifications with sound organization. In other words, even for the professional analyst meanings are always built in a web of personal history, memory, and subjectivity.

I spoke earlier of the connection between the piece and my father; I end with a meditation on my son's life. A quiet and articulate man, whose speech combines the southern drawl of his Chicago beginnings, the New England clip of his formative years in Boston, and the edgy force of his finishing-school, coming-of-age years in inner-city West Philadelphia. As of this writing he is in his early twenties; indeed, his "physical frame is celebrated 'cause he made it." Although his father is a scholar and jazz musician, hip-hop forms the soundtrack of his life. In our own dialogues I've learned of his budding interest in a career as a music producer, the challenges of life, his anxieties over losing peers to violent deaths, and the vexed relationship between all-American manhood and capitalism, among other themes articulated in "Life's a Bitch."

Recently he revealed that, during a college music appreciation course, a lecture on the twelve-bar blues form spurred a memory of me teaching him as a youngster to play the blues as part of our daily routine practicing his Suzuki cello lessons. He dumped this activity at age twelve with the declaration, "Dad, I'm an outside kind of boy." But I know that if he pursues one of his dreams of producing hip-hop, inevitably he'll discover my vintage vinyl collection, dig in my crates, and, perhaps, stumble onto some of my father's favorite recordings and complete our circle.

As Nas taught us in 1994, the year Pops died, musical dialogue is both Illmatic and authentic. "Life's a Bitch."

10 A New Kind of Blue

THE POWER OF SUGGESTION AND THE PLEASURE OF
GROOVE IN ROBERT GLASPER'S *BLACK RADIO*

"Changing the game!" exclaimed the press photographer at pianist Robert Glasper's standing-room-only appearance at World Cafe Live in Philadelphia in the spring of 2012. "Yeah, no doubt," a middle-aged man shot back in enthusiastic agreement. The midsized auditorium was filled with an interracial, intergenerational crowd of listeners enveloped in the mesh of sound worlds that Glasper presented with both commitment and ease.

The audience's enthusiasm for the Robert Glasper Experiment's landmark 2012 release *Black Radio* (Blue Note)—and its accompanying promotional tour—was affirmed by the American music industry's arbiters of taste. To much surprise, *Black Radio* received a Grammy Award nomination in two categories: Best R & B Performance for "Gonna Be Alright (F.T.B.)," featuring Ledisi, and Best R & B Album. Even before it debuted, there was steady buzz about what the recording's aesthetic approach and its critical reception might mean to the future of jazz. Now, in the wake of

"A New Kind of Blue: The Power of Suggestion and the Pleasure of Groove in Robert Glasper's *Black Radio*," *Daedelus* 142: 4 (American Academy of Arts and MIT Press: Fall 2013): 120–25. The essay had its genesis as a lecture given to a history of jazz course that I was teaching when Glasper's influential project dropped.

its release, it is clear that *Black Radio*'s influence extends well beyond the jazz world, as evidenced by the R & B branding. Like Miles Davis's pivotal 1959 album *Kind of Blue*, which signaled a new direction for modern jazz, *Black Radio* may indeed qualify as a game changer.

New York Times music critic Nate Chinen wrote that *Black Radio* was "the rare album of its kind that doesn't feel strained by compromise or plagued by problems of translation."[1] Such a synthesis of styles is quite a feat given that jazz, R & B, and hip-hop have developed dissimilar social contracts with audiences, a chasm made glaringly clear by hip-hop's emergence as a commodity in the 1980s and the almost contemporaneous "young lions" movement that shot Wynton Marsalis and his co-conspirators of young, mostly male jazz musicians to stardom. In public and private discourse, these neoclassicist hard boppers were pitted against the sample-filled digital soundscapes of hip-hop producers ("they are not even 'real' musicians") and their rapping, rhyming counterparts ("they are *really* not musicians"). Although some critics could engage with each of these sound worlds, many listeners remained wedged between polarizing aesthetic discussions that inspired a politics of division.

That was the 1980s. Dramatic changes in the recording industry over the last fifteen years have opened up new creative opportunities for artists, and musicians are taking full advantage of them. Talented independent engineers and producers, armed with relatively high-quality personal recording studios, have increased exponentially; it's now a literal cottage industry. And because of the digital revolution, which provided cost-effective access to cutting-edge technologies, many musicians have become astute in engineering and production in addition to their more traditional competencies in composition and performance, as well as in marketing and promotion. This newfound freedom has allowed ambitious musicians and producers to break out of genre boxes and craft conceptually adventurous projects. Some creators intentionally share their work free of charge on the social media sites Facebook, Twitter, and YouTube before they actually "drop" through traditional commercial avenues. Many recordings appear only in these online outlets and attract thousands of listeners without the help of a record label.

A new music economy has been established in which record and marketing executives no longer exclusively determine what music is entitled to widespread dissemination. One of the most exciting results of this shift is that informal musical collectives have begun to work across genre lines (those imaginary sonic boundaries that exclude more than they invite), creating new audience alliances as well. Although he is contracted with Blue Note, the label historically associated with "straight-ahead" jazz, Glasper proves himself in his latest release to be in the avant-garde of this exciting new aesthetic wave.

That is not to say that there are not sonic precursors to *Black Radio's* appealing new sounds. Chinen's article mentions a few such milestone performers: Miles Davis, Guru, A Tribe Called Quest, De La Soul, and Roy Hargrove. Each artist/group has produced projects that blend elements of jazz with those of other popular styles. We can push the list back further in time to include innovators like pianist Ramsey Lewis, the father of "soul-jazz," who has continued to build a vibrant career, sliding effortlessly across the jazz/pop continuum. The clearheaded and creative adventurer Herbie Hancock, too, stands as a towering inspiration to genre-crossing artists, both in spirit and in technical execution.

And we must not overlook, as is all too often the practice, the important women contributors to this aesthetic shape-shifting sensibility. Gospel great Elbernita "Twinkie" Clark's songwriting, singing, and Hammond B-3 playing did much to set that genre on an unapologetic and sonically ecumenical path throughout the 1980s and beyond. Pianist and composer Patrice Rushen's work boasted a prescient eclecticism that surely provided neo-soul rhythm and acid jazz tracks some of their harmonic approaches. Bassist and songwriter Meshell Ndegeocello's virtuosic musicianship and fluency in hip-hop, pop, funk, soul, and jazz—and the singular and courageous way she combines the genres—must be considered a signpost in this discussion.

As a subject of written criticism and promotion, as a live performance event, and as a recording, *Black Radio* deserves our careful attention. But precisely what part of the *Black Radio* project suggests that we are in the midst of a post-genre moment, a wholesale realignment of the traditional social contracts governing music creation, dissemination, and consumption in the industry? *Black Radio's* sense of aesthetic balance—of getting it just right—is key to our understanding, and it may be derived from two provocative musical choices: (1) a self-conscious foregrounding of digital technology in the soundscape, including tricked-out mixes and effects, among other techniques; and (2) a harmonic palette drawn from the progressive post-bop vocabulary, featuring close, infectious harmonies that pivot around common tones and shifting tonal centers. The songs are otherwise characterized by the careful alignment of sonic symbols from across the historical black popular music soundscape. Here, Glasper's aesthetic strategy positions him to assuage the traditionalist criticism of his dual pedigree in hip-hop and jazz while also providing ample space for experimentation.

Beginning with an impressive set of trio recordings in the tradition of, most obviously, bebop pianist Bud Powell (always a litmus test for the modern jazz pianist), Glasper's recorded output gradually moved into other conceptual and sonic territories. Brands are powerful entities, particularly in the music industry. Although he claims roots in gospel, R&B, jazz, and hip-hop, Glasper entered into public awareness as a "jazz pianist," and it is hard to break away from that rubric once it sticks. The same is true for any artist whose work is marketed in a system that makes money from rigid predictability. This "agreement" becomes a social contract that ultimately seeks to dictate what artists produce, how companies sell content, and the spending and listening habits of specific demographics. Although Glasper was branded as a jazz musician, he has also maintained highly visible collaborations with the revered hip-hop producer and beat-maker J Dilla (James Dewitt Yancey) and the rapper Q-Tip (of the critically acclaimed group A Tribe Called Quest).

What we think of as the essence of jazz today developed during the 1940s bebop revolution. As historian Scott DeVeaux has explained:

> In the wake of bebop, we no longer think of jazz improvisation as a *way* of playing tunes but as an exacting art form in itself that happens, as a rule, to use popular music as a point of departure. In the hands of a jazz improviser, a copyrighted popular song is less text than pretext. Its crucial identifying feature—melody—is erased in the heat of improvisation, leaving behind the more abstract and malleable level of harmonic pattern. Out of the ashes of popular song comes a new structure, a new aesthetic order, shaped by the intelligence and virtuosity of the improviser; and it is to that structure, and that structure alone, that our attention should be drawn.[2]

This aesthetic order, grounded in virtuoso spectacle, has been both a blessing and a curse; it is an ideal that has, on the one hand, created expressions of sublime beauty and, on the other, eroded the economic base of the once popular music with exercises in abstraction that some claim are too difficult to decipher.

The world of hip-hop, Glasper's other pedigree, has its own social contract and historical groundings, though some of its more infamous themes of nihilism, misogyny, and political confrontation have tended to eclipse the dynamism of its defining musical traits. Nonetheless, as a system of organized sound, it has (like contemporary gospel music) flaunted an irreverent and irrepressible voracious muse, absorbing sound elements as quickly as they appear in the public sphere. Likewise, hip-hop has demonstrated similar senses of portability together with the reinforcement and transcendence of ethnic identities as they have been bound to specific sound organizations.

Glasper's *Black Radio* project intelligently and artfully indexes these histories. Indeed, all of the sonic and social agreements of hip-hop, jazz, and gospel (Glasper grew up playing in church) congeal in thoughtful, groove-based arrangements on the album (and in the live shows, though in different ways). When we consider the crafty details of the songs, their conceptual and technological framing, their harmonic environment and relationship to popular song, their virtuosic performances, and their accessibility and even spirituality, we can better understand *Black Radio* as an example of "post-genre" black music. The project plays with sonic, social, and iconic symbols in a way that recalibrates calcified, boring ideas about genre and turns them on their head with a good sense of funky adventure.

As the music scholar and cultural critic Mark Anthony Neal has written in his insightful review of *Black Radio*, the use of the terms "post-genre" and "black music" might seem oxymoronic.[3] What Neal is indicating, of course, is that the concept "genre" operates as an index of sound *and* the social ideas assigned to it. In other words, people socially agree on what sounds mean, to what community they "belong," and what extramusical connotations they might convey. So if it is post-genre, where does blackness fit in?

Neal's meditation on the project situates Glasper's *Black Radio* in the historical context of black American radio stations, which reinforced the personal connection between Glasper's album and my experiences growing up listening to the Chicago-based station WVON (Voice of the Negro).

Chess Records executives Leonard and Phil Chess owned the AM station from 1963 until Leonard's death in 1969. They programmed it all: gospel, blues, jazz, R&B, pop, and, because it was Chicago, some more blues. Musical eclecticism defined the station's community of listeners, linking the generations with an "open-eared," aesthetically patient temperament: one of *your* songs was surely coming up next. Tellingly, when I visited Glasper's hometown of Houston a few years back, I noticed the same ecumenical historical consciousness on its radio stations.

But we have largely lost our expansive tastes to the corporate pressures put on program directors to maintain the strict social contracts of genre. And this is the very reason that audiences (and, ironically, the industry) have enjoyed *Black Radio*'s nod to that more eclectic time, and why I use the forward-looking term "post-genre" to capture the project's pulse, contour, and impact.

Every track on *Black Radio* rewards—a high standard not often met these days, particularly with projects of this size. The most attractive sonic features, as I have stated above, derive from how the digital aspects of the recording share the foreground with Glasper's signature harmonic approach. Another feature that departs from the jazz social contract, as laid out by DeVeaux, is how the project is consciously not dominated by heroic virtuoso solos. These fresh elements, of course, also contributed to *Black Radio*'s Grammy nominations in the R&B category, rather than in Glasper's "brand" category, jazz.

Glasper's individualized progressive post-bop vocabulary is instantly recognizable. The project collapses this approach, however, with another aesthetic: gospel music. One cannot help but associate the way that his talented band—Derrick Hodge (bass), Casey Benjamin (vocoder, flutes, saxophone), and Chris Dave (drums)—hit strong pocket grooves with all the deep soul of a sanctified Pentecostal band. They languish over the rhythmic and harmonic possibilities of these grooves, subtly twisting, turning, and burning as if these manipulations were the point of the whole endeavor. With all the dramatic innovations that have recently occurred in gospel music, one quality has held strong: the love of repetitive grooves that work the spirit, providing a platform for some of the most moving singing and instrumental improvisations in the industry. *Black Radio* brims with this groove-centered aesthetic.

Take Glasper's rendition of "Cherish the Day," a cover of the chanting groove-tress herself, Sade. The original, released in 1993, is emblematic of a core aesthetic of urban pop styles of the last twenty years: verse/chorus song forms built on identical chord structures. This quality has become ubiquitous in R&B/urban soul songwriting because of the spillover effect of hip-hop's cyclic loops. What separates Glasper's interpretation of this overused technique, however, is that his ensemble has taken the concept—an analog interpretation of a digital concept—and injected the improvisational freedom of the jazz/fusion/funk sonic complex. Consider Casey Benjamin's unpredictable and expressive synth solo on "Cherish the Day"—doubled in parallel intervals throughout. It is a husky statement reminiscent of Chick Corea's Elektric Band of the 1980s. How the band keeps the groove pitched just hotter than a simmer beneath his improvisation is a marvel of group interplay. It sounds like a very hip church fanning up some community spirit. Why rush through it for radio's sake? Moving the spirit takes time.

With regard to female singers, there is plenty here to appreciate. There is the newcomer Ledisi, the firebrand vocalist with grit, riffs, and range; Meshell Ndegeocello's warm molasses presentation; Chrisette Michele's breathy and sensuous croon; Erykah Badu, the priestess of the neo-soul movement of the 1990s; and Lalah Hathaway, daughter of the iconic singer Donny Hathaway, who possesses her father's appealing melismatic execution. Hathaway's reworking of "Cherish the Day" exhibits the best qualities of her vocal presentation: an open-throated, well-supported, and sultry alto voice, captured effectively by the studio engineer. Breathy vowels abound as she moves through tasty melodic lines, working over chord changes like her father, but with much more economy. Lesser-known female singers, sisters Amber and Paris Strother and Anita Bias, offer further neo-soul-ish warmth to the project.

The stylistic inclusivity is not limited to the performers; note how Chris Dave's drum sound is engineered in places to throw back to early 1990s hip-hop samples. Meanwhile, the lavish background vocals on the old-school slow jam "Oh, Yeah," featuring Musiq Soulchild and Chrisette Michele, harken back to R&B duet sensations Donny Hathaway and Roberta Flack, but with the complexities of a Jaguar Wright multitrack vocal symphony. And Glasper's acoustic solo after minute four of the track—a tasty ride over a Fender Rhodes–drenched soundscape—suggests how this recording might have sounded if long instrumental solos had been the emotional focal point of this project.

Scattered and unusual mixes, electronic effects, stylistic juxtapositions, fade-ins, oral declamations, and rhythmic chants combine to frustrate efforts to "place" this music. The most experimental tracks, showcasing the male voices of Lupe Fiasco, Bilal, Shafiq Husayn, Stokely, and Mos Def, crisscross generic markers with dizzying aplomb. Packaged with a statement by writer Angelika Beener—less liner notes than manifesto— the album announces itself as something new, a turn toward breaking out of the sonic/marketing formulas so prevalent in today's industry offerings. The most important aspect of this "announcement," however, is this: *Black Radio* allows the music to do the real preaching. Thus, we hear the band's "post-genre" gesture as a suggestion, not a mandate. In other words, only the music in the *totality* of our experience, music that is boundaryless, market-resistant, artistically adventurous, and conceptually focused, can take black music back. Free black music!

11 Free Jazz and the Price of Black Musical Abstraction

"If you don't experiment, you'll die."

Jack Whitten, personal communication, 2005

Free jazz, the development in American music that shook jazz's traditional relationship to popular song form, controlled improvisation, blues tonality, and rhythmic regularity, rose simultaneously with other social upheavals during the 1960s. Even bebop, a musical turn in jazz that transformed the genre into an "art," or America's classical music, seemed like a tame venture in comparison to the New Thing, as free jazz was called. The lightning-fast melodic, rhythmic, and harmonic inventions of Charlie Parker, Dizzy Gillespie, Bud Powell, and others became key signs of an Afro-modernism at midcentury linked to numerous social, economic, and political developments. Among these changes was a massive migration of southern blacks north and westward, a demographic shift that created an atmosphere for advances in education, economics, and culture. Although

"Free Jazz and the Price of Black Musical Abstraction," in *Energy/Experimentation: Black Artists and Abstraction, 1964–80* (New York: Studio Museum in Harlem, 2006), 72–77; reprinted as "Free Jazz and the Price of Black Musical Abstraction," in Kellie Jones, ed., *EyeMinded: Living and Writing Contemporary Art* (Durham, NC: Duke University Press, 2011), 353–61. This essay represents my first writing for museum catalogs. The exhibition, "Energy/Experimentation: Black Artists and Abstraction, 1964–80," curated by Kellie Jones, was on display April 5 to July 2, 2006.

these shifts formed the foundation for the civil rights victories of the 1950s and early 1960s, the free jazz movement remains linked to black power, a similar revolutionary push for African American freedom.

The influence of the black power movement was considerable. It represented "the dominant ideological framework through which many young, poor, and middle-class blacks made sense of their lives and articulated a political *vision* for their futures."[1] The black power era—roughly from the mid-1960s to the mid-1970s—symbolized for many a new social order, a new radicalism. This social movement was not, however, a unified, static affair. Numerous political currents and agendas formed this new expression of "blackness": violence was advocated by some, peaceful resistance by others; a wide variety of new organizations appeared, each influenced by a wide range of philosophies; leftist-leaning ideologues clashed with black middle-class sensibilities; black feminism critiqued the overwhelmingly male centricity of the movement; and international concerns about black and Latin folk around the globe resisted a solely African American focus of the freedom struggle. What emerged was a highly politicized and quite diverse blackness that reclaimed, and in some instances reformed, black history, transformed its present, and informed Afro-America's future. And it all took place under the slogan "black power."

During the 1960s, the northern and western cities to which previous generations of southern black migrants had fled during the 1940s began to collapse around them. As the capital base of these urban spaces rapidly progressed toward a stifling postindustrialism that would mark the 1970s, they imploded in riots, joblessness, and structural decay. It became clear that the land of promise had not, in fact, kept its word. African Americans responded to black hopelessness with black power—an expression that, as we have learned, meant many things to many people.

Out of this multifarious, conflicted blackness exploded an array of cultural expressions in poetry, visual arts, theater, and music and its criticism. Dubbed the Black Arts Movement, its concerns formed a complex of radical spiritual, ideological, and political priorities. One never gets the sense that it was ever a "culture for culture's sake" project. It had a razor's edge, and it cut to the bone. Although the masses of working-class African Americans sought pleasure in the activities of the mainstream culture industry, such as rock and R&B (musical works that white Americans adored as well), many writers, musicians, and artists believed that free jazz formed the perfect soundtrack for black power. In their minds, a social revolution required a musical one as well.

And a musical revolution it was. What began as heady experiments among a smattering of musicians in more prosperous and socially stable times slowly gathered force and became a creative storm. But like black power, free jazz represented a particularly wide range of musicians and stylistic developments.

Jazz historians often trace the origins of free jazz to a long line of subtle innovations that date back as early as Duke Ellington's experiments with colorful timbres and long-form composition in the 1930s. During the 1940s and 1950s, in the long shadow of the bebop era, Lennie Tristano, Thelonious Monk, Miles Davis, and Charles Mingus all stood out among their peers for their unorthodox approaches to jazz composition and improvisation. Many trace the foundations of free jazz to divergent musical precursors that displayed what might be called an experimental impulse.

Beginning in the late 1950s, the jazz idiom took its most dramatic departure from its time-honored conventions. Ornette Coleman, John Coltrane, Cecil Taylor, Albert Ayler, the Association for the Advancement of Creative Musicians (AACM) and Eric Dolphy all emerged as leaders of the New Thing, indeed, a thing so brutally new that in the ears of many it threatened the "natural" organic development of the genre. In other words, people wondered if free jazz was jazz at all, or even music for that matter. If bebop exaggerated melodic contour, harmonic extension, and rhythmic disjuncture to the brink of abstraction, certainly free jazz broke through the genre's common-practice sound barrier, wreaking musical havoc, building controversial careers, mystifying old-school critics, and attracting reverent converts.[2]

On the formal level, free jazz comprised a number of sweeping experiments in sound organization that broke with the past. Because the music was more collectively improvised than either swing or bebop, the division of labor between soloist and accompanists was often obscured. Each competed for the listeners' attention because the music did not include a single emotional focal point, as is the case with, say, a pop singer backed by an orchestra or even a bebop soloist center stage in the soundscape of a virtuoso jazz trio. The New Thing's introduction of unconventional timbral approaches pushed the envelope of what was expected in African American music in general and jazz specifically. Popular song-form harmonic patterns were shunned in favor of open structures that denied listeners familiar landmarks and placed new demands on musicians. Two other significant breaks with past styles could be felt in tonality and rhythm. Exploitation of the tonal system marked bebop as singular; the flatted fifth together with abundant ninth, eleventh, and thirteenth scale degrees made it a harmonically rich modernism. Free jazz took this tendency and pushed it further out, almost completely liberating the genre from the restrictions of functional harmony. Finally, free jazz tended to move through time unevenly, undermining the sense of swing that perhaps represented jazz's most distinctive feature.

Did free jazz—this radical experiment in sound—merely reflect the politically charged moment, or did it fuel it? Both. Evidence suggests, however, that because both sides of the equation, the musical and the social, were eclectic and diverse, drawing one-to-one homologies between the art and the times can be imprecise at best. Yet we can say this much: the political commitments of musicians such as Archie Shepp and writers such as Amiri Baraka (aka LeRoi Jones) made the connections unavoidable. At the same time, we must always think about agency. Artists, no matter how political, are rarely motivated by a singular idea. Rather, they are usually responding to a variety of factors. The forces of the culture industry and the search for an individual, immediately recognizable voice within a set field of musical parameters (e.g., the formal qualities of free jazz) have, for example, always provided inspiration for creativity.

Qualifications aside, the free jazz movement represents the most insistent consummation of social, cultural, and identity politics in jazz's history. There was undeniable cross-fertilization of performance rhetoric. During the 1960s, Amiri Baraka's recitation style was heavily influenced by Albert Ayler's cultivated saxophone yelps. Charlie Mingus and Sun Ra both experimented with poetry, and Archie Shepp was both a playwright and poet. Music was a central preoccupation, as the poets were often accompanied by jazz and R&B. The mutual influence among black artists of all stripes could also be seen in their similar attempts to control the modes of production of their work. Coltrane, for example, spearheaded efforts to start a record label and booking agency, and Baraka founded the Black

Arts Repertory Theatre/School, sponsored concerts for prominent free jazz artists, and claimed that the cultural politics of identity should be central to jazz criticism. Such efforts demonstrated how these artists formed an unprecedented community of social and cultural activism.[3]

Free jazz's musical conventions can claim two streams of influence. There existed during the 1960s a huge investment in the claim that by rejecting many of the melodic, harmonic, rhythmic, and even timbral tenets of common-practice Western art music, the New Thing was returning black music to its African roots. The spirit behind this idea was a well-traveled one. In fact, scholars and cultural critics of the African American experience have long sought to find continuities among the lives of black people throughout the African diaspora, especially as they manifest in cultural expressions such as music, literature, cuisine, religion, visual arts, and dance.

The forced migration of Africans throughout the Atlantic world spawned myriad cultural forms, which, though displaced and transformed, share a core set of distinctive and unifying attributes that link them to the (black) Old World. Art historian Robert Farris Thompson called it a "flash of the spirit." The term describes for him "*visual and philosophic* streams of creativity and imagination, running parallel to the massive musical and choreographic modalities that connect black persons of the western hemisphere, as well as the millions of European and Asian people attracted to and performing their styles, to Mother Africa. . . . The rise, development, and achievement of Yoruba, Kongo, Fon, Mande, and Ejagham art and philosophy fused with new elements overseas, shaping and defining the black Atlantic visual tradition."[4] Religious scholar Albert Raboteau sees this continuity in religion as well, despite efforts to remove the cultural memory of slaves: "In the New World slave control was based on the eradication of all forms of African culture because of their power to unify the slaves and thus enable them to resist or rebel. Nevertheless, African beliefs and customs persisted and were transmitted by slaves to their descendants. Shaped and modified by a new environment, elements of African folklore, music, language, and religion were transplanted in the New World."[5] These notions were adopted by free jazz artists to tie their musical works to both historic Africa and the struggles of black people around the globe. As early as 1964, Marion Brown insisted, for example,

that because many black musical forms were passed down from generation to generation orally, he could discern African tribal musics in the riffs
and runs of contemporary black music such as jazz and R&B, an idea that
many others began to champion.[6]

The push to locate continuity with the African past was central to black
power rhetoric, and for its architects, black music underscored this coherence poignantly. This strain of thinking has been so influential in Black
Nationalist rhetoric that blues and jazz have continued to provide engaging metaphors, models, and themes for a host of studies aimed at elucidat-
ing black cultural production and even larger issues in American culture,
especially literature.[7]

Indeed, exploration of the dynamic relationship between black Old and
New World practices traditionally has been regarded as a valuable way to
explain the power and especially the *difference* in black music making.
Historically, this subject has attracted considerable attention, from the
antebellum writings of American journalists, missionaries, foreign travelers, and schoolteachers to the twentieth-century work of critics and scholars.[8] Conflicting notions about African American music's Africanness
(blackness) or its hybridity (Afro/Euro-ness) fuel this continuing debate.
The Black Arts Movement championed the idea that black musical creativity was the result of its engagement of African ways of "musicking," ways
that revealed themselves in a range of techniques, styles, and repertoires.
The musical styles born of this seemingly endless capacity to codify the
stuff of Others into something with a black difference, to cross-pollinate
real and imagined boundaries, have proceeded throughout the years without reflecting the conflict expressed in the discourse *about* these musical
texts.

At the same time, however, one cannot dismiss as irrelevant the strain
of experimentation in Western art music that also discarded the tonal system and other familiar qualities of "classical music." Musicologist Susan
McClary has brilliantly identified the economy of prestige within which
avant-garde composers such as Roger Sessions, Arnold Schoenberg,
Milton Babbitt, and Pierre Boulez worked. Difficulty, audience alienation,
disdain of the popular, and dismissal of signification grounded in social
meaning—the meaning that makes music compelling to most listeners—
were worn like badges of honor and consigned their work to a condition

she calls "terminal prestige." While classical musics have long functioned as repositories for aristocratic and then middle-class sensibilities, desires, struggles, and fulfillment, they (and particularly the classical avant-garde) have become invested in denying the idea that the most prestigious forms of instrumental music signify social meaning.[9]

The formal qualities of this "Western" avant-garde and the jazz avant-garde discussed here may strike many casual listeners as possessing a number of similarities. But a comparison of the claims that each group made about itself is instructive. As literary scholar Henry Louis Gates once argued, "Anyone who analyzes black literature must do so as a comparativist, by definition, because our canonical texts have complex double formal antecedents, the Western and the black."[10] The same is obviously true of black music.

If the Western avant-garde (so-called for my purposes here) subscribed to what McClary called the "difficulty-for- the-sake-of-difficulty" attitude, free jazz was assigned more politically charged meanings.[11] Don't get me wrong. Jazz has over the last fifty or so years actively sought upward mobility on the ladder of cultural hierarchies, and it has done so with challenging music. Critics and musicians have fought for the legitimacy of the genre, working to change its status to a bona fide art, replete with anxieties about popular culture. But, as we learned above, the difficulty of free jazz was invested with a social function. Furthermore, because the composers of the Western avant-garde were subsidized by prestigious university and college music departments, they could afford to shun commercialism outside of their protected circle. Jazz musicians, on the other hand, have always had to cultivate careers within the culture industry, competing for their share of the pie to survive. Indeed, the economy of prestige was quite different for free jazz musicians.

Both, however, were masculinist discourses. Male musicians formed the core of each, with seemingly little room for the creative work of women. If female musicians had made inroads into the ranks of early jazz, swing, and bebop, free jazz was categorically a boys' club. As I noted above, the black feminist agenda that emerged in the 1960s and 1970s was not considered central to the thrust of black power, and, according to some, this undermined the scope and potential of the project. Thus, the free jazz movement reflected this lacuna. Yet at the same time, musicologist David

Ake has recently drawn attention to, and complicated, the view of free jazz as simply masculinist. Ornette Coleman, he argues, provided a new paradigm for black male jazz musicians by expanding what were acceptable representations of masculinity in jazz. Coleman achieved this in his nonteleological compositions, his preppy, nonslick demeanor in cover art photographs, his vegetarianism, and his nonwomanizing reputation, all of which challenged the conventional codes of jazz masculinity in the late 1960s.[12]

Cornel West has recently argued that the black power era revealed a crack in what was once considered a monolithic equal rights struggle. As an emergent black middle class grew apart from the black working class and the working poor, the resulting stratification within Afro-America threatened traditional alliances. This stratification, of course, could be seen in the jazz world, as musicians with diverse educational and social backgrounds began to constitute the community to a greater degree than they had before. Musical diversity followed. No longer could one assume that, say, jazz and R&B or even gospel were the musics of the black working class exclusively. As free jazz showed us especially, the rich diversity of experiences spawned experimentation. And as Jack Whitten reminds us in the epigraph at the beginning of this chapter, there is much at stake both artistically and socially if one ceases to experiment.

But free jazz musicians paid a price for their experiments. Although their connections to the freedom struggle were clear, there is little indication that the black masses fully embraced the form as their own, as their flag, so to speak. By challenging the arbiters of taste in both Western music and the bebop old guard, free jazz musicians pushed the envelope and themselves out of the cherished circle of common-practice jazz. But the price of not freeing jazz would have been more costly, indeed. Jazz could have died.

12 Jack Whitten's Musical Eye

When I met Jack Whitten in 2005, his work was on view at the Studio Museum in Harlem in the exhibition *Energy/Experimentation*, a show focused on African American artists who worked in the language of visual abstraction.[1] As a musician and musicologist, I became fascinated with these artists' work, especially Whitten's, because of its astounding beauty and how it resonated with my thinking about mid-twentieth-century jazz musicians of the bebop era. I had just published a book on modern jazz pianist Bud Powell (1924–66). The long arch of the bebop movement was, indeed, a moment in which he found inspiration. Whitten paid homage to jazz musicians from this era in paintings that highlighted his idiosyncratic use of abstraction. Powell was memorialized, for example, in *Five Lines Four Spaces (An Updated Version of the Broadway Boogie Woogie, for Bud Powell)* from 2011, which Whitten furthermore saw as an

"Jack Whitten's Musical Eye," in *Jack's Jacks*, exhibition catalogue on Jack Whitten (Berlin: Hamburger Bahnhof—Museum für Gegenwart, 2019), 89–102. The painter Jack Whitten's abstraction work, particularly his homages to influential musicians, is a great source of inspiration for me. "Jack Whitten: Jack's Jacks," the exhibition for which this essay was written, was on view from March 29 to September 1, 2019, at the Hamburger Bahnhof—Museum für Gegenwart.

updated version of Mondrian's iconic painting "but from a black perspective," which for him meant to "warp the grid [and] make it curve"; he
concluded, "I don't mind if a little Hip-Hop got in!"[2] Whitten's artistic
ruminations, while singular and illuminous, are part of a larger conversation between music, musicians, and visual artists.

During the so-called Jazz Age of the 1920s, for example, the Mexican-
born painter Miguel Covarrubias evoked the notion of "the modern" in
American culture through black-and-white images that captured the essence
of jazz clubs and popular dance. Archibald Motley's bold, colorful paintings,
like *Blues* from 1929, can barely contain the exuberance and adventure listeners felt as the underground music from a beleaguered subculture became
all the rage of an era. The music even lent the epoch its moniker. Whitten
would recognize the jazz genre's importance to the world as a cultural marker
of change in the grand tripartite painting *The Birth of Jazz (Point/Wave/
Point)* (2015), in which he reconciled his two signature painterly techniques,
combining intricate flanking panels constructed of acrylic tesserae with a
central swath of pigment pulled deftly across the canvas.

In the 1930s, swing music became both a commercial force and the
most popular style in the American music industry. As Americans jitter-
bugged their way through an economic depression, the visual language of
social realism became a prominent expression among black artists of the
period. Art historian Richard J. Powell describes the prototypical subject
matter of these works as "the human figure conceptually placed within a
'social narrative.'"[3] Artists celebrated the laboring working class as folk
heroes possessing the powers to connect the ancient agricultural past, the
industrial present, and a technological, skyscraper-filled future. The repetitious trope of working-class folk has an analogy in the formulaic tendencies in swing music. Indeed, the repeating riffs, ubiquitous twelve-bar
blues patterns, predictable song forms, accessible melodies, and danceable rhythms combined to make a statement about how musical cliché
could act as a powerful social organizer. Swing's formal conventions and
the mass-mediated dancing black bodies that became synonymous with
them were, for me, aligned with Social Realism's depictions of laboring
black people. Whitten would look back at one of this era's greatest singers,
Ella Fitzgerald, in *Ella II (For Ella Fitzgerald)* (1997). And the next year,
with *Cultural Shift (Let's Celebrate Lena Horne) AKA The Lena Horne*

Jubilee, Whitten recognized a singing actress whose career began in the swing era and who became one of the first crossover black starlets. This, indeed, represented a cultural shift. For many, composer, pianist, and bandleader Duke Ellington was one of most emblematic musicians of the Swing Era of jazz. His compositional technique might even be described as painterly. He would use his orchestra's repertory as a canvas, twisting and turning his musicians' varied approaches to improvisation and timbre into kaleidoscopes of tone colors, infectious melodies, and danceable rhythms. Whitten recognized Ellington's singular achievements in two paintings: *Black Table Setting (Homage to Duke Ellington)* (1974) and *The Predominance of Tan, Black and Blue (The Duke of Ellington's Centennial Celebration)* (1999).

The years spanning the 1940s and 1960s brought new challenges and, of course, produced new art. The times were harsh but changing. In politics, economics, and culture many developments occurred that held consequences for African Americans, especially within their expressive cultural practices. As I have written elsewhere, the times held many tensions and contradictions: "On the one hand, the Jim Crow system that appeared after Reconstruction seemed to be drawing its last breath because of political, legal, and economic pressure mounted by African-Americans in grass roots protests. On the other hand, the shifting maze of discriminatory practices constantly undermined these various struggles for equality. These cultural dynamics played themselves out in postwar African-American literature, visual arts, and music."[4] It was, perhaps, the virtuosity of modern jazz musicians that seemed to attract deep identifications from artists who projected their dreams of freedom onto the technical excellence of the musicians. Even the unusual song titles like Charlie Parker's "Ornithology" and Thelonious Monk's "Epistrophy" evoked a brave new world for black artists.[5] The great figures of classic bebop style improvisation were memorialized by Whitten, for example in the paintings *Sassy: For Sarah Vaughn* (1990), *Cosmic Bopper: For Diz* (1993) (referring to Dizzy Gillespie), *El Nino: For Charlie Parker* (1998), *Flying High for Betty Carter* (1998), *Brilliant Corners (For Thelonious "Sphere" Monk)* (1998), and *Vibrations for Milt "Bags" Jackson* (1999).

Indeed, freedom was the goal as thousands of black citizens left the South and migrated to cities like New York, Chicago, and Los Angeles, among other destinations. Jack Whitten was one of them when he moved from Louisiana to New York City in 1960 to study at Cooper Union, escaping what he called the "American apartheid" of the South. Clearly art and activism were joined somehow in his mind. Whitten was committed to both artistic expression and to the civil rights of black people and relished all the opportunities that living in New York afforded him to pursue both of them.

A former junior high and high school musician, Whitten was keenly aware of, and completely enamored by, the exciting musical, literary, and social activism culture of New York's Lower East Side, where he lived and worked. There he met poet and playwright LeRoi Jones (Amiri Baraka), who would become a major cultural influencer in the coming decades. As a student at Cooper Union Whitten took in all the art being created around him. His student piece *The Blacks*, an acrylic collage, was inspired by Jean Genet's play *The Blacks: A Clown Show* (1958), which had a run at St. Mark's Playhouse while he was a student. In 1963 Whitten joined his voice and body to the movement for equal rights as he participated in Martin Luther King Jr.'s March on Washington.[6]

The real (and symbolic) cerebral profile of the new jazz Whitten was hearing in New York was inspiring not only to musicians but to writers and visual artists as well. Icons like composer Quincy Jones and poet Amiri Baraka said that bebop musicians gave them a paradigm for what it meant to be an intellectual, young black artist in America. Jazz continued along this path of artistic freedom during the 1950s and 1960s, when it took another dramatic departure into further abstraction, moving away from its roots in popular song. Ornette Coleman, John Coltrane, Cecil Taylor, Albert Ayler, Eric Dolphy, and members of the Association for the Advancement of Creative Musicians (AACM), among others, pushed the music into something called "free jazz," or the New Thing. As I have written elsewhere, "If bebop exaggerated melodic contour, harmonic extension, and rhythmic disjuncture to the brink of abstraction, certainly free jazz broke through the genre's common practice sound barrier, wreaking musical havoc, building controversial careers, mystifying old school critics, and attracting reverent converts."[7] Many writers adopted the New Thing as a political statement of freedom by the musicians. Whitten himself apparently believed that Ornette Coleman was a cultural flashpoint outside of the jazz world and recognized this status in 2015, allotting the musician a place in his series of cultural and political icons, the *Black Monoliths,* with the work *Black Monolith, IX (Open Circle for Ornette Coleman).*

Whitten understood his artistic life as linked to restless experimentation, and he must have recognized that impulse among the musicians he admired and to whom he paid homage. If black visual artists like Romare Bearden and Norman Lewis moved away from what Lowery Stokes Sims called an "aesthetic system of figuration" that visually represented "black identity," then post-bop and free jazz musicians would do the same for music during Whitten's formative years as a student. Black musical figuration—diatonic melodies, blue notes, popular song forms, repeating riffs, and danceable rhythms—gave way to an abandonment of these procedures. It is important to mention here that although jazz music is known as a site of experimentation and as "America's classical music," that is not to say that Whitten did not recognize other forms of black music as influential. Blues, rock, soul, and funk were treated with as much respect by Whitten in paintings that paid homage to the icons of black musical figuration, including James Brown, John Lennon, Michael Jackson, Prince, B. B. King, and Chuck Berry.

As a former saxophonist, Whitten understood well the discipline it took to perpetually experiment with and master a musical language. His own dual training in his high school's marching band and in a gigging jazz band (The Dunbar Jazzettes) provided him two ways to experience the commitment it took. Could these experiences have been the lens through which he would comprehend the dual sites of his art training—inside Cooper Union's classrooms, and from his mentors Romare Bearden and Norman Lewis outside of school? Could music have been, in fact, his portal into which he understood painting itself as a language? Because of music's nonrepresentational character and its allegorical capacity, visual abstraction offered Whitten a similar expressive mode as music does.

Whitten's "musical" paintings were often prompted by a musician's passing, but sometimes they were simply a look back at an artistic subject that he respected, as is the case with his works dedicated to John Coltrane. Salim Washington has described Coltrane's ever-evolving creative process as tied to his relentless experimentation with sonic materials, particularly in his use of long modal vamps over which he seemingly could improvise endlessly, the use of nontempered tuning, and dramatic techniques like shrieks, honks, screams, and glissandi-like smears. Likewise, Whitten's ceaseless search to develop his painterly language involved experimentation with opticality, materials, space, tools, and surface, as did the works of many of his generation. Kellie Jones describes this creative force as "energy," which for her is the exploration of "new materials and technologies, including new formulas of acrylic paint, light, electronics, photography and a translation of photographic thinking."[8]

Light would be particularly important.

Whitten describes New York's jazz scene as formative to his processes as an artist. He hung out in the jazz clubs like Birdland, the Five Spot Café, and Minton's Playhouse constantly and knew some of his musical heroes: Thelonious Monk, Art Blakey, Cecil Taylor, Sonny Rollins, Miles Davis, Eric Dolphy, Sonny Rollins, Jackie McLean, and Coltrane. The high quality of musicianship that he experienced in the clubs of that era made him aware that his calling lay elsewhere: "[It] destroyed any notion of my being a Jazz musician."[9] Although Whitten's relationships with both Blakey and Davis (and their long careers that nurtured generations of talent) were celebrated in *The Messenger: For Art Blakey* (1990) and *Homecoming: For Miles* (1992), both acrylic on canvas, it is his interactions with Coltrane that appear to have been the most generative. In one conversation with the artist, Coltrane described his "sheets of sound" improvising technique as a "wave." Whitten never forgot it. He said in an interview with Robert Storr, "I connected that in terms of painting, in my second show at Allan Stone, which came out of that conversation with John Coltrane. I called these paintings *Light Sheets*. They were paintings that were tacked directly to the wall, without a stretcher. . . . What I was talking about was a plane of light, light operating as a plane. I saw that directly related to Coltrane's sound. The plane of light is synonymous with wave and sheet; this is what led me to the 1970s slab paintings."[10] Without doubt, Whitten's kaleidoscopic *Totem 2000 VI Annunciation: For John Coltrane* (2000) looks back on Coltrane's instructions with care and devotion, even after his painting technique had developed away from the slabs into his later fragmented, mosaic style constructed of acrylic tesserae and found material.

Like the music of Coltrane and Miles Davis, who both had decades-long careers that were marked by dramatic evolutions of style, Whitten's musical paintings were linked to some greater painterly problem that he was deliberating continuously. Although the musical expertise of the virtuosos he met on New York's jazz scene in the 1960s dissuaded him from pursuing a musical career, he clearly continued to strongly identify with the art form as a central impulse in his practice. In his published studio log, titled *Notes from the Woodshed,* Whitten drew links between his deliberations in the studio and during his summers carving wood on Crete, and jazz musicians' notion of the "woodshed," the strict and demanding practice habit in which one works out ideas and their technical execution. Throughout the notes Whitten makes many equivalences to music: his visual structures were "polyrhythmic" and tied to the layers of light in his painting. Indeed, he wanted his art objects to be like jazz. Primarily listening to jazz in his studio, he saw his painting as him improvising by himself (like a solo pianist?).[11] For Whitten free jazz meant a no-limits freedom, one that he sought to convey in his innovative art practice, particularly in how he approached abstraction.[12]

It's no wonder, then, that when I saw some of Whitten's paintings firsthand I experienced them as musical works. From a distance across the room, one is always taken by their large-scale form and overall structure. But there's something about them that compels you to pause and plunge into the restless details—the theme and variations, the tempo, tone colors, staccato and legato lines, the relief, the broad contours and heterophony of timbres, indeed, the waves of light, shadows, and visual chromaticism. And you patiently remain there transfixed in the face of Whitten's art as you take in the sound of his unconscious. You hear through his music eye until the final virtuoso strain is sounded.

13 Out of Place and Out of Line

JASON MORAN'S ECLECTICISM AS CRITICAL INQUIRY

From the late nineteenth to the early twentieth centuries, African American musicians inhabited a world of hustle on ecumenical fronts. Long before our present-day ideas about genre had become stubborn, calcified categories, a more porous performance culture existed. And black musicians rarely "stayed in their place" but rather worked across invisible boundaries. Opera singers like Sissieretta Jones, who had a legendary career on the international concert stage, could find easy work on the minstrelsy circuit. The classically trained violinist Will Marion Cook unapologetically wrote, in collaboration with poet Paul Laurence Dunbar, the pioneering musical-comedy sketch *Clorindy; or, The Origin of the Cakewalk*, which premiered on Broadway in 1898. Scott Joplin, the ragtime pianist/composer who got American audiences dancing their way out of Victorianism, also composed the groundbreaking opera *Treemonisha* in 1911. You get the picture; it was all about stretching, as they say. So every time I read Jason Moran tagged simply as "jazz pianist,"

"Out of Place and Out of Line: Jason Moran's Eclecticism as Critical Inquiry," in *Whitney Biennial Catalogue* (New York: Whitney Museum of American Art, 2012). This essay was written for Alicia Hall Moran's and Jason Moran's historic performances at the 2012 Whitney Biennial.

I think: "Wait a minute—he's so much more." He's genius personified, and he never stays in his place.

Moran, a newly minted recipient of a John D. and Catherine T. MacArthur "genius" award, has done much in his career thus far to challenge the idea of category, indeed, to push out at the edges of jazz's sometimes defensive palisade by crisscrossing artistic media and by turning this family of idioms on its head. Some would indeed call such audacious attitude "genius." The term is such a slippery concept. It's a label that gets tossed around musical circles, usually to describe an artist with a highly visible and prolific output. We also use it to talk about people with an unusually profound endowment of technical facility through which they express something that audiences perceive as "universal," "timeless," or transcending the moment in which they experience them. But musical genius is always in the ears, hearts, and heads of the beholder. Experiencing it, in my view, is not a matter of transcendence. It's about using one's mechanics of delivery and sense of social constitution—knowledge of how musical codes "work"—to anchor listeners in a deep sense of the "present tense." Genius, despite its reputation, is never a matter of isolated, rugged individualism. As Moran demonstrates time and time again, it can also be a collaborative affair, one in which artistic communities in motion become living models of thoughtful and meaningful social interaction, something that we all, I believe, are born to desire and witness.

How does he do it? Moran's artistic palette encompasses more than music. It interrogates how all of the arts—music, film, poetry, architecture, dance, and painting—can directly inform each another. Because of his ecumenical approach, his work has helped to expand not only the language but also the large possibilities of the contemporary jazz scene. Over the last ten years his recordings as both leader and sideman have traced the development of an artist exploring new and eclectic sound worlds. In his performance rhetoric—one that is instantly recognizable—you can hear many of his wide influences: the Southwest blues, traditional jazz, contemporary modal, and even traces of Berg, Monk, Webern, and more. I can think of no other young pianist on the jazz scene today who seems to be in perpetual artistic motion—constantly searching, forever challenging and chiding his muse. He has engaged in collaborations with museums, choreographers, art historians, poets, and performance artists, and the result has been adventurous projects that embrace the power derived from unusual juxtapositions. He is, arguably, the most critically engaged pianist to emerge on the jazz scene in years.

Recently I caught Moran live in performance with his band of ten years, the Bandwagon, and even that highlighted both boundary crossing and collaboration. Surrounded by a clutter of written scores, they moved up something serious through an adventurous set of compositions from past projects and their latest CD, *Ten*. They opened with a powerful reading of a song written by Alicia Hall Moran, Jason's talented and very soprano spouse. "Blessing the Boats" was packed with sly ostinato figures in the piano, pushy pop musical gestures, and sinewy melodies winding through tricky harmonic environments. It was an exploration of composition in process that worked well, preparing us for the meal in the guise of a meaningful gracing of the table.

The empathetic and telepathic virtuosity demonstrated by his colleagues, drummer Nasheet Waits and bassist Tarus Mateen, simply astounded. These very strong musical personalities are not simply a backdrop for Moran's musings: they are part and parcel of the sonic mosaic that has become his vehicle in much the same way as Duke Ellington's orchestra was for his. Moran's compositional signature and improvisational rhetoric also leave a lasting impression long after the last strains are heard.

Throughout the set Moran's performance rhetoric included full-voiced gospel-style chords in the right hand with single note doublings with Mateen; Earl Hines's "trumpet style"; Bud Powell–esque bebop lines; Cecil Taylor–like passages of dissonant, florid pianism; and gutsy tremolo passages that sound like vocalized field hollers straight out of the ring shout rituals of black expressive culture. His most intense solos move rapidly between arpeggios superimposed over dissonant harmonic structures and spirited scales. As Moran combines this rhetoric over the course of several songs, one experiences in real time a white-knuckled virtuosity awash in dizzying counterpoints of melodies, timbres, and polyrhythms that ebb and flow with apparent spontaneity.

His compositions are studies in the economic use of emotional momentum. Many move from precious, pithy statements into grand pronouncements and back again. Some leave you on the mountaintop, breathless. The Bandwagon achieves these in the context of grooves that, while infectious, are not easily digested. That is, one has to concentrate to perceive the large structures of their form. They are built not on smallish cyclic harmonic patterns but on larger-scale patterns of repetition. Moreover, because of their length, they can sound like seamless multimovement jazz suites. Their grooves take on many rhythm configurations, from soupy, down-home blues to hard bop swing or rhythm rhetoric from more contemporary sound worlds. Moran's occasional use of onstage prerecorded sounds give the effect of an installation art piece, where we in the audience are snapped out of our typical listening positions and drawn into a more intense listening and visual relationship with the band.

And speaking of art pieces, Moran's various collaborations with artists such as Adrian Piper, Kara Walker, and Glenn Ligon together with his impressive commissions in the museum world recall and extend black American musical cultures of the past in which artistic expression was a way to transgress boundaries, not reify them. Maybe it was the tenor of times, but in the decades leading up to the high and heavy years of the civil rights and Black consciousness movements, African American artists across the board believed that their work could collectively engage, interrogate, and challenge the status quo. This quote from the late poet Gwendolyn Brooks captures this energy:

> My husband and I knew writers, knew pianists and dancers and actresses, knew photographers galore. There were always weekend parties to be attended where we merry Bronzevillians could find each other and earnestly philosophise sometimes on into the dawn, over martinis and Scotch and coffee and an ample buffet. Great social decisions were reached. Great solutions for great problems were provided. . . . Of course, in that time, it was believed, still, that the society could be prettied, quieted, cradled, sweetened, if only people talked enough, glared at each other yearningly enough, waited enough.

I've attended a Jason and Alicia Hall Moran house party and can testify that this kind of energy still thrives. There's more at stake in his circle than socializing and collaborating for the hell of it; it's even larger than making art objects for their own sake. Rather, the whole enterprise—the art, the music, the building of a collective—is about what art historian and curator Kellie Jones has recently called "community archive," a quest for a larger meaning through art. For her, the idea describes "how artistic communities—be they families of origin [or families by marriage], groups, movements, neighborhoods, and so on—create and theorize their pasts, illuminating the dialogic among individuals and the collectives to which they belong, and in which artistic meaning is derived." (But please don't think there's not good food and music, too!)

Jones was asked in *ARTnews* back in 2007 to predict who the art world would be looking at 105 years hence. She said Jason Moran, and many of us agreed. Since that time he's continued to experiment, traversing sonic, literary, and visual art worlds, and then comes back to share what he's learned. Like his predecessors from well over a century ago, Moran's approach obliterates boundaries, colors outside the lines, and poses a critical question: "Whose art worlds are they anyway?"

14 African American Music

A term applied to distinct configurations of sound organization linked historically and socially to people of African descent living within the United States. While scholarship has identified a shared body of conceptual approaches to sound among the numerous idioms of African American music, musicians have employed them across various functional divides in American culture such as written and oral, sacred and secular, art and popular. Although African American people have been the primary innovators among these idioms, due to mass mediation, the contiguous nature of culture sharing among American ethnic groups, an ever developing and sophisticated global market system, technological advances, and music's ability to absorb the different meanings ascribed to it, people of all backgrounds have shaped, contributed to, and excelled in this fluid yet distinct body of music making. In addition, many historians

"African American Music," in *New Grove Dictionary of American Music and Musicians* (New York: Oxford University Press, 2012), https://doi.org/10.1093/gmo/9781561592630 .article.A2226838. My assignment, as I imagined it for this general reference article, was to build on the previous foundational contributions of Eileen Southern and Portia Maultsby, who both wrote the African American article for previous editions of the *New Grove Dictionary of Music*, in 1980 and 1986, respectively. I wanted to expand on their groundbreaking works with new insights from subsequent scholarship and for a broad audience.

of African American music have included the activities of blacks that participated as performers and composers in the Eurological concert tradition under this rubric.

SLAVERY, CULTURE, AND THE BLACK ATLANTIC

Between the fifteenth century and mid-nineteenth century close to twelve million Africans were captured and transported to the New World, with the greatest number imported to Brazil and other locations in the Caribbean sugar industry. Reaching its apex between 1700 and 1820 when 6.5 million Africans were taken, the Atlantic slave trade represented one of the largest forced migrations in world history. Only 6 percent of the total number exported came directly to what is known now as the United States. These captured Africans were distributed along the eastern seaboard from New England to the mid-Atlantic colonies to the Southeast, but the greatest concentration landed in the South.

The nature of slavery in the United States was a singular enterprise, categorically different from various iterations of the "peculiar institution" throughout South America and the Caribbean. These distinct qualities shaped the development of African American cultural forms in dance, literature, visual culture, and especially music. Despite the ingenious and hideous development of laws and social practices designed to keep black slaves subservient, they nonetheless asserted their aspirations, their senses of beauty and the sublime, their frustrations, pain, and humanity through sound organization.

North America began its philosophically "Western" existence as commercial and religious extensions of European powers. As such early black music making in this context must be understood in its relationship to European-derived musical practices. Although early religious music in the colonies represented a direct transplant from the Old World, it was soon indigenized by the Pilgrims, whose music became rooted and influential. Musically simplistic and textually derivative, early American religious music would through a series of sonic and ideological developments become wholly "American," though in a persistent relationship—adaptations, rejections, and importations—with European models.

African American musical traditions mirrored these processes with respect to their relationship to the growing musical practices of the larger culture. These traditions constituted a confluence of broad African-derived approaches to sound organization and European-derived song structures and musical systems in a constant state of dynamic and historically specific interactions. What emerged is a composite: an indigenized conceptual framework of music making that has functioned through the years as a key symbol of an African American cultural identity.

The paradox of living as slaves and later as second-class citizens in a society founded on the principles of democracy and freedom produced a social structure in which black cultural production was mapped on a continuum between participation in what the scholar George Lewis has conceptualized as Eurological traditions and those reflecting Afrological aesthetic and structural priorities. Blacks who received training in Colonial-era singing schools are part of a long tradition of participating in Eurological practices that continues into the twenty-first century. Black music scholarship has generally included such musical activities by African Americans under the rubric "African American music." From New Orleans to the mid-Atlantic to New York, the historical record indicates a robust and varied musical culture among a new people created by forced mass migration, social domination, and heroic cultural resilience.

In letters from missionaries, slave advertisements, runaway slave notices, personal travel journals, and memoirs, white observers noted both the musical talents of and the distinct body of music making taking place among the slaves. Their writings, permeated in some instances with the desire to sensationalize what was considered "barbaric" in these practices, described the sounds they heard in rich and colorful detail. An 1867 account of a Pinkster festival held in the 1770s describes an annual days-long celebration among slaves in Albany, New York. A conglomeration of dance, drum, and song, the musical components of the event provide a telling example of the cultural priorities of a people enjoying themselves during a rare time of repose from their lives as the "nonhuman" tools of their masters:

> The dance had it peculiarities, as well as everything else connected with this august celebration. It consisted chiefly of couples joining in the performance at varying times, and continuing it with their utmost energy until extreme

fatigue or weariness compelled them to retire and give space to a less
exhausted set; and in this successive manner was the excitement kept up
with unabated vigor, until the shades of night began to fall slowly over the
land, and at length deepen into the silent gloom of midnight.

The music made use of on this occasion, was likewise singular in the
extreme. The principal instrument selected to furnish this important portion of the ceremony was a symmetrically formed wooded article usually
denominated an *eel-pot*, with a cleanly dressed sheep skin drawn tightly over
its wide and open extremity.... Astride this rude utensil sat Jackey
Quackenboss, then in his prime of life and well known energy, beating lust-
ily with his naked hands upon its loudly sounding head, successively repeating the ever wild, though euphonic cry of *Hi-a-bomba, bomba, bomba,* in
full harmony with the thumping sounds. These vocal sounds were readily
taken up and as oft repeated by the female portion of the spectators not
otherwise engaged in the exercises of the scene, accompanied by the beating
of time with their ungloved hands, in strict accordance with the eel-pot melody. (James Eights, 1867)

Researchers have historically stressed the "functionality" of black music
in comparison to that of the larger society and as a viable link to its
"African past." Nonetheless, Anglo-Saxon Protestant religious expression
was functional as well in Colonial America and as such became an important structural space for the development of African American music. As
early New Englanders debated the value of oral and written modes of ped-
agogy and dissemination in their churches and singing schools well into
the nineteenth century, African Americans codified their own musical
sensibilities within the framework of their gradual acculturation into
American Christianity. These qualities included performance practices
with a predilection for antiphonal response, timbral heterogeneity, rhythmic variety, improvisation, corporeal activity, and open-ended structures
encouraging endless repetition as well as oral dissemination. In 1819,
John F. Watson, a black northern minister, criticized integrated camp
meetings in which black musical practices were absorbed into the white
church world, and his comments pointed toward a long-term pattern of
cultural interdependence:

In the blacks' quarter, the coloured people get together and sing for hours
together, short scraps of disjointed affirmations, pledges, or prayers, length-
ened out with long repetition choruses. These are all sung in merry chorus-

manner of the southern harvest field or husking frolic method, of the slave blacks. (Watson, 1819)

These practices made sonically porous the boundaries separating secular and sacred realms as slave festivals, holidays, and even revolts were accompanied by similar musical components, although the degree of "Africanisms"—those musical qualities with analogous connections to the historical (and, in some cases, recent) homeland of the slaves—varied according to regional differences determined by the density of the black population in relation to that of the white ruling classes. Music became an iconic symbol of black difference and a recognized source of communal identity and thus inspired the passing of laws in selected states to control the social environment for fear of white safety.

Between 1650 and 1750, the idea that African peoples formed a unified racial unit flourished in Europe as plantation slavery and its cultures shaped race ideology, trade economies, and social practices on both sides of the Atlantic. This construction of African identity was further entrenched in North America as black people founded churches, schools, and fraternal institutions during the decades surrounding 1800, many including the term "African" in their designations. The 1816 founding of the African Methodist Episcopal Church in Philadelphia formally established a black religious tradition in the United States that would continue to develop within the institutional and structural systems of the larger society. The publication of an ex-slave, Reverend Richard Allen's hymnal *A Collection of Spiritual Songs and Hymns,* in 1801 affirms that the desire to engage in musical practices of their own making was part of the reason for the establishment of separate denominations. Following the tradition of printed metrical psalters of the New England compilers, Allen's hymnal contains songs by Isaac Watts and others whose forms encourage antiphonal response among participants.

BLACK CULTURAL DIVERSITY IN THE NORTH AND THE SOUTH

Among free blacks in the North, black brass bands that played popular songs of the day could be found in Philadelphia, New York, and Boston as well as in the Midwest and in New Orleans. Some of the music performed by these groups was their own and, thus, a school of composition written for popular consumption emerged employing the styles, tastes, and conventions of their white counterparts.

Nonprofessional black itinerant musicians and vendors also roamed public urban spaces peddling their wares with street cries and song fragments analogous to those heard in the fields of southern plantations. The African Grove Theater in New York City began as a private tea garden in 1816 and opened its doors to the public in 1821. In spite of constant hostility from the neighboring whites, the theater nonetheless remained open until around 1829, mounting productions that typically included overtures, ballad operas, ballets, and intermittent dances and "fashionable" songs or marches.

Francis Johnson, another pioneer Philadelphian, was central in establishing a black instrumental band tradition as a composer, virtuoso musician on the violin and keyed bugle, a bandleader, music instructor, entrepreneur, community organizer, a master music promoter, and the first African American to have his musical works published. He was among the first American musicians to take a band to Europe. Johnson received music instruction from a white teacher who thoroughly grounded him in music theory, composition, and performance. He formed his ensemble between the years 1819 and 1821, playing for many occasions among Philadelphia's white elites. He traveled with equally talented black musicians whose performance practices surely set them apart because of their ability to "distort" the notes on the written page into a dynamic style that was drawn from musical traits from black culture. The overwhelming popularity of Johnson's contribution to the various traditions of American band music in his time foreshadowed that of John Philip Sousa, another towering giant in this realm.

During the first sixty years of the nineteenth century, the United States continued its expansion across the continent, and slavery continued even though an 1808 Congressional act officially ended the lawful importation of slaves. The demand for slaves in the interior South increased with the dramatically growing plantation economy, solidifying the interdependence of both institutions. Communities of both free and enslaved blacks, the numbers of which rose from three quarters of a million in 1790 to well over four million by 1860, continued their resistance to their status in American society. The formation of the Free People of Color, the courageous slave revolts, the establishments of black newspapers, and the growth of independent black churches affirm the presence of a vital black cultural agency.

In the South, the internal slave trade destabilized traditional familial and communal ties, but cultural practices such as music making became crucial sites of resistance and community building. With the overwhelming majority of blacks living in the plantation culture of the South in the nineteenth century, it was natural that their musical practices would become widespread and recognized for their extraordinary qualities. The music of slave religious expression and secular work songs reveal their preferred sonic ideals. In their public working and festival settings sanctioned by the masters, the slaves were encouraged to perform "cultural difference" according to practices from their African cultural heritage and as such expressed their own perspectives toward time, work, and their status as human beings. The new cultural formations that emerged had a tremendous impact on white southern culture as well, a pattern that would continue in subsequent centuries.

Nonreligious music making flourished among slave populations and free blacks in all regions. Documentary evidence shows that the talented fiddlers and players of the banjo, an instrument of African origin, provided dance music for both black and white populations. Reports of musicians "pattin' juba," a rhythmic technique involving striking the hands on various parts of the body while stamping the feet and singing, detail a propensity for rhythmic complexity. Dancing and drumming often went hand in hand in various festivals or weekend occasions for leisure. Work songs, children's game and ring songs, corn-husking songs, and songs of protest offer convincing evidence of the rich variety of secular music making taking place in slave populations. Broadly speaking, the creative processes underlying these widespread and varied musical practices operated on a continuum between newly composed materials and those that transformed existing material into something uniquely African American.

During the antebellum period, local customs and laws, black population patterns, and the distinct political histories of various regions determined the shape and geographic diversity of African American musical expression. Where free blacks were in the minority, such as they were in the North, a musician such as Johnson could get training and compete in an integrated, though still unequal, environment. In some regions of the slave-holding South, where blacks were subjected to more harsh and extreme control measures, Christianity strongly shaped the development of a distinctive system of black musical expression. Some areas restricted black music making by suppressing drumming at various historical moments. In New Orleans, part of a larger region with strong French and Spanish cultural roots, a rich heritage of Creole of color, black, and white cultural mixing distinguished the city's musical profile. The Marigny Theater, for example, opened in 1838 for Creoles of color to enjoy light comedies in French together with other kinds of variety shows that included music. New Orleans's black musical life was among the most vibrant in the nation, boasting special seating for free blacks and slaves at opera houses, freelance instrumentalists, brass bands and orchestras, and the Negro Philharmonic Society, formed during the 1830s to present concerts by local and visiting musicians.

THE NEW POPULAR CULTURE

New musical expressions continued to emerge among black populations during the nineteenth century. In the larger world of popular entertainment, blackface minstrelsy emerged as a complex set of performance genres—songs, sketches, dances, novelty acts—whose conventions and functions changed over time and whose influence remained intact for many years. At the peak of its popularity between 1850 and 1870, it featured white men in blackface executing caricatures of expressive practices observed among slaves, black street vendors, and roving musicians in cities. Minstrelsy's sensational stereotypes and popularity became a paradigm with which black performers would have to contend publicly well into the twentieth century. Nineteenth-century periodicals ran articles that disparaged the popularity of minstrelsy, which was understood as a uniquely American form of entertainment at a time when the country's cultural elite still looked to European performers, repertoire, and practice as the measure of "good" music. Important to black music history is the fact that contemporary audiences collapsed minstrelsy with musical styles developed by African Americans themselves. Minstrelsy set the tone for "black" performance as a "guilty pleasure," an act of transgression against established social mores for an expanding white middle class with anxiety about upward mobility and distinguishing themselves from those lower on the social ladder.

By the middle of the nineteenth century, Americans could pursue a number of occupations in the music industry such as performing, composing, teaching, concert management, and publishing. While black amateur musicians abounded, professional opportunities that appeared after Emancipation offered rapid advancement for these musicians whose talents became a growing component of the nation's musical profile. As the century proceeded, musical practice began to settle into categories of valuation: art, mass or popular, and traditional or folk. Issues of repertoire, training, heritage, patterns of consumption, and venue were factors determining the pedigree of a musical practice. As blacks made their sociopolitical transition from slavery to freedom, their musical culture continually transformed and was transformed by the structures that governed the creation, dissemination, and interpretation of artistic production in America.

For the African American performer after the Civil War, participation in theater could involve three related forms: musical theater, minstrel shows, and vaudeville. The black musical theater tradition began when the Hyers Sisters, two women who had already built careers on the concert stage, created together with the white writer Joseph Bradford the musical comedy *Out of Bondage* in 1876. *Out of Bondage* was the first of many such productions, whose plots included plantation scenes and topics of racial progress within a format that featured plantation songs, ballads, operatic numbers, and folk dances.

In the realms of performance and composition, the minstrel show became a crucial route to financial security for many black musicians, even those trained in classical music. What was often billed as Ethiopian minstrelsy created the amplest opportunities for African Americans to break into show business, with more than one hundred black minstrel troupes formed between 1865 and 1890. Their entertainment comprised a traveling one-hour-and-forty-five-minute variety show consisting of three general categories of songs: ballads, comic songs, and specialty numbers. Representative shows featured singers and a small ensemble of instrumentalists who performed the works of such black songwriters as James Bland, Gussie Davis, and Samuel Lucas, as well as Stephen Foster, a white writer. The repertory of the typical black minstrel show also included religious songs and operatic arias.

It was perhaps because of this range of stylistic possibilities on the minstrel stage that black female concert singers such as Sissieretta Jones (popularly known as Black Patti) and others of her ilk could transition from the concert stage to the minstrelsy trope circuit when "black prima donnas" fell out of vogue around the turn of the century. Nonetheless, the years after the Civil War saw the rise and popularity of many black women on the concert stage singing European art music. Touring widely in the United States and Europe, Black Patti, soprano Marie Selika Williams, and the Hyers Sisters, among others, maintained active careers with good management and engagements in prestigious concert halls.

Black male instrumentalists achieved significant popularity during this time. Born a slave, the unsighted pianist and composer Thomas Bethune (1849–1909), known as "Blind Tom," received musical training from his masters, learning thousands of works of the classical repertory by ear. Routinely subjected to tests of his powers of extraordinary musical memory, Bethune toured Europe, the United States, and South America for thirty years under the aegis of his owners, who continued to manage his career even after slavery ended. Other black male pianists, organists, and violinists trained as concert artists, breaking new ground first by obtaining formal training in conservatories and next by building reputations in the art world.

SPIRITUALS, BLACK CULTURE, AND THE ART IDEA

A musical development that countered the pervasiveness of black cultural stereotypes in minstrelsy occurred when the Fisk Jubilee Singers, a group of eleven men and women under the directorship of George L. White, began performing art songs designed for the concert stage. Founded in 1866, six months after the end of the Civil War, Fisk University was established to educate newly freed slaves. White, being charged by the school's administration to provide music instruction to promising students, provided lessons that included musicianship, classical repertory, and music from their own culture: spirituals. With the melodies of the "folk" spirituals as an emotional focal point, these songs were arranged into strict part singing and were performed vocally in bel canto style. A new American genre was born. When White took the group on a tour in 1871 to raise funds for the struggling institution, they performed a program similar to that of white singers but that also included spirituals.

Other black colleges would follow suit, using singing groups to raise funds, a tradition that has continued to the present. The Fisk Jubilee Singers and subsequent groups created a new framework for understanding black musical performance. The creation and popularity of the concert spiritual fit into the larger functions of commercialism, religion, and structural integration through education that has long defined African American culture. It also represented another example of the indigenization of culture seen in the initial "invention" of the spiritual in which Eurological poetic and song forms were transformed into a new genre through Afrological performance practice. In this latest turn, however, the Eurological ideas about the fully composed and bounded musical "work," bel canto singing techniques, and concert decorum and praxis were applied to an African American body of song, producing a new form of indigenization that would become an important symbol of history, progress, and the idea of an expansive African American identity.

As awareness of black music continued its surge into the public sphere, it inspired numerous responses across the American culture industry. The anthology *Slave Songs of the United States*, published in 1867, compiled 136 melodies with lyrics collected and edited by northern abolitionists William Francis Allen, Charles Pickard Ware, and Lucy McKim Garrison. Transcribed from songs collected from various geographical locations in the South, the book was the first of its kind, designed to share with readers the mostly religious songs heard by the book's authors. According to the editors, standard notation could not capture all the qualities of performance of these sacred and plantation songs. Represented in print as monophonic melodies, they in fact were performed as improvised heterophony. The compilers desired to capture slave culture's "difference" in written form, an act that for them would at once save a sonic world for posterity and represent the nobility of an enslaved people in the contemporaneous moment.

James Monroe Trotter's *Music and Some Highly Musical People* (New York, 1878) represented another approach to disciplining black musical activity in the United States through literary means. Written by a black amateur musician and impresario, Trotter's book, although focusing exclusively on nineteenth-century African American musicians, is the first general survey of American music of any kind, making it a landmark in American music historiography. The book contains an appendix with the scores of compositions by black writers, the act of which intended to instill racial pride, a sense of cultural nationalism, and "relations of mutual respect and good feeling" between the races.

In the concert world, the pursuit of establishing a language of American musical nationalism came to an apex among composers, patrons, and institutions in the 1890s. This goal was explored along many lines—aesthetic, historical, political, and stylistic. When Bohemian composer Antonín Dvořák visited America as director of the National Conservatory between 1892 and 1895, he created a stir when he pronounced that composers could use African American and Native American melodies to build an indigenous art music culture because of their beauty.

Henry T. Burleigh (1866–1949), one of Dvořák's black students, published *Jubilee Songs of the United States* (1916), arranged for piano and voice, a landmark collection that created the genre of solo black art song. A concert artist, arranger, music editor, and composer, Burleigh wrote more than three hundred works, many of which were popular in their time among singers of all backgrounds. While the large-scale impact of Dvořák's proclamations may be debated, the fact that Burleigh and many other composers—both black and white—responded creatively to his admonition and wrote music that began an important tradition confirms its importance.

The last years of the nineteenth century saw the rise of "public amusements," an explosion of commercialized leisure that indexed America's turn from Victorian sensibilities. Advances in technology, the emergence of cultures of consumerism, and unprecedented black mobility together with increasing educational opportunities created a social milieu in which black musicians became a strong presence in the culture industry. As the specter of minstrelsy still prevailed, many black musicians would have to engage its practices in order to gain opportunities in the newly emerging mass-market enterprise.

BLACK MUSIC AND THE MODERN POP CULTURE INDUSTRY

The new technology of recording, pioneered by Thomas Edison in 1877, began as an experiment to reproduce the spoken word and soon became a way to disseminate music. When George W. Johnson, a former slave, recorded "The Whistling Coon" in 1890 for the New Jersey Phonograph Company, it made him the first African American recording artist. As a child, he was assigned to be the "body servant" to his master's young son, to whom he was close in age. Johnson sat in on his young master's flute lessons, imitated the notes, and could eventually whistle any tune he heard. He was "discovered" as an adult by the New Jersey Phonograph Company, which was looking for something "cheap and loud." Johnson recorded a coon song written by the white vaudevillian Sam Devere and filled with lyrics poking fun at physical stereotypes of African Americans.

Close to a decade later black musicians countered these coon song stereotypes when Bert Williams and George Walker recorded songs from the new tradition of the black musical theater for the Victor Talking Machine Company in 1901. The jubilee and quartet singing tradition, made popular by the touring Fisk singers a generation prior, also attracted the attention of the company the following year as they recorded the Dinwiddie Colored Quartet and the Fisk Jubilee Quartet. Nonetheless, distancing themselves from the coon aesthetic of minstrelsy and at the same time riding the crest of its popularity for financial gain proved to be an arduous balancing act for the black musician.

As African Americans became an increasing presence in the popular sphere, traveling troupes began to produce bona fide stars that gained international fame. Bob Cole (1868–1911) and Billy Johnson (ca. 1858–1916) both left Black Patti's Troubadours to produce *A Trip to Coontown*, which debuted in 1898 and toured successfully for two years. That same year, Will Marion Cook (1869–1944), violinist, composer, choral and orchestral director, and organizer, debuted his *Clorindy; or, The Origin of the Cakewalk* (cowritten by poet Paul Laurence Dunbar) on Broadway, a landmark in the history of black musical theater.

Cook had already established himself as a presence as early as 1890 while directing a touring chamber orchestra and composing for *Scenes from the Opera of Uncle Tom's Cabin* in 1893. Like Burleigh, he was a student of Dvořák and wrote numerous works for voice and chorus, some of which were published in the 1912 anthology *A Collection of Negro Songs*. Cook belonged to a group of institutionally trained nationalistic composers devoted to using materials from black vernacular culture in a wide range of music from the concert stage to theater. Others included J. Rosamond Johnson, R. Nathaniel Dett, and Clarence Cameron White.

BLACK MUSICAL WORLDS IN ART AND POP

Musical activities among concert musicians during this period moved in two directions: attempts to break the color line in the established art world and numerous acts of institution building among African Americans for their own constituents. Black singers and instrumentalists continued to make inroads through their artistic endeavors by touring and concertizing in prestigious venues throughout America, the West Indies, and Europe. Emma Azalia Hackley (1867–1922), R. Nathaniel Dett (1882–1943), Carl Diton (1886–1962), Hazel Harrison (1883–1969), and Helen Hagan (1891–1964) were among the pioneers who toured extensively and built careers of which both the black and white press took notice. Although their careers were progressive in many ways, these artists met many obstacles because of the racial climate. As such, together with teaching at historically black colleges, they began to build their own institutions—concert series, music schools and studios, opera companies, chorale societies, symphonies—that perpetuated the performance and study of art music in African American communities.

The combination of commercial markets, individual innovations, and communal sensibilities continued to produce a rich variety of musical forms beyond the concert stage from the 1890s onward. Circulating through written and oral means of dissemination and gathering stylistic coherence gradually over time, ragtime, blues, and early gospel music can all be considered products of eclectic heritages and performance practices. Each would prove to be foundational to many forms of twentieth-century music making.

EXPANDING THE BLACK VERNACULAR: RAGTIME, BLUES, JAZZ, AND GOSPEL

In the 1890s the term "ragtime" embraced a wide range of music, including syncopated coon songs from minstrelsy, arrangements of these songs for large ensembles, any syncopated music for dancing, and solo piano music. As early as 1876 one finds reference to a stylistic precursor named "jig time" in the musical theater production *Out of Bondage*. Describing an energetic music played on the piano, it was also known as "jig piano," which simulated the rhythms and melodic phrasings of banjo and fiddle dance music. It was the coon song, however, that was more ubiquitous in American society due to minstrelsy's popularity and its association with the cakewalk dance. The publication of William Krell's *Mississippi Rag* (actually a cakewalk) and African American composer Thomas Turpin's *Harlem Rag*, both in 1897, promoted a definition of ragtime as a solo piano composition that codified in score form the elements of the improvised versions. However, the idea of "ragging" an improvisation of a popular song still remained a living tradition alongside the new "classic ragtime." Scott Joplin became particularly well known as a composer of piano ragtime, writing syncopated pieces with multiple strains or themes similar to the march. Sheet music and piano rolls allowed ragtime composers to reach a broad swath of the American public.

The melodic sources of the blues grew from the same moans, field hollers, and timbral qualities upon which the spirituals were built. Popular ballads from the Eurological tradition provided the song form models, and they were performed in a variety of nonreligious venues and public spaces such as cafes, saloons, streets, theaters, and railroad stations, among other places where money could be earned for performances. The lyrics of the blues, usually performed in first-person narrative form, address a large variety of specific everyday experiences, often with irony and humor. Guitars, pianos, and small ensembles with a variety of instruments provided the accompaniment for singers in a tightly interactive manner. The genre's codified poetic structure (A-A-B) and the repeating twelve-bar harmonic form that became convention has become one of the most important practices of twentieth-century American music. Like "ragtime," the term "the blues" once denoted a variety of expressions, although it was first developed in the interior South. Women performers like Mamie Smith, who became the first black singer to record the blues with "Crazy Blues" (1920), pioneered the new race record phenomenon, which targeted African American consumers. It should be noted as well that sheet music by individuals like W. C. Handy (1873–1958) and touring vaudeville stage shows also played a large role in circulating the blues widely.

While the African American church remained the principal venue for early gospel music in the years leading up to the 1930s, it shared with ragtime and blues similar relationships to vernacular cultural sensibilities and to the culture industry. Many rural and urban churches maintained the energetic, kinetic, and vocally dramatic conventions established in the spirituals tradition. A shift occurred when composers such as the minister Charles A. Tindley began to write and publish religious songs made specifically for his own services, innovating the gospel hymn with accompaniment, verse/chorus structure, and improvisation. Recordings began to circulate other forms of early twentieth-century religious music as well, including the energizing blues-shouting vocals and "jig time" piano of singer Arizona Dranes and rural church music for solo vocalist and guitar accompaniment. All three streams would inform the genre of gospel music that emerged in Chicago in the 1930s.

American involvement in World War I, a boom in northern industry, and the restriction of foreign immigration from Europe created unprecedented opportunities for African Americans living in the South. During the so-called "Great Migration," up to one million southern blacks left for the urban north. This mass movement created a cultural milieu in which new musical forms appeared and older styles continued to transform as a result of this move from rural to urban and agrarian to industrial lifestyles. In all aspects of the culture industry—recording, publishing, performance, teaching, and composition—an African American presence made an indelible mark.

One of the most dramatic developments occurred in the continued ascendancy of instrumental improvised music as the ragtime era led into the Jazz Age. Jazz, also a genre developed through black musical innovation, grew from many sources, including jig or ragtime piano, the blues, popular song, wind bands, and social dance music. New Orleans, the site of most early jazz activity, supported a strong tradition of wind bands and dance orchestras, many of which emphasized a wide range of styles and fully scored arrangements that included "hot" improvisational techniques. Charles "Buddy" Bolden (1877–1931), a popular bandleader, was legendary for his highly idiosyncratic approach on the cornet. From these beginnings, jazz would continue to develop into a dynamic amalgam of tributaries from a continually evolving range of sources, including blues, various popular song forms, marching band instruments together with electric and non-Western ones, other contemporaneous genres from the popular sphere, and art world conceptualizations. These sources, when taken together, would come to symbolize both African American ingenuity and a broader American sensibility that privileged the notion of cultural crosscurrents.

By the 1920s New York had become the center of the music industry, drawing black musicians to its numerous cabarets, dance halls, nightclubs, and recording opportunities; its lively community of musicians forged new ideas that would attract worldwide attention. Musicians such as bandleaders James Reese Europe (1881–1919), composer and arranger Will Vodery (1885–1951), and William C. Handy, together with many others, had laid the foundation in the preceding decade for the subsequent sharp demand for black entertainment. Many of the most influential musicians moved between activities in the black theater and the creation of syncopated music for large orchestras that became America's dance soundtrack. Improvising ragtime pianists such as Eubie Blake, Jelly Roll Morton, Willie "the Lion" Smith, Luckey Roberts, and James P. Johnson wrote and performed piano dance music that became foundational to what would be known as the "Jazz Age." Although they have until recently been largely written out of this history, female musicians such as Hallie Anderson (1885–1927) and Marie Lucas (1880s–1947) were abundantly present on the scene.

Something labeled "jazz" made its debut on recordings in 1917 when the Original Dixieland Jazz Band, a group of white musicians from New

Orleans, released "Livery Stable Blues" and "Dixie Jass Band One-Step."
Teeming with novelty sounds—including simulated animal noises—these
recordings managed to excite enough interest from the public to usher in
an era of recording that encompassed a wide range of idioms grouped
under the rubric "jazz." The music of black musicians such as King Oliver,
Jelly Roll Morton, and Louis Armstrong—all from New Orleans—
introduced a culturally commingled sound into the musical landscape,
one grounded in blues and robust polyphony and based on various dance
forms. Indeed, the words "jazz" and "modern" became linked and stretched
at this time to describe many idioms. Paul Whiteman, a popular white
bandleader who once claimed that jazz "sprang into existence . . . from
nowhere in particular," infused his music with jazz feeling. A notable contribution was George Gershwin's stylishly grand *Rhapsody in Blue* (1924),
a work commissioned by Whiteman that channeled referents from an
array of musical tributaries, including jazz.

Between World Wars I and II jazz grew from a localized phenomenon
into an internationally known genre. Musicians on both sides of America's
racial divide—Duke Ellington, Louis Armstrong, Count Basie, Bix
Beiderbecke, Benny Goodman, Mary Lou Williams, and many others—
became well-known jazz figures, and in some cases true icons. Ellington's
career in particular was symbolic of jazz's ascendance on many levels. His
idiosyncratic approach to composition, arranging, and orchestration demonstrated the artistic potential of popular music. The impact of jazz could
be measured not only in record sales—it would become by the late 1930s
America's popular music choice—but also by its emergent (and international) written criticism, which over time bloomed from discographical
surveys for collectors to record reviews, essays, and book-length studies.

With the rise of modernism in the United States, black music, particularly in the hands of black musicians, became a point of debate and speculation. Its value in the public sphere took on a variety of non-mutually
exclusive configurations: as an expression of cultural nationalism; as an
avenue for commercial gain; as propaganda in the fight for equal rights;
and in a variety of other ideas imposed by record companies, critics,
"slumming" white audiences, and black intellectuals. Similarly to other
expressive arts—film, photography, and literature—black music in the
1920s and 1930s informed and was influenced by large, sometimes

incongruent, cultural movements such as primitivism, the Harlem Renaissance, and Negritude. This, together with the overwhelming popularity of popular dances like the cakewalk, the Charleston, the jitterbug, and the lindy hop—all of which became international sensations—worked to saturate the sensibilities of black popular music into all sectors of global society—in mind, body, and spirit.

BLACK CLASSICAL MUSIC IN THE ART WORLD

In the concert world, other ideas about musical modernism beyond the jazz revolution were taking shape. The establishment of first-rate schools of music in America, the growth of urban, in-residence symphony orchestras and opera companies, and a new avant-garde musical language that turned away from diatonicism all created a larger chasm between art and popular realms. Some black performers with designs on concert careers responded by specializing in art music and by dabbling less in the popular arena than in years past. Some continued to make a living in both realms. From 1921, when Eubie Blake's and Noble Sissle's production *Shuffle Along* premiered, black musical theater produced an aesthetic middle ground as its conventions embodied a mixture of popular song, blues, ballads, choral number, expert arrangements, and symphonic orchestrations. Duke Ellington's *Symphony in Black: A Rhapsody of Negro Life* (1935) extended this musical language of entertainment that was shared by composers across racial lines.

The National Association of Negro Musicians, chartered in 1919, has up until the present provided a haven of institutional support for black performers, teachers, and composers whose work remains primarily situated in the art world. Singers Roland Hayes, Marian Anderson, Paul Robeson, and Dorothy Maynor built careers that took them to concert stages around the world in recitals, with opera companies, and before symphony orchestras. They developed a large following among black audiences and therefore developed repertory that featured art songs based on black thematic materials. The Negro String Quartet, the National Negro Opera Company, the Negro Symphony Orchestra, and professional choruses formed by Hall Johnson and Eva Jessye continued the legacy of institution building among musicians who continued to face varying degrees of discrimination in the concert world. In 1935 Jessye was appointed the choral director for Gershwin's iconic opera *Porgy and Bess*, a work that would become a major platform for black opera singers for decades to come. Dubbed "An American Folk Opera," *Porgy and Bess* embodied the spirit of black vernacular music, evocations that were based on Gershwin's research in South Carolinian black communities.

The 1930s saw the emergence of full-fledged symphonic works based on thematic material derived from black culture. William Grant Still's *Afro-American Symphony* premiered in 1931 and made history as the first work of its kind by a black composer to be played by a major symphony orchestra, the Rochester Philharmonic Orchestra. Still's prolific output spanned popular music, orchestral work, film and television work, opera, and chamber works, all contributing to his designation as "Dean of Afro-American composers." Florence Bea(trice) Price (1888–1953), one of the few female composers at this time to find acclaim, wrote pedagogical pieces, radio commercials, and serious concert works, including the *Piano Concerto in One Movement* and Symphony in E minor (1932). Many of the pieces written by black composers during this time expressed what might be called an "Afro-Romanticism," using black thematic materials couched in the language of nineteenth-century Romanticism. William Levi Dawson's *Negro Folk Symphony*, which premiered in 1934 with the Philadelphia Orchestra, was such a work. Shirley Graham, the versatile and dynamic musician who later married W. E. B. Du Bois, composed and wrote the libretto for *Tom-Tom* (1932), an opera in three acts that made history as the first of its kind by an African American woman.

MUSIC IN THE BLACK CHURCH

Within the community theater of the black church, one of the most vibrant and autonomous institutions in African American communities, publications such as *Gospel Pearls*, which first appeared in 1921, served to canonize the "on the ground" musical tastes of congregations. The collection is drawn from several origins: standard Protestant hymns, hymns from the lining-out tradition, spirituals, and songs by Charles Tindley and other black writers. From the 1930s on, songwriters Lucie Campbell (1885–1963) and W. Herbert Brewster Sr. (1897–1987), singer and music publisher Sallie Martin (1896–1988), and pianist, singer, and publisher Roberta Martin (1907–69) all contributed to creating gospel music, a newly formed genre that combined the melodic inflection of the blues, the ragged rhythms of "jig" piano, the fervor and intensity of the ring shout, and the entrepreneurial instincts of popular music. At the center of this creative force was Thomas Dorsey (1899–1993), a preacher's son who moved to Chicago from Atlanta in 1916 while pursuing an active career in show business. Dorsey maintained performing and songwriting activities in both the church and entertainment worlds, but he also organized two firsts: in 1931 he founded a "gospel" choir and later established a publishing company devoted to original gospel compositions. Dorsey also accompanied a singer who became arguably the first gospel performer to become a star outside the church, Mahalia Jackson (1911–72), a performer whose blues-based vocal singing style became the gold standard of the genre for decades.

Since the codification of ragtime piano, pianists developed highly idiosyncratic approaches to solo and ensemble-based improvisation that constituted key elements in the generic codes of various black popular musics. The stride piano of James P. Johnson and Fats Waller, the boogie-woogie style of Meade "Lux" Lewis, and the rollicking "keyboard style" of Roberta Martin's gospel piano would come to define genres and also supply rhetorical gestures for subsequent styles. Likewise, the conventions of both male and female quartet singing styles moved across the porous boundaries of secular and sacred contexts. Not only did quartet singing continually expand its conventions, but groups like the Soul Stirrers, Swan Silvertones, Dixie Hummingbirds, Original Gospel Harmonettes of Birmingham, Southern Harps Spiritual Singers, the well-known Five Blind Boys of Alabama, and the Five Blind Boys of Mississippi stood as paradigms for popular singing groups across genres and up to the 1990s.

NEW AMALGAMATIONS: BEBOP AND RHYTHM AND BLUES

Although commercial markets thrived on strategies of categorization and containment—"race records" for blacks, country or "hillbilly" music for southern whites, and the hit parade for middle-class whites—musicians and audiences, in truth, borrowed and listened across these social and sonic categories, creating new styles and extending audience bases as a matter of course. The steady migration of southerners to the North exploded once again during the years surrounding World War II and, together with a surge toward the abandonment of Jim Crow practices and laws, new social patterns emerged, and with them new musical forms. The infectious swing music of the 1930s, perhaps best personified in the bands of Count Basie, would influence and be supplanted by two new musical styles—bebop and rhythm and blues—each articulating various, though not competing, views about leisure, entrepreneurism, art practice, modernism, and identity.

Bebop, also known as modern jazz, emerged in the early to mid-1940s as an instrumental approach to the swing dance aesthetic, an innovation that abstracted some of swing's core conventions. Drummers disrupted the steady dance beat by dropping offbeat, dramatic accents called "bombs." In order to sidestep paying copyright fees, musicians wrote compositions by writing new, more challenging melodies on the harmonic structures of existing popular songs. The harmonic structures themselves featured a sophisticated approach that exploited the upper partials—ninths, elevenths, and thirteenths—and put a strong emphasis on the tritone relationships and flatted fifths. The virtuosic improvisations of instrumentalists Charlie Parker, Dizzy Gillespie, Bud Powell, and Max Roach set jazz on a new artistic and demanding course. Vocalists Sarah Vaughan and Betty Carter influenced legions of singers with their command of bebop techniques. Pianist Thelonious Monk's idiosyncratic compositional approach and acerbic solo approach emerged as the quintessential voice of new era in jazz.

If bebop abstracted swing and popular song then early rhythm and blues—an umbrella label for a constellation of black vernacular styles that appeared somewhat contemporaneously—took swing aesthetics and intensified its dance feeling with a heavier backbeat, a proclivity for twelve-bar blues form, repetitious and riff-based melodies, and lyrics whose subject matter comprised all of the earthiness and humor of traditional blues, though, with an urbane twist. Perhaps best exemplified by Ruth Brown and Louis Jordan, the style was sonically related to rock and roll, which emerged in the 1950s as a way to market the new dance music to white teenagers during the beginning years of the civil rights movement and fears of desegregation. Although black performers such as Little Richard, Chuck Berry, and Fats Domino certainly counted among early rock stars (many believed rock to be another strain of rhythm and blues), as the style became codified as a genre with its own race-specific social contract, it became understood as primarily "white." The mainstream of rhythm and blues styles featured elements from gospel, blues, and jazz, an imaginative repertoire of lyrics employing vivid imagery from black life, and qualities derived from specific locations such as the "urban blues" sound from Chicago and Los Angeles. Independent record labels were primarily responsible for recording and disseminating early rhythm and blues.

BLACK MUSIC IN THE ACADEMY

An important generation of black composers would benefit from opportunities that opened up in education for African Americans as a result of the civil rights movement. As a result of this shifting tide, many would secure professorships at American universities in addition to securing major prizes and commissions. Their works, ranging from neoclassical styles to uses of more avant-garde materials, were written for chamber groups, opera, solo singer, and symphonies, among other settings. Howard Swanson, Ulysses Kay, George Walker, Hale Smith, and T. J. Anderson were among those who led the way, establishing reputations within the academy and the larger art music world. In the realm of performance, black musicians continued to build active careers, although relatively fewer inroads were gained in the nation's symphony orchestras, still the most prestigious vehicles for concert instrumentalists. African American conductors found greater success abroad, securing positions in Europe after obtaining rigorous training in American institutions. By contrast, the opera and concert stage proved more generous to singers such as Robert McFerrin, Leontyne Price, George Shirley, Grace Bumbry, Shirley Verrett, and Jessye Norman, all of whom made history by singing roles traditionally assigned to white singers. The predominance of black male composers in this period was striking. Julie Perry, despite formidable fore-runners such as Florence Price and Shirley Graham, was singular in her prominence as a black female composer of her generation.

POST–WORLD WAR II: BLACK MUSIC INTO THE MAINSTREAM

From the mid-twentieth century on, stimulated in part by another South-to-North mass migration during and after World War II, black music with roots in the popular sphere—jazz, gospel, rhythm and blues, and all their multifarious sonic iterations—defined, for many, the aesthetic core of what was singular about American music culture. Despite their divergent social functions in the public sphere, they shared qualitative and concep-tual characteristics. Independent record labels were key in disseminating the music as their owners sought to maximize profits as major labels ini-tially ignored these styles. Ultimately major labels would seek out, record, and distribute the music, and by doing so facilitate their dominant national and international impact. Black popular music came to be seen as an important expressive force for the richness of African American culture, as a metaphor for the processes of creativity in such fields as literature, visual arts, and dance, and as a key symbol for the structural integration of black people into the mainstream of American society.

These genres moved along a trajectory that combined a sturdy ground-ing in historical traditions with a perpetual avant-gardism, the latter describing how musicians constantly pushed stylistic conventions into new configurations. Gospel music, while continuing its relationship to the aesthetics of the spiritual and the blues and to the combination of religion and entrepreneurialism that characterized the colonial and antebellum eras, developed into an important incubator of talent for other genres. Gospel singing techniques developed in the black church proved espe-cially impactful as by the end of the twentieth century they defined how many "pop" singers would approach a song. As the decades progressed, innovators such as Rosetta Tharpe, James Cleveland, Edwin and Walter Hawkins, and Elbernita "Twinkie" Clark, among others, built on the earlier contributions of pioneers Lucie Campbell, Willie Mae Ford Smith, and Roberta Martin to establish gospel music as a bastion of cutting-edge creativity, marketing savvy, and stylistic influence. It is important to note the centrality of female musicians in gospel music, which in many ways remains singular in the realm of modern African American music production. Beginning in the 1990s, other cities beyond the recognized centers of Chicago, Detroit, Los Angeles, and Philadelphia became important producers of gospel music, including Houston, Charlotte, and Atlanta.

Ray Charles, Sam Cooke, James Brown, and Aretha Franklin were all important throughout the 1950s and 1960s in infusing the techniques of gospel into the mainstream. Their contributions to the emergent styles dubbed "soul music" and "funk" defined an era that might be considered the "Afro-Americanization" of global pop culture as their conventions shaped music making internationally in styles ranging from West African High Life to Trinidadian "Gospelypso." Like gospel and rhythm and blues, jazz also continually regenerated itself, sometimes by absorbing the qualities of other styles, including rock and funk. Developments such as free jazz and fusion—both representing the reframing of improvisation in rhythmic and harmonic structures and qualities of interaction that departed significantly from previous conventions in the genre—inspired intense debates about the stability of the art form. The various bands of drummer Art Blakey and trumpeter Miles Davis proved to be incubators for an impressive string of performers who became leading figures in the 1970s, 1980s, and 1990s.

Beginning in the 1960s academic research on African American music laid the groundwork for the explosion of university-sponsored work appearing throughout the 1990s and into the millennium. Writings by LeRoi Jones (Amiri Baraka), Dena Epstein, Charles Keil, Portia Maultsby, Albert Murray, Samuel A. Floyd Jr., Olly Wilson, Josephine Wright, and especially Eileen Southern all contributed to a literature that considered the historical, ethnological, and sonic dimensions of black music. Wilson's dual career as an experimental composer and author of key writings on black musical aesthetics was an exemplar of the "observing participant" that would define many scholars of African American music of the last twenty-five years.

If early rhythm and blues began its existence in the margins of the music industry, by the 1960s and 1970s its family of idioms had moved to the center of the mainstream. Against the backdrop of the civil rights and black power movements, rhythm and blues, soul, and funk addressed on the levels of both style and message many of the ideals, aspirations, and urgent sense of sociopolitical efficacy that marked the moment. At the same time, mass mediation also played a key role in the ubiquity of black popular music in the public sphere as television shows from *American Bandstand* to *Soul Train* and later the appearance of *BET* broadcast the music into American homes on a large scale. Black films in the early 1970s such as *Shaft* and *Superfly* contained scores by Isaac Hayes and Curtis Mayfield respectively, thus providing another platform for the dissemination of the music. The output of record labels such as Curtom and Chess (Chicago), Stax (Memphis), and Motown (Detroit), to name but a few, demonstrated the continued significance of regional difference in the styles despite the potential for homogenization in the mass mediation context.

Subsequent to the high years of protests and legal challenges for equal rights by African Americans, urban centers decayed into postindustrial spaces fraught with poor educational systems, drug epidemics, and widespread economic depression. Even as superstars such as Michael Jackson, Prince, Whitney Houston, Janet Jackson, and others had careers that "crossed over" into the pop charts, a growing disaffection and creative surge within urban communities spawned new forms of music directed at their own communities. Hip-hop, a popular genre appearing in the late 1970s and coming of age in the 1980s and 1990s, represented a dramatic sonic development based on the inventive manipulation of previously recorded music and semi- to nonmelodic oral declamation as its emotional focal point. Attention to and understanding of the genre has benefited from a generation of scholars who grew up as fans and wrote about it within a paradigm of literary and cultural studies, a framework that moved easily among journalistic, ethnographic, and scholarly modes of discourse.

The digital age of musical creativity and dissemination, of which hip-hop is perhaps most emblematic, triggered debates about the relativism of musicianship, ownership and copyright, and cultural authenticity. Despite these tensions, musicians have continued to mix genres: hip-hop symphonies, jazz-inflected hip-hop, and gospel's "holy hip-hop" demonstrate the intermusicality of black musical practices. At the same time, contemporary musicians—whether jazz neoclassicists, revivalist black string bands, or neo-soul artists—continue to turn to musical practices of previous decades to both honor the past and to cultivate new audiences.

Onward

AN AFTERWORD

Shana L. Redmond

Not too long ago I was confronted by my own date of expiry in the professoriate. It is not a determined date or time but it is a feeling, one with which I am becoming more and more familiar every day. It's an aching, heavy antagonism that I can't shake. There are many reasons for this weight, much of it structural and some of it powerfully rendered in the previous pages, but suffice it to say that inclusion for Black scholars within the University "ain't been no crystal stair." When the preeminent historian of my lifetime, Robin D. G. Kelley, announced in 2015 that universities are "incapable of loving [Black students]—of loving anyone, perhaps," I nodded in sad recognition of that obvious truth's gravity. Over the course of my relatively short career I'd been confronted amply with the fact that I was too Black or feminine or working-class or queer or precise or assertive or . . . or . . . or to blend in. And because I'd made little effort toward that expectation—an impossibility—I was all the more an institutional outsider, even to the sounds and knowledges that are distinctly and perfectly mine.

Unsurprisingly, my love for Black music grew from a desire to know myself. A quiet, withdrawn child, I relied on the grooves and breaks to help me understand why I felt and thought as I did. Songs were my consolation and friend when resources and people were taken away—and they were always being taken away. As my troubles expanded, so too did my catalog and its influence. The music was a guide that opened unto me, revealing more than a song of myself—it became a lush, dramatic story of We. "The Music, The Music," as Amiri Baraka wrote, "this is our history." We rely on and trust in Black music because this is where we hear ourselves, for ourselves—imperfect and glorious—even if others listen in (and they always do). It's not policy that can be won and lost or the athleticism that inevitably fades with time. The music is permanent, even if ephemeral, for its ability to be in and of our bodies and carried throughout this life and into the next. I learned through living and hearing as a Black woman that the music held promises that could not be found elsewhere nor could it be taken from me, and so I chased it. As a performer and scholar I took vulnerable leaps, knowing that I would be richly rewarded by my people for the time and study that I gave to that infinite force.

Becoming an academic has challenged my ability to hold onto this possibility. Two things that I find incredible pleasure in—listening and writing—have become increasingly mechanized and, to some extent, inconsequential when fed through the racial calculus and cold discernment of the university. Being dispossessed of what I love by a workplace that, ostensibly, hired me to continue caring about and for those very things, is a particular violation that is compounded by the fact that this is not only what or how I study—it is what and how I live. I am in and of a body and mind, community, and culture uncontained by scholarly discourse or popular criticism, both of which are spheres of influence with little or no regard for my—Our—unique talents and ways of knowing. More than twenty years after Guthrie first asked "Who Hears Here?," Black Black music scholars continue to be minoritized in its study, which begs again a follow-up: "Will we achieve signifying difference without significant blackness?"

Never. Indeed, as Guthrie argues, "our experiences and productive biases *do* matter." All of them. And it's not for the myth of essentialism or purity that this is true. What we mean by "significant blackness" is as complicated and capacious as that of which we sing, speak, and write. Yet whatever our unique intersections, there is something inherently risky about our work when our very bodies are the terrain of knowledge and struggle. When our loved ones are implicated. When safety and survival are not guaranteed. This reality incites the passion and rage behind the writing that makes one walk away from the page for breath. This reality provokes the curiosity and experimentation that force the weary to compose and practice, day after day, in search of meaning or flight. We know these things and it works on us as much as we work on it. For these reasons and more, they won't and *can't* go when or where We go. A degree is a minimum qualification for the study of the universe. What else and how else do you know? To whom are you looking and conceding space? "What," as my Black feminist mentor asked me, "is at stake?"

Over the course of his influential career Guthrie has beautifully answered, and continues to answer, these questions in his scholarship and music, modeling along the way how to gather and hold close all pieces of ourselves. It proves a difficult exercise to return, with all that we carry, to the inexhaustible questions and marvels, but it is bracing as well. I may not be long for the job, but the work will always call and to it I will always respond.

Notes

INTRODUCTION. WHO HEARS HERE NOW?

1. See Christopher Small, *Music of the Common Tongue: Survival and Cele-bration in Afro-American Music* (London: John Calder Publishers, 1987).

2. Marlon T. Riggs, "Unleash the Queen," in *Black Popular Culture,* ed. Gina Dent (Seattle, WA: Bay Press, 1992).

3. Riggs, "Unleash the Queen," 101.

4. Riggs, "Unleash the Queen," 103.

5. Katherine McKittrick, *Dear Science and Other Stories* (Durham, NC: Duke University Press, 2020).

6. Riggs, "Unleash the Queen," 105.

7. See Richard Crawford, *The American Musical Landscape* (Berkeley: University of California Press, 1993).

8. Susan McClary, "Paradigm Dissonances: Music Theory, Cultural Studies, Feminist Criticism," *Perspectives of New Music* 32, no. 1 (Winter 1994): 69.

9. See David Brackett, "The Question of Genre in Black Popular Music," *Black Music Research Journal* 25, no. 1 (2005); Fabian Holt, *Genre in Popular Music* (Chicago: University of Chicago Press, 2007); Jeffrey Kallberg, "The Rhetoric of Genre: Chopin's Nocturne in G Minor," in *Chopin at the Boundaries: Sex, History, and Musical Genre* (Cambridge, MA: Harvard University Press, 1996); and Keith Negus, *Music Genres and Corporate Cultures* (New York: Routledge, 1999).

10. For excellent work on Black cultural forms in twentieth-century Chicago, see Davarian L. Baldwin, *Chicago's New Negroes: Modernity, the Great Migration, and Black Urban Life* (Chapel Hill: University of North Carolina Press, 2007); Wallace D. Best, *Passionately Human, No Less Divine: Religion and Culture in Black Chicago, 1915-1952* (Princeton, NJ: Princeton University Press, 2005); Adam Green, *Selling the Race: Culture, Community, and Black Chicago, 1940-1955* (Chicago: University of Chicago Press, 2007); William Howland Kenney, *Chicago Jazz: A Cultural History, 1904-1930* (New York: Oxford University Press, 1993); and Jacqueline Najuma Stewart, *Migrating to the Movies: Cinema and Black Urban Modernity* (Berkeley: University of California Press, 2005).

11. Dena Epstein, *Sinful Tunes and Spirituals: Black Folk Music to the Civil War* (Urbana: University of Illinois Press, 1977); LeRoi Jones, *Blues People Negro Music in White America* (New York: W. Morrow, 1963); Charles Keil, *Urban Blues* (Chicago: University of Chicago Press, 1966); and Eileen Southern, *The Music of Black Americans: A History* (New York: W. W. Norton, 1971). These journals included *Black Perspective in Music, Ethnomusicology*, and *Black Music Research Journal*.

12. See Portia K. Maultsby, "Influences and Retentions of West African Musical Concepts in U.S. Black Music," *Western Journal of Black Studies* 3, no. 3 (Fall 1979), for an example one of her early articles that inspired a generation of scholars and made space for Black music study, particularly in the discipline of ethnomusicology.

13. For an example of the breadth and depth of his brilliant historical work and criticism, see Robin D. G. Kelley, *Race Rebels: Culture, Politics, and the Black Working Class* (New York: The Free Press, 1994).

14. Farah Jasmine Griffin, *Who Set You Flowin'? The African American Migration Narrative* (New York: Oxford University Press, 1995).

15. Gina Dent, ed., *Black Popular Culture* (Seattle, WA: Bay Press, 1992).

16. Tricia Rose, *Black Noise: Rap Music and Black Culture in Contemporary America* (Hanover, NH: Wesleyan University Press, 1994); Greg Tate, *Flyboy in the Buttermilk: Essays on Contemporary America* (New York: Simon and Schuster, 1992); and Cornel West, *Race Matters* (Boston: Beacon Press, 1993).

17. Ronald M. Radano, *New Musical Figurations: Anthony Braxton's Cultural Critique* (Chicago: University of Chicago, 1993); David Brackett, *Interpreting Popular Music* (Cambridge: Cambridge University Press, 1995); Samuel A. Floyd Jr., "Ring Shout! Literary Studies, Historical Studies, and Black Music Inquiry," *Black Music Research Journal* 11, no. 2 (1991); Ingrid Monson, *Saying Something: Jazz Improvisation and Interaction* (Chicago: University of Chicago Press, 1996); and Robert Walser, *Running with the Devil: Power, Gender, and Madness in Heavy Metal Music* (Hanover, NH: Wesleyan University Press, 1993).

18. I'm thinking here of Ronald Radano, Mark Tucker, Jeffery Magee, and Jeffery Taylor.

19. For discussions of post–World War II music culture in Black Chicago, see George Lewis, *A Power Stronger Than Itself: The AACM and American Experimental Music* (Chicago: University of Chicago Press, 2008); Ronald M. Radano, *New Musical Figurations: Anthony Braxton's Cultural Critique* (Chicago: University of Chicago Press, 1993); and Guthrie P. Ramsey Jr., *Race Music: Black Cultures from Bebop to Hip-Hop* (Berkeley: University of California Press, 2003).

20. See Felicity D. Scott, *Architecture or Techno-Utopia: Politics after Modernism* (Cambridge, MA: MIT Press, 2007).

21. See, for example, Roger D. Abrahams, *Deep Down in the Jungle . . . : Negro American Folklore from the Streets of Philadelphia* (Hatboro, PA: Folklore Associates, 1964); Matthew J. Countryman, *Up South: Civil Rights and Black Power in Philadelphia* (Philadelphia: University of Pennsylvania Press, 2006); and W. E. B. Du Bois, *The Philadelphia Negro* (New York: Cosimo, 2007).

22. Carol Oja, "Race and the American Musicological Society: Founding the Committee on Cultural Diversity," *Musicology Now* (April 30, 2021), assessed January 16, 2022, https://musicologynow.org/race-and-the-american-musicological-society-founding-the-committee-on-cultural-diversity/.

CHAPTER 1. COSMOPOLITAN OR PROVINCIAL?

1. Samuel A. Floyd Jr. coined this apt descriptor in his essay "Eileen Jackson Southern: Quiet Revolutionary," which outlines Southern's early life and scholarly contributions to the field of black music scholarship. Samuel A. Floyd Jr., "Eileen Jackson Southern: Quiet Revolutionary," in *New Perspectives on Music: Essays in Honor of Eileen Southern*, ed. Josephine Wright with Samuel A. Floyd Jr. (Warren, MI: Harmonie Park Press, 1992).

2. Eileen Southern, *The Music of Black Americans: A History*, 2nd ed. (New York: W. W. Norton, 1983).

3. See, for example David Brackett, "James Brown's 'Superbad' and the Double-Voiced Utterance," *Popular Music* 11, no. 3 (1992); Hazel V. Carby, "In Body and Spirit: Representing Black Women Musicians," *Black Music Research Journal* 11, no. 2 (1991); Samuel A. Floyd Jr., "Ring Shout! Literary Studies, Historical Studies, and Black Music Inquiry," *Black Music Research Journal* 11, no. 2 (1991); Paul Gilroy, "Sounds Authentic: Black Music, Ethnicity, and the Challenge of a 'Changing' Same," *Black Music Research Journal* 11, no. 2 (1991); Eric Lott, "Double V, Double-Time: Bebop's Politics of Style," *Callaloo* 11, no. 3 (1988); Ingrid Monson, "Doubleness and Jazz Improvisation: Irony, Parody, and Ethnomusicology," *Critical Inquiry* 20 (Winter 1994); Timothy D. Taylor, "His Name Was in Lights: Chuck Berry's 'Johnny B. Goode,'" *Popular Music* 11 (1992); Gary Tomlinson, "Cultural Dialogics and Jazz: A White Historian Signifies," *Black Music Research Journal* 11, no. 2 (1991); and Robert Walser, "Out of

Notes: Signification, Interpretation, and the Problem of Miles Davis," *Musical Quarterly* 77 (Summer 1993), and "Rhythm, Rhyme, and Rhetoric in the Music of Public Enemy," *Ethnomusicology* 39, no. 2 (Spring/Summer 1995). Other outstanding efforts in this regard include two book-length studies, Ronald M. Radano, *New Musical Figurations: Anthony Braxton's New Cultural Critique* (Chicago: University of Chicago Press, 1993), and especially Samuel A. Floyd Jr., *The Power of Black Music: Interpreting Its History from Africa to the United States* (New York: Oxford University Press, 1995), which offer an extensive application of contemporary critical theory to black music research. Floyd's groundbreaking work addresses "the absence of a thorough and specific aesthetic for the perception and criticism of black music; suggests a viable, valid, and appropriate way of inquiring into the nature of black music; suggests a basis for discourse among intellectuals on musical difference; and helps break down the barriers that remain between 'high art' and 'low art'" (5). Floyd, Brackett, Monson, and Walser make use of Henry Louis Gates's (1988) theory of signifyin(g) by extensive and convincing application of his ideas to formal musical analysis grounded in black cultural aesthetics. Henry Louis Gates, *The Signifying Monkey: A Theory of African-American Literary Criticism* (New York: Oxford University Press, 1988). Other studies that include notable use of critical theory on various aspects of black music include a special issue of *Black Music Research Journal* (vol. 11, Fall 1991; guest editor Bruce Tucker) and Krin Gabbard's recent collected anthologies on jazz, *Jazz among the Discourse* (Durham, NC: Duke University Press, 1995) and *Representing Jazz* (Durham, NC: Duke University Press, 1995).

4. In a study on the growth of black history and its relationship to the profession of history, Meier and Rudwick (73) write that Afro-American historiography can arguably be "divided into five periods of unequal length: (1) from the ASNLH's [Association for the Study of Negro Life and History] founding in 1915 and up into the 1930s; (2) the Roosevelt era of the New Deal and World War II; (3) the decade and a half between the war's end and the opening of the 'Civil Rights Revolution' of the 1960s; (4) the brief half-dozen years marked by the apogee of the direct-action phase of the black protest movement; and (5) the climax of scholarship that followed, 1967–80." Each category, Meier and Rudwick observe, is marked by "distinct patterns of socialization that shaped the outlook of the historians who entered the field." Southern's *The Music of Black Americans* appeared in Meier's and Rudwick's last period. August Meier and Elliott Rudwick, *Black History and the Historical Profession, 1915–1980* (Urbana: University of Illinois Press, 1986).

5. On the spirituals controversy, see, for example, George Pullen Jackson, *White and Negro Spirituals: Their Life and Kinship* (New York: Da Capo Press, 1975); Eileen Southern, "An Origin for the Negro Spiritual," *Black Scholar* 2 (Summer 1972); and William H. Tallmadge, "The Black in Jackson's White Spir-

ituals," *Black Perspective in Music* 9, no. 2 (1981). For representative literature on jazz's stylistic debates, see Leonard Feather, "Goffin, Esquire and the Moldy Figs," in *The Jazz Years: Earwitness to an Era* (New York: Da Capo Press, 1987); Bernard Gendron, "Moldy Figs and Modernists: Jazz at War (1942–1946)," *Discourse* 15 (1993); Peter Watrous, "Yes, It's improvised. But Is It Really Jazz?," *New York Times*, October 10, 1993, 33; and Kevin Whitehead, "Jazz Rebels: Lester Bowie and Greg Osby," *Down Beat* (August 1993). The idea of "race" in classical compositions by African American composers is discussed in T. J. Anderson, "Black Composers and the Avant-garde," in *Readings in Black American Music*, 2nd ed., ed. Eileen Southern (New York: W. W. Norton, 1983); Joseph Hunt, "Conversation with Thomas J. Anderson: Blacks and the Classics," *Black Perspective in Music* 1, no. 2 (1973); Hale Smith, "Here I Stand," in *Readings in Black American Music*, ed. Eileen Southern (New York: W. W. Norton, 1983); and Olly Wilson, "The Black-American Composer," *Black Perspective in Music* 1, no. 1 (1973). For scholarly literature on rap, see Jeffrey Louis Decker, "The State of Rap: Time and Place in Hip Hop Nationalism," in *Microphone Fiends: Youth Music and Youth Culture*, ed. Andrew Ross and Tricia Rose (New York: Routledge, 1994); Michael Eric Dyson, *Reflecting Black: African-American Cultural Criticism* (Minneapolis: University of Minnesota Press, 1993); Robin D. G. Kelley, *Race Rebels: Culture, Politics, and the Black Working Class* (New York: Free Press, 1994); Tricia Rose, *Black Noise: Rap Music and Black Culture in Contemporary America* (Hanover, NH: University Press of New England, 1993); and Robert Walser, "Rhythm, Rhyme, and Rhetoric in the Music of Public Enemy," *Ethnomusicology* 39, no. 2 (Spring/Summer 1995).

6. Scholarly journals whose focus is black music include *The Black Perspective in Music* (1973–1990), edited by Eileen Southern; and *Black Music Research Journal* (1980–present), edited by Samuel A. Floyd Jr. For secondary literature on scholarly periodicals, see Ron Byrnside, "'The Black Perspective in Music': The First Ten Years," *Black Music Research Journal* 6 (1986). Important bibliographic and reference works include Dominique-René De Lerma, "Black Music: A Bibliographic Essay," *Library Trends* 23, no. 3 (January 1975); Dominique-René De Lerma and Jessie Carney Smith, *Bibliography of Black Music* (Westport, CT: Greenwood Press, 1981–84); Samuel A. Floyd Jr. and Marsha J. Reisser, *Black Music in the United States: An Annotated Bibliography of Selected Reference and Research Materials* (Millwood, NY: Kraus International, 1983); Portia K. Maultsby, "Selective Bibliography: U.S. Black Music," *Ethnomusicology* 19 (1975); JoAnn Skowronski, *Black Music in America: A Bibliography* (Metuchen, NJ: Scarecrow Press, 1981); Eileen Southern, *Biographical Dictionary of Afro-American and African Musicians* (New York: Greenwood Press, 1982); and Eileen Southern and Josephine Wright, *African-American Traditions in Song, Sermon, Tale, and Dance, 1600s–1920: An Annotated Bibliography of Literature, Collections, and Artworks* (New York: Greenwood Press, 1990).

7. Many definitions exist for the term "ideology." I use it after Rose Rosengard Subotnik's formulation to describe a "general philosophical orientation," a "specific philosophical viewpoint," and as a "conceptual context that allows the definition of human utterances." Rose Rosengard Subotnik, *Developing Variations: Style and Ideology in Western Music* (Minneapolis: University of Minnesota Press, 1991), 4–5.

8. Gary Tomlinson, "Cultural Dialogics and Jazz," x.

9. Houston A. Baker Jr., *Blues, Ideology, and Afro-American Literature: A Vernacular Theory* (Chicago: University of Chicago Press, 1984), 17–18.

10. Richard Crawford, *The American Musical Landscape* (Berkeley: University of California Press, 1993), 6–7.

11. St. Clair Drake, *Black Folk Here and There: An Essay* in *History and Anthropology*, vol. 1 (Berkeley: University of California Press, 1987), 1.

12. Sterling Stuckey, *The Ideological Origins of Black Nationalism* (Boston: Beacon Press, 1972).

13. Robert Stevenson, "America's First Black Music Historian," *Journal of the American Musicological Society* 26, no. 3 (1973): 403.

14. James Monroe Trotter, *Music and Some Highly Musical People* (New York: Charles T. Dillingham, 1881), 3.

15. Trotter, *Music and Some Highly Musical People*, 4.

16. For more information on Trotter's family background, see Stephen R. Fox, *The Guardian of Boston: William Monroe Trotter* (New York: Atheneum, 1971), 388–89. I thank Gerald Gill for this reference.

17. Quoted in Stevenson, "America's First Black Music Historian," 392. See also Joseph T. Wilson, *The Black Phalanx* (New York: Arno Press, 1968), 506.

18. Trotter, *Music and Some Highly Musical People*.

19. Frédéric Louis Ritter, *Music in America* (London: W. Reeves, 1884); and Stevenson, "America's First Black Music Historian." It should be noted that American music historiography, according to Richard Crawford, has always been marked with a "strain of randomness," a lack of consensus in scope, method, and emphasis. Crawford, *The American Musical Landscape*, 6.

20. Henry Louis Gates, "Canon-Formation, Literary History, and the Afro-American Tradition: From the Seen to the Told," in *Afro-American Literary Study in the 1990s*, ed. Houston A. Baker Jr. and Patricia Redmond (Chicago: University of Chicago Press, 1989); and Stuckey, *The Ideological Origins of Black Nationalism*.

21. Alfred A. Moss, *The American Negro Academy: Voice of the Talented Tenth* (Baton Rouge: Louisiana State University Press, 1981), 24.

22. Stevenson, "America's First Black Music Historian," 400.

23. Trotter, *Music and Some Highly Musical People*, 4, 112.

24. Southern and Wright, *African-American Traditions*, xxii–xxiii.

25. In April 1852 John Sullivan Dwight (1813–93), called America's "first major music critic," founded *Dwight's Journal of Music*, a journal that published such writings. Thomas Riis, "The Cultivated White Tradition and Black Music in Nineteenth-Century America: A Discussion of Some Articles in *J. S. Dwight's Journal of Music*," *Black Perspective in Music* 4, no. 2 (1976): 156–57. Riis lists all articles on black music topics that appeared in the journal's almost thirty-year run.

26. Southern and Wright, *African-American Traditions*, xxiv, note that in the nineteenth century the *Journal of American Folk-lore* and *Hampton Institute's Southern Workman* published folksongs regularly, with and without extensive comment (see the special issue of *Black Perspective in Music* 4 [July 1976], which reprints some of these articles). Portia Maultsby's survey of literature on the spiritual identifies four theories with which various authors have addressed the song's origin: (1) imitation of European composition; (2) original compositions by slaves; (3) African origin; and (4) acculturation. Portia K. Maultsby, "Africanisms Retained in the Spiritual Tradition," in *International Musicological Society, Berkeley 1977*, ed. Daniel Heartz and Bonnie Wade (Basel: Bärenreiter, 1981).

27. William Francis Allen, Charles Pickard Ware, and Lucy McKim Garrison, *Slave Songs of the United States* (New York: Peter Smith, 1951).

28. Dena J. Epstein, *Sinful Tunes and Spirituals: Black Folk Music to the Civil War* (Urbana: University of Illinois Press, 1977), 304.

29. See Southern and Wright, *African-American Traditions*, xxxiii–xxxiv, for information about other such collections from this period. See also Irene V. Jackson-Brown, "Afro-American Song in the Nineteenth Century: A Neglected Source," *Black Perspective in Music* 4, no. 1 (1976).

30. Ronald M. Radano, "Denoting Difference: The Writing of the Slave Spirituals," *Critical Inquiry* 22, no. 3 (1996), provides an astute analysis of the cultural politics of producing nineteenth-century spirituals transcriptions.

31. William E. Terry, "*The Negro Music Journal*: An Appraisal," *Black Perspective in Music* 5, no. 2 (1977): 146.

32. J. Hillary Taylor, "Music in the Home," *Negro Music Journal* 1, no. 1 (1902): 10.

33. Riis, "The Cultivated White Tradition and Black Music," 158.

34. Richard Crawford, "Sonneck and American Musical Historiography," in *Essays in Musicology: A Tribute to Alvin Johnson*, ed. Lewis Lockwood and Edward Roesner (Philadelphia: American Musicological Society, 1990), 270–71.

35. Quoted in Crawford, "Sonneck and American Musical Historiography," 277.

36. On the treatment of black music, see Maud Cuney-Hare, *Negro Musicians and Their Music* (New York: Da Capo Press, 1974). See also, for example, Natalie

Curtis-Berlin, "Black Singers and Players," *Musical Quarterly* 5 (1919), and "Negro Music at Birth," *Musical Quarterly* 5 (1919).

37. Floyd compares the impact of Woodson's scholarly and entrepreneurial efforts in the field of history to Eileen Southern's work in musicology. Floyd, "Eileen Jackson Southern," 14–15.

38. August Meier and Elliott Rudwick, *Black History and the Historical Profession, 1915–1980* (Urbana: University of Illinois Press, 1986), 1.

39. Meier and Rudwick, *Black History and the Historical Profession*, 2–3.

40. Meier and Rudwick, *Black History and the Historical Profession*, 2.

41. John Hope Franklin, "Afro-American History: State of the Art," *Journal of American History* 75 (1988): 163.

42. Meier and Rudwick, *Black History and the Historical Profession*, 74–75.

43. Crawford, "Sonneck and American Musical Historiography," 279.

44. Samuel A. Floyd Jr., "Music in the Harlem Renaissance: An Overview," in *Black Music in the Harlem Renaissance: A Collection of Essays*, ed. Samuel A. Floyd Jr. (New York: Greenwood Press, 1990), 4.

45. Although Dvořák's sentiments have been widely reported in this way, Charles Hamm, in an essay titled "Dvořák in America: Nationalism, Racism, and National Race," argues that the composer was actually referring to what was known as the "popular" music of its day, namely the songs of Stephen Foster. Charles Hamm, *Putting Popular Music in Its Place* (New York: Cambridge University Press, 1995).

46. On the issue of aesthetics and performance practice, they write, "The Spirituals possess the fundamental characteristics of African music. . . . I think white singers, concert singers, *can* sing Spirituals—if they *feel* them. . . . In a word, the capacity to *feel* these songs while singing them is more important than any amount of mere artistic technique." James Weldon Johnson and J. Rosamond Johnson, *The Books of American Negro Spirituals: Including The Book of American Negro Spirituals and The Second Book of Negro Spirituals* (New York: Da Capo Press, 1989), 19, 29.

47. August Meier, *Negro Thought in America, 1880–1915: Racial Ideologies in the Age of Booker T. Washington* (Ann Arbor: University of Michigan Press, 1988), 51.

48. Johnson and Johnson, *The Books of American Negro Spirituals*, 17.

49. Henry Edward Krehbiel, *Afro-American Folk-Songs: A Study of Racial and National Music* (New York: Frederick Ungar, 1962), v.

50. James Weldon Johnson presented this view in his collection of poetry from 1922: "The final measure of the greatness of all peoples is the amount and standard of the literature and art that they have produced. The world does not know that a people is great until that people produces great literature and art. No people that has produced great literature and art has ever been looked upon by the world as distinctly inferior" (quoted in Henry Louis Gates, "Canon-Formation," 33).

51. Stevenson, "America's First Black Music Historian," 384–85.

52. Cuney-Hare, *Negro Musicians and Their Music*, xii; Rayford W. Logan and Michael R. Winston, eds., *Dictionary of American Negro Biography* (New York: W. W. Norton, 1982); Eileen Southern, *The Music of Black Americans*, 444.

53. Cuney-Hare, *Negro Musicians and Their Music*, 1–2.

54. Cuney-Hare, *Negro Musicians and Their Music*, vi.

55. Alain Locke, *The Negro and His Music* (Salem, NH: Ayer Company, 1991), 4.

56. Locke, *The Negro and His Music*, 4.

57. Paul Burgett, "Vindication as a Thematic Principle in the Writings of Alain Locke on the Music of Black Americans," in *Black Music in the Harlem Renaissance*, 29. Burgett writes that two conflicting forces influenced Locke: his education and "the exigent harshness of the racial experience in America" (39). Locke was twice a Harvard graduate: in 1907 he graduated magna cum laude with Phi Beta Kappa honors, and in 1918 he received his PhD in philosophy. Locke was also the first black Rhodes scholar to Oxford.

58. Locke, *The Negro and His Music*, 137.

59. For more on Trotter, Locke, Cuney-Hare, and other early writers on black music, see Guthrie P. Ramsey Jr., "The Art of Bebop: Earl 'Bud' Powell and the Emergence of Modern Jazz" (PhD diss., University of Michigan, 1994).

60. Arnold Rampersad, "Introduction," in *The New Negro: Voices of the Harlem Renaissance*, ed. Alain Locke (New York: Atheneum, 1992), xxii–xxiii.

61. J. A. Rogers, "Jazz at Home," in *The New Negro*, ed. Alain Locke, 224.

62. Langston Hughes, "The Negro Artist and the Racial Mountain," in *The Black Aesthetic*, ed. Addison Gayle Jr. (Garden City, NY: Anchor Books, 1972), 168.

63. Locke, *The Negro and His Music*, 94.

64. Cuney-Hare, *Negro Musicians and Their Music*, 154.

65. Zora Neale Hurston, "Spirituals and Neo-Spirituals," in *Negro: An Anthology*, ed. Nancy Cunard (New York: Frederick Ungar, 1970), 223–25.

66. See Glenn Watkins, *Pyramids at the Louvre: Music, Culture, and Collage from Stravinsky to the Postmodernists* (Cambridge, MA: Harvard University Press, 1994), for a discussion of what he calls the "Cunard Line."

67. Rampersad, "Introduction," xxvi, xv.

68. Richard Crawford, "On Two Traditions of Black Music Research," *Black Music Research Journal* 6 (1986): 1.

69. W. E. B. DuBois's *The Souls of Black Folk* carries the first scholarly consideration of the spiritual by a black nationalist. W. E. B. Du Bois, *The Souls of Black Folk* (New York: New American Library, 1982). See Ronald M. Radano, "Soul Texts and the Blackness of Folk," *Modernism/Modernity* 2, no. 1 (1995), for an extensive discussion of Du Bois's treatment of the spiritual.

70. Richard A. Long, "Interactions between Writers and Music during the Harlem Renaissance," in *Black Music in the Harlem Renaissance*, 129.

71. James Lincoln Collier, *The Reception of Jazz in America: A New View* (Brooklyn: Institute for the Study of American Music, 1988), 10. See also Crawford, "Sonneck and American Musical Historiography"; Scott DeVeaux, "Constructing the Jazz Tradition: Jazz Historiography," *Black American Literature Forum* 25 (1991); Roger Pryor Dodge, "Consider the Critics," in *Jazzmen*, ed. Frederic Ramsey Jr. and Charles Edward Smith (New York: Limelight Editions, 1985); John Gennari, "Jazz Criticism: Its Development and Ideologies," *Black American Literature Forum* 25 (1991); and Ronald Welburn, "The Early Record Review: Jazz Criticism's First-Born Child," *Annual Review of Jazz Studies* 3 (1985), "Jazz Magazines of the 1930s: An Overview of their Provocative Journalism," *American Music* 5, no. 3 (1987), and "James Reese Europe and the Infancy of Jazz Criticism," *Black Music Research Journal* 7 (1987).

72. The term "essentialist" is used here to denote the belief that some things (races, in this case) have essences that serve to define them.

73. Henry Louis Gates Jr., ed., *"Race," Writing and Difference* (Chicago: University of Chicago Press, 1986), 5.

74. Quoted in Eileen Southern, *Readings in Black American Music*, 2nd ed. (New York: W. W. Norton, 1983), 239.

75. Kwame Anthony Appiah, "Racisms," in *Anatomy of Racism*, ed. David Theo Goldberg (Minneapolis: University of Minnesota Press, 1990), 4.

76. "Jazzing Away Prejudice," *Chicago Defender*, May 10, 1919, 20. I have quoted this editorial at some length because it is a contemporary written black source that openly supports jazz—and such sources are rare for the time. The *Chicago Defender*, unlike the *New Negro*, was designed primarily for a black readership, and it was not above publishing searing commentary on the musical preoccupations of the black middle class. At the same time, however, the newspaper's music columnists wrote more about classical music than other forms until the 1940s, when they began giving more attention to jazz and rhythm and blues.

77. Henry O. Osgood, *So This Is Jazz* (Boston: Little, Brown, and Company, 1926), 11.

78. Osgood, *So This Is Jazz*, 26.

79. John Gennari, "Jazz Criticism: Its Development and Ideologies," *Black American Literature Forum* 25 (1991); and Ted Gioia, *The Imperfect Art: Reflections on Jazz and Modern Culture* (New York: Oxford University Press, 1988).

80. Gioia, *The Imperfect Art*, 29.

81. Gioia, *The Imperfect Art*, 33.

82. Ronald Welburn, "Jazz Magazines of the 1930s: An Overview of their Provocative Journalism," *American Music* 5, no. 3 (1987): 261.

83. Winthrop Sargeant, *Jazz: Hot and Hybrid* (New York: Da Capo Press, 1975), 7.

84. Sargeant, *Jazz: Hot and Hybrid*, 22–23.

85. Sargeant, *Jazz: Hot and Hybrid*, 211.

86. Frederick Ramsey Jr. and Charles Edward Smith, *Jazzmen: The Story of Jazz Told in the Lives of the Men Who Created It* (New York: Limelight Editions,1985), 9.

87. Lawrence W. Levine, "Jazz and American Culture," *Journal of American Folklore* 102 (1989): 8–9.

88. Quoted in Levine, "Jazz and American Culture," 12.

89. Levine, "Jazz and American Culture," 6–7.

90. Levine, "Jazz and American Culture," 18.

91. David Levering Lewis, *When Harlem Was in Vogue* (New York: Oxford University Press, 1989), 163.

92. LeRoi Jones, *Black Music* (New York: William Morrow, 1967), 11.

93. Lewis, *When Harlem Was in Vogue*, 175.

94. Quoted in Martin Bauml Duberman, *Paul Robeson* (New York: Alfred A. Knopf, 1988), 177.

95. Henry Louis Gates, *Loose Canons: Notes on the Culture Wars* (New York: Oxford University Press, 1992), 26.

96. Crawford, *The American Musical Landscape*, 3.

CHAPTER 2. WHO HEARS HERE?

1. Philip Gossett, "New York—1995," *American Musicological Society Newsletter* [hereafter *AMS Newsletter*] 26, no. 1 (February 1996): 1. One can get some sense of the official, yet somewhat marginal, "diversity discourse" in musicology by reading the AMS newsletters, especially from 1992 to the present. Since that time, the newsletter has chronicled how various AMS presidents, board members, and the rank and file have responded to various issues surrounding diversity, including the status of women, the curriculum, methodology, gay and lesbian studies, and ethics. Grassroots protest from within the society has inspired the leadership to address diversity issues directly. Writing in 1993, for example, Ellen Rosand, Gossett's predecessor, said in her presidential message, "I have to confess becoming aware of a certain amount of grumbling within the membership of the Society. Many of the negative vibes resonated on one issue: the sense of disenfranchisement felt by a number of you. In the Council it was the perception of the Board of Directors as an elite group drawn from the 'Eastern establishment' and therefore supposedly removed from—insensitive to—the concerns of 'the people.' In the Committee on Cultural Diversity it was a sense of alienation from many of the topics on the program." To these complaints Rosand responded, "We try very hard to achieve geographical, biological, philosophical, cultural, and ideological balance on every committee, but we need your

input." See "Presidential Message," *AMS Newsletter* 23, no. 1 (February 1993): 3. In 1995 Rosand wrote about the "new musicology," a term that had become a way to describe certain shifts in the intellectual terrain of the discipline. The new musicology was "a good thing," Rosand wrote, because it validates "the widest range of musical expression as worthy of serious study, [and] it is opening the field to students whose musical experience may lie outside the classical canon." See "The Musicology of the Present," *AMS Newsletter* 25, no. 1 (February 1995): 10. With the exception of the February 1994 issue (vol. 24, no. 1), some aspect of diversity was discussed in every newsletter from volume 22 to volume 27.

2. It is understandable why the Simpson saga and racial crisis weighed heavily on Gossett's mind at that time. The ubiquity of the televised double-murder trial of O. J. Simpson, combined with the veritable cottage industry of cable talk shows and books it spawned, rank it as arguably the most fantastic media spectacle of the late twentieth century. If we put stock in the daily news polls, many Americans took sides during the trial, and the divide separating black and white Americans grew sharp and remained consistent. Thus, in my view, Gossett's reference to the trial in this context accented a racial element in the discussion of "diversity" in musicology. Catchy terminology circulated furiously in the American vernacular as we spoke frankly about race in America during the trial. One such term is "race card." The race card is something to be "played," as in "playing the race card." During an interview with the journalist Barbara Walters on October 2, 1995, Robert Shapiro, Simpson's former friend and now disgruntled defense attorney, accused Johnnie Cochran, the lead attorney on Simpson's defense team, of "playing the race card from the bottom of the deck." The phrase described what Shapiro saw as the defense team's unfair tactics. See Johnnie L. Cochran Jr. (with Tim Rutten), *Journey to Justice* (New York: Ballantine Books, 1996), 355. As an always-already trump for African Americans, in particular, to use against all manner of adversity, the term "race card" is tailor-made for the age of political correctness. Run into a difficult situation, flash your race card like a bus pass, and the job is yours, the mortgage will be granted, and the neighbors will not be alarmed when you move in. Sentiments such as these created a tangible divisiveness, especially in the contexts of contemporary fire-hot affirmative action debates and the various legislative actions concerning race preferences in the state of California.

3. See, for example Katherine Bergeron and Philip Bohlman, eds., *Disciplining Music: Musicology and Its Canons* (Chicago: University of Chicago Press, 1992); Philip Brett, Gary Thomas, and Elizabeth Wood, eds., *Queering the Pitch: The New Gay and Lesbian Musicology* (New York: Routledge, 1994); Susan McClary, *Feminine Endings: Music, Gender, and Sexuality* (Minneapolis: University of Minnesota Press, 1991); and Ruth A. Solie, *Musicology and Difference: Gender and Sexuality in Music Scholarship* (Berkeley: University of California Press, 1993).

4. If I might be allowed one more reference to the O. J. Simpson trial, the infamous phrase "if it doesn't fit, you must acquit" presents a related case in point. The rhyme and the black-preacherly turn of phrase it conjures, together with other factors, combined to make it a memorable vernacular (some would say "vulgar," which, according to the *Oxford Dictionary*, is part of the original meaning of the word) utterance at an intensely scrutinized moment of America's criminal justice system. Black speech rhetoric of this kind and the black presence it has come to symbolize continually shape and influence the dynamic evolution of American vernacular "languaging" at large. But conventional wisdom dictates that when the stakes are high, as they were in the Simpson trial, the rhetorical practice is perhaps best left to the black comedians during prime time. These kinds of expressions are known as "street talk"; they do not belong in the formal arenas of one's life. My use of vernacular language in this essay, for example, might seem to some readers to be an unusual strategy in the present forum.

5. Publication dates for these journals include *Black Perspective in Music* (1975–90), *Black Music Research Journal* (1980–present), and *Journal of Black Sacred Music* (1987–95).

6. In an unusual move, *Black Perspective in Music,* founded and edited by the musicologist Eileen Southern, would identify African American contributors to the journal. The following editorial comment appeared on the contributors page of each number of the journal: "It is germane to the purpose of this journal to identify black-American writers. Accordingly, the symbol (+) is used for such identification."

7. For an explicit definition of the "black vernacular," see Robert G. O'Meally, "The Vernacular Tradition," in *Norton Anthology of African American Literature,* ed. Henry Louis Gates Jr. and Nellie Y. McKay (New York: W. W. Norton, 1997).

8. See *Chronicle of Higher Education* 44, no. 34, May 1, 1998, A16–A22.

9. A recent correspondence from the AMS's Committee on Cultural Diversity, for example, informed members of the society of the recent efforts to recruit minority scholars into the field of musicology: "For the past several years the American Musicological Society has actively recruited minority students into the field of musicology. As you may be aware, minorities are significantly underrepresented in our field. To give one example: fewer than twenty African Americans have received the Ph.D. in musicology during the last twenty-five years. To better expose students to the field, sixteen students, primarily from historically black colleges, were invited to attend the 1995 AMS National Conference in New York City; a similar number of students attended the 1996 conference in Baltimore. Students attended sessions, met with senior scholars in the field, and were invited to a reception (in 1995) and a luncheon (in 1996) held in their honor. We have seen encouraging results from these efforts: several of these students have subsequently elected to pursue doctoral degrees at major universities in the

United States." Personal files, Committee on Cultural Diversity, September 21, 1998.

10. With respect to this issue, it would be instructive to compare the growth of scholarship on feminist issues or gay and lesbian studies in musicological discourse to the increased number of scholars claiming membership in those constituencies.

11. My present argument is not meant in any way to diminish the larger and important issue of job availability in musicology. Writing in 1996, Peter Jeffery addressed the paucity of new musicology jobs and the abundance of "independent scholars" in the field: "In a word, they are the new generation of American musicologists: groomed to be university teachers, yet forced to earn a living outside their chosen field. How much longer can they persevere? How much longer should we, as a consistent member of the American Council of *Learned* Societies, ignore or evade the ethical issue that we are preparing our graduate students for nonexistent academic careers?" See "Report from the Committee on Career Related Issues: Musicology in Crisis," *AMS Newsletter* 26, no. 1 (February 1996): 9.

12. Doris Evans McGinty, "Black Scholars on Black Music: The Past, the Present, and the Future," *Black Music Research Journal* 13, no. 1 (Spring 1993).

13. McGinty, "Black Scholars on Black Music," 2. See also Alfred A. Moss Jr., *The American Negro Academy* (Baton Rouge: Louisiana State University Press, 1981), and James Monroe Trotter, *Music and Some Highly Musical People* (New York: Johnson Reprints, 1968).

14. McGinty, "Black Scholars on Black Music," 9.

15. Richard Crawford, "On Two Traditions of Black Music Scholarship," *Black Music Research Journal* 6, no. 1 (1986): 5 (quoted in McGinty, "Black Scholars on Black Music," 9).

16. McGinty, "Black Scholars on Black Music," 9.

17. The notion that black scholars were positioned to know a "truth" about African American people and culture has generated sustained critiques. Some of the more recent thinking on this topic has come from black female scholars who study African American literature. See, for example Ann duCille, "Phallus(sies) of Interpretation: Toward Engendering the Black Critical 'I'," *Callaloo* 16, no. 3 (1993); and Deborah E. McDowell, *"The Changing Same": Black Women's Literature, Criticism, and Theory* (Bloomington: Indiana University Press, 1995). DuCille, writing about African American fiction and its surrounding criticism, warns us that "because art is invention, 'truth' is generally held to be a false standard by which to evaluate a writer's work. This should be the case whether the issue is Alice Walker's representation of black men or Spike Lee's treatment of black women. Yet . . . this is precisely the leap of faith that critics of African American literature continue to make. Texts are transparent documents that must tell the truth as I know it. Failure to tell *my* truth not only invalidates the text, it also discredits, de-authorizes, and on occasion deracializes the writer.

Truth, however, like beauty, is in the eye and perhaps the experience of the beholder" (560).

18. Nellie Y. McKay, "Naming the Problem That Led to the Question 'Who Shall Teach African American Literature?' or Are We Ready to Disband the Wheatley Court?," *PMLA* (May 1998).

19. McKay, "Naming the Problem," 361.

20. McKay, "Naming the Problem," 363.

21. McKay, "Naming the Problem," 364.

22. McKay, "Naming the Problem," 364–65.

23. McKay, "Naming the Problem," 366. This essentialism cuts both ways, however. McKay notes that "African American scholars seeking appointments in more-traditional fields for which they were trained confront an automatic assumption that they are better able to teach, say, [Toni] Morrison than Milton. Such blatant disrespect and contorted logic, such reluctances to learn about African American literature, its background and long history of serious scholarship, and to understand what Toni Morrison calls its structures, moorings, and anchors . . . cause major distress for black scholars and discredit the integrity of our profession" (365).

24. For a relevant discussion in the field of anthropology, see Virginia R. Dominguez, "A Taste for 'the Other': Intellectual Complicity in Racializing Practices" (with commentary), *Current Anthropology* 35, no. 4 (August–October 1994). See also the critical debates anthologized in Houston A. Baker Jr. and Patricia Redmond, eds., *Afro-American Literary Studies in the 1990s* (Chicago: University of Chicago Press, 1989), and Angelyn Mitchell, ed., *Within the Circle: An Anthology of African American Literary Criticism from the Harlem Renaissance to the Present* (Durham, NC: Duke University Press, 1994).

25. Ann duCille, "Who Reads Here? Back Talking with Houston Baker," *Novel* 26, no. 1 (Fall 1992): 101.

26. I borrow the term "generational shift" from the literary scholar Houston A. Baker Jr., who uses it to describe "an ideologically motivated movement overseen by young or newly emergent intellectuals dedicated to refuting the work of their intellectual predecessors and to establishing a new framework for intellectual inquiry." See Baker, *Blues, Ideology, and Afro-American Literature: A Vernacular Theory* (Chicago: University of Chicago Press, 1984), 67. Historiographical work on jazz criticism and scholarship has recently received attention from many different perspectives. See, for example, Richard Crawford, *The American Musical Landscape* (Berkeley: University of California Press, 1993); Scott DeVeaux, "Constructing the Jazz Tradition: Jazz Historiography," *Black American Literature Forum* 25 (Fall 1991); David A. Franklin, "A Preliminary Study of the Acceptance of Jazz by French Music Critics in the 1920s," *Annual Review of Jazz Studies* 4 (1988): 1–8; Krin Gabbard, introduction, "The Jazz Canon and Its Consequences," in *Jazz among the Discourses* (Durham, NC: Duke University

Press), 1–28; John Gennari, "Jazz Criticism: Its Developments and Ideologies," *Black American Literature Forum* 25 (Fall 1991); Bruce Johnson, "Hear Me Talkin' to Ya: Problems of Jazz Discourse," *Popular Music* 12 (1993); and Ronald Welburn, "Jazz Magazines of the 1930s: An Overview of Their Provocative Journalism," *American Music* 5 (Fall 1987), "The Early Record Review: Jazz Criticism's First-Born Child," *Annual Review of Jazz Studies* 3 (1985), and "James Reese Europe and the Infancy of Jazz Criticism," *Black Music Research Journal* 7 (1987). For a discussion on how early jazz writings are positioned relative to black musical research, broadly conceived, see my "Cosmopolitan or Provincial? Ideology in Early Black Music Historiography, 1867–1940," *Black Music Research Journal* 16, no. 1 (Spring 1996). A very useful survey of the literature is Portia K. Maultsby, "Music in African American Culture," in *Mediated Messages and African-American Culture,* ed. Venise T. Berry and Carmen L. Manning-Miller (Thousand Oaks, CA: Sage Publications, 1995).

27. See, for example *Black Music Research Journal* 11, no. 2 (Fall 1991), for samples of the use of contemporary theory on black musical topics.

28. LeRoi Jones, *Black Music* (New York: William Morrow & Company, 1967), 20.

29. James Brown, *Star Time,* disc 2, Polygram Records, 849 111-2 (1993).

30. James Weldon Johnson and J. Rosamond Johnson, "Lift Every Voice and Sing," in *Songs of Zion* (Nashville, TN: Abingdon Press, 1981), 32.

31. See my discussion of Afro-modernism in "'We Called Ourselves Modern': Music and Afro-Modernism in 1940s America," in my *Race Music: Black Cultures from Bebop to Hip-Hop* (Berkeley: University of California Press, 2004).

32. In *Race Music* I describe how my family of origin would also reward our young neighbor, who "did the James Brown" for us, in similar fashion—by whooping, hollering, and tossing change at his feet across the waxed hardwood floor. After the performance, he eagerly collected his pay for a job well done. Everybody was satisfied. For a while, at least. When our little neighbor's capitalist sensibilities developed, he began to request a set fee for performances. The new arrangement dispirited some of the innocence and appeal of our ritual, but we continued to enjoy the spectacle nonetheless.

33. James Brown, "Santa Claus, Go Straight to the Ghetto," *James Brown's Funky Christmas,* Polygram, 31452 7988-2 (1995); originally released in 1968.

34. The term "color-struck" refers to a once-prevalent intrablack attitude of bigotry in which fairer-skinned African Americans are valued more than those with darker complexions. Although these attitudes still exist to some extent among some African Americans, they were exposed during the 1960s black power revolution. This intrablack color prejudice may also be harbored by darker-skinned blacks against those with lighter skin.

35. David Brackett, *Interpreting Popular Music* (Cambridge: Cambridge University Press, 1995), 121.

36. On the "cut" in black music, see James A. Snead, "Repetition as a Figure of Black Culture," in *Black Literature and Literary Theory*, ed. Henry Louis Gates Jr. (New York: Routledge, 1984).

37. Zora Neale Hurston, "Characteristics of Negro Expression," in *Within the Circle: An Anthology of African-American Literary Criticism from the Harlem Renaissance to the Present*, ed. Angelyn Mitchell (Durham, NC: Duke University Press, 1994), 80.

38. My performing experience in both these accompaniment practices confirms for me that accompanying funk and bebop presents a set of idiom-specific challenges for musicians. Diligent practice and discipline are required in order to capture the spirit and nuance in each.

39. Ronald Welburn, "The Black Aesthetic Imperative," in *The Black Aesthetic*, ed. Addison Gayle Jr. (Garden City, NY: Anchor Books, 1971), 133.

40. At least two writers have characterized James Brown's "race man" status as conflicted and contradictory. Both Nelson George and Brian Ward point out that Brown's belief in bootstrap mentality led him to blind support of Richard Nixon's "black capitalism as black deliverance" mantra. George critiques Brown's machismo attitude, which paralleled that of other male black power advocates of the time. In my view, these factors, in truth, make Brown a pretty typical example of a race man.

41. Ann duCille, "The Occult of True Black Womanhood," *Signs* 19, no. 3 (Spring 1994): 593.

42. Madhu Dubey, *Black Women Novelists and the Nationalist Aesthetic* (Bloomington: Indiana University Press, 1994), 4. I thank Farah Jasmine Griffin for this reference.

43. Samuel A. Floyd, "Eileen Southern: Quiet Revolutionary," *New Perspectives on Music: Essays in Honor of Eileen Southern*, ed. Josephine Wright with Samuel A. Floyd Jr. (Warren, MI: Harmonie Park Press, 1992), 6–7. Southern's subsequent research developed into a book-length project and has since encouraged additional work in the field, including musical biography and autobiography, archival and oral histories, systematic research on jazz and blues, the compilation of bibliographies and indices, ethnographic studies, critical editions, and much more. Southern's *The Music of Black Americans: A History* (New York: W. W. Norton, 1971), now in its third edition, stands as an important symbol of the epoch in which it first appeared, even as it filled a glaring lacuna in American musical scholarship as a whole.

44. Southern, *The Music of Black Americans*, xv.

45. A suggestive sample of this work can be found in Eileen Southern, ed., *Readings in Black American Music*, 2nd ed. (New York: W. W. Norton, 1983), which has several instructive essays by black composers such as Olly Wilson, T. J. Anderson, and Hale Smith. See also Addison Gayle Jr., ed., *The Black Aesthetic* (Garden City, NY: Anchor Books, 1971).

46. Floyd, "Quiet Revolutionary," 14.

47. Floyd, "Quiet Revolutionary," 7.

48. Southern, *The Music of Black Americans*, xvi.

49. Southern, *The Music of Black Americans*, xvi.

50. For an excellent comparison of *Blues People* and *The Music of Black Americans*, see Richard Crawford, "On Two Traditions of Black Music Research." Each of these works, Crawford writes, "seems the most complete embodiment of its approach to the subject" (2).

51. Sidney Finklestein, *Jazz: A People's Music* (New York: Da Capo Press, 1975), also treats political economy but it does not deal with the history of black music.

52. Bruce Tucker, "Editor's Introduction: Black Music after Theory," *Black Music Research Journal* 11, no. 2 (Fall 1991): v; see also Gennari, "Jazz Criticism."

53. Ralph Ellison, *Shadow and Act* (New York: Vintage Books, 1972). In a brilliant essay titled "Looking for the 'Real' Nigga: Social Scientists Construct the Ghetto," the historian Robin D. G. Kelley provides an excellent critique of "ghetto ethnographers" of the 1960s through 1980 by questioning the "scientific" quest for and the creation of "authentic" black culture; *Yo' Mama's Disfunktional! Fighting the Culture Wars in Urban America* (Boston: Beacon Press, 1997). Although Kelley does not engage Jones's work in the essay, many aspects of *Blues People* flatten out difference within urban black musical culture. As Kelley writes, "By conceiving black urban culture in the singular, interpreters unwittingly reduce their subjects to cardboard typologies who fit neatly into their own definition of the 'underclass' and render invisible a wide array of complex cultural forms and practices" (17). In my view, Jones was more successful in capturing a more nuanced black culture in his fictional writing, such as the short story *The Screamers*, in which he describes a social dance. See *The LeRoi Jones/Amiri Baraka Reader*, ed. William J. Harris (New York: Thunder's Mouth Press, 1991).

54. Jones, *Black Music*, 20.

55. Charles Keil, *Urban Blues* (Chicago: University of Chicago Press, 1966), 1. Keil's work used the tools of his home discipline, anthropology, but it was also informed by the tenets of black cultural nationalism, ideals that the author embraced.

56. Keil, *Urban Blues*, vii.

57. Keil, *Urban Blues*, 225.

58. Keil, *Urban Blues*, 236.

59. Gunther Schuller, *Early Jazz: Its Roots and Musical Development* (New York: Oxford University Press, 1968), ix.

60. Schuller, *Early Jazz*, ix.

61. Dena Epstein, *Sinful Tunes and Spirituals: Black Folk Music to the Civil War* (Urbana: University of Illinois Press, 1977); Lawrence Levine, *Black Cul-*

ture, Black Consciousness (New York: Oxford University Press, 1977), xi; Schuller, *Early Jazz*, ix.

62. Keil, *Urban Blues*, 236.

63. Levine, *Black Culture, Black Consciousness*, xiii.

64. See, for example, Portia K. Maultsby, "Music of Northern Independent Black Churches During the Ante-bellum Period," *Ethnomusicology* 19 (September 1975), and "Black Spirituals: An Analysis of Textual Forms and Structures," *Black Perspective in Music* 4 (Spring 1976).

65. See, for example, Horace Clarence Boyer, "An Overview: Gospel Music Comes of Age," *Black World* 23 (November 1973): 42–48, 79–86, and "Contemporary Gospel Music: Sacred or Secular?," *Black Perspective in Music* 7, no. 1 (Spring 1979): 5–54.

66. For information on the black literary magazines of the black arts movement, see Abby Arthur Johnson and Ronald Maberry Johnson, *Propaganda and Aesthetics: The Literary Politics of African-American Magazines in the Twentieth Century* (Amherst: University of Massachusetts Press, 1991).

67. Jacqueline Cogdell DjeDje, *American Black Spiritual and Gospel Songs from Southeast Georgia: A Comparative Study* (Los Angeles: University of California Center for Afro-American Studies, 1978).

68. For an extensive listing of this area of scholarship, see Irene V. Jackson, *Afro-American Religious Music: A Bibliography and Catalogue of Gospel Music* (Westport, CT: Greenwood Press, 1979).

69. Olly Wilson, "The Significance of the Relationship between Afro-American Music and West African Music," *Black Perspective in Music* (1972); Pearl Williams-Jones, "Afro-American Gospel Music: Crystallization of the Black Aesthetic," *Ethnomusicology* 19 (1975). Kofi Agawu questions the validity of earlier conceptions of rhythm in conventional views of "African music" and forwards one he believes is "phenomenologically truer to the African experience" in "The Invention of African Rhythm," *Journal of the American Musicological Society* 48, no. 3 (Fall 1995): 395.

70. See "Criticism," in *The Oxford Companion to African American Literature*, ed. William L. Andrews, Frances Smith Foster, and Trudier Harris (New York: Oxford University Press, 1997), for an overview of the various paradigms employed by scholars in the study of black literature.

71. See Brackett, *Interpreting Popular Music;* Kyra D. Gaunt, "African-American Women between Hopscotch and Hip-Hop: 'Must Be the Music (That's Turnin' Me On)'," in *Feminism, Multiculturalism, and the Media: Global Diversities*, ed. Angharad Valdivia (Thousand Oaks, CA: Sage Publications, 1995); Ingrid Monson, *Saying Something: Jazz Improvisation and Interaction* (Chicago: University of Chicago Press, 1996); John P. Murphy, "Jazz Improvisation: The Joy of Influence," *Black Perspective in Music* 18 (1990); Ronald Radano, *New Musical Figurations: Anthony Braxton's Cultural Critique* (Chicago:

University of Chicago Press, 1993); Timothy D. Taylor, "His Name Was in Lights: Chuck Berry's 'Johnny B. Goode'," *Popular Music* 11, no. 1 (January 1992); Gary Tomlinson, "Cultural Dialogics and Jazz: A White Historian Signifies," *Black Music Research Journal* 11 (Fall 1991); and Robert Walser, "Out of Notes: Signification, Interpretation, and the Problem with Miles Davis," *Musical Quarterly* 77, no. 2 (1993), and "Rhyme, Rhythm, and Rhetoric in the Music of Public Enemy," *Ethnomusicology* 39, no. 2 (Spring–Summer 1995).

72. Monson, *Saying Something*, 73; Walser, "Out of Notes," 358; and Brackett, *Interpreting Popular Music*, 156.

73. Marcia J. Citron, *Gender and the Musical Canon* (Cambridge: Cambridge University Press, 1994), 15.

74. Susan Cook and Judy Tsou, eds., *Cecilia Reclaimed: Feminist Perspectives on Gender and Music* (Urbana: University of Illinois Press, 1994), 5.

75. Jon Michael Spencer, *Re-Searching Black Music* (Knoxville: University of Tennessee Press, 1997).

76. I do not treat the work of all these scholars here. For a discussion of Ingrid Monson's and Ronald M. Radano's books, see my "Who Matters: The New and Improved White Jazz-Literati, A Review Essay," *American Music* 17, no. 2 (1999).

77. Shelley Fisher Fishkin, "Interrogating 'Whiteness,' Complicating 'Blackness': Remapping American Culture," *American Quarterly* 47, no. 3 (1995): 428–29.

78. Tomlinson, "Cultural Dialogics and Jazz."

79. "The Signifyin' Monkey," as told by Oscar Brown Jr., in *Talk That Talk: An Anthology of African-American Storytelling*, ed. Linda Goss and Marian E. Barnes (New York: Touchstone Book, 1989), 457.

80. Samuel A. Floyd Jr., *The Power of Black Music* (New York: Oxford University Press, 1995), 95.

81. This revealing of my personal and professional relationship with Professor Tomlinson is intentional. Despite all the talk about cultural politics in the academy, few scholars are willing to admit in print the degree to which professional and personal jealousies, allegiances, and political maneuvering shape our "objective" narratives. One of the first things one learns (and very quickly) as a minority in the field, however, is that these factors should never be taken for granted or ignored. I would be remiss if I did not point out as well that I began thinking and writing about this topic before taking my present appointment at the University of Pennsylvania.

82. Tomlinson, "Cultural Dialogics and Jazz," 230.

83. Robert Walser, "Out of Notes," in Krin Gabbard, ed., *Jazz among the Discourses* (Durham, NC: Duke University Press, 1995), 167. Page number references for the Walser article from here to the end of this chapter refer to the Gabbard anthology.

84. Miles Davis, *My Funny Valentine: Miles Davis in Concert*, recorded February 12, 1964, Columbia-CS 9106.

85. Floyd, *The Power of Black Music*, 273, also notes this trend in jazz literature. Floyd argues against "the exclusive use of positivistic analysis," linking this work to the vindication imperative. He writes further, "The zeal for jazz among some musicologists and musicologically oriented scholars and critics, who feel that they have to justify black music to the larger scholarly community, has been both fortunate and unfortunate for African-American music."

86. Walser, "Out of Notes," 169.

87. Walser, "Out of Notes," 168

88. Walser, "Out of Notes," 172.

89. Walser, "Out of Notes," 173.

90. Walser, "Out of Notes," 168.

91. See William "Billy" Taylor, "Jazz: America's Classical Music," *Black Perspective in Music* 14, no. 1 (Winter 1986), and "Jazz in the Contemporary Marketplace: Professional and Third-Sector Economic Strategies for the Balance of the Century," in *New Perspectives on Jazz*, ed. David N. Baker (Washington, DC: Smithsonian Institution, 1990), 89.

92. Walser, "Out of Notes," 170.

93. Ralph J. Gleason, *Celebrating the Duke* (New York: Delta Books, 1975), xviii.

94. Gleason, *Celebrating the Duke*, 17.

95. Billy Taylor, *Jazz Piano: History and Development* (Dubuque, IA: Wm. C. Brown, 1982).

96. Taylor, *Jazz Piano*, 9.

97. Walser, "Out of Notes," 169, 178.

98. Walser, "Out of Notes," 169.

99. Pearl Cleage, "Mad at Miles," in *The Miles Davis Companion: Four Decades of Commentary*, ed. Gary Carner (New York: Schirmer, 1996). If Cleage begged the question about Davis's "woman question," the respected feminist critic and literary scholar Hazel Carby tries to provide us with answers. In *Race Men* (Cambridge, MA: Harvard University Press, 1998), Carby provides a full-scale critique of Davis's problems with women. She explains the implications and social constitution of Davis's attitudes toward women and the tension between his startling musical accomplishments and "the devastation rendered by patriarchal codes of domination" (144). While Cleage's essay is in my view one of the most penetrating critiques of music I have read—her personal responses give her essay power—Carby's misses the mark on some levels. Although we learn that she perceives a lack of the phallocentric markers of closure and climax in the musical organization of Davis's important recording *Kind of Blue*, we never learn precisely why what she perceives as its erotic pulse, circularity, democratic sensibility, vulnerability, openness, ambiguity, and intimacy should be considered a

challenge to gendered social conventions. Are these qualities innately feminine as Davis's wife beating was essentially masculine?

100. Cleage, "Mad at Miles," 214.

101. See Anthony Appiah's discussion of the traps of racial essentialism in "The Uncompleted Argument: Du Bois and the Illusion of Race," in "*Race," Writing, and Difference*, ed. Henry Louis Gates Jr. (Chicago: University of Chicago Press, 1985). See also Kwame Anthony Appiah, *In My Father's House: Africa in the Philosophy of Culture* (New York: Oxford University Press, 1992), for a broad discussion of the role that historic and mythic Africa has played in the social construction of blackness.

102. Brackett, *Interpreting Popular Music*, 119.

103. See, for example Roger Abrahams, *Deep Down in the Jungle: Negro Narrative Folklore from the Streets of Philadelphia* (Hawthorne, NY: Aldine, 1963); William Labov, Paul Cohen, Clarence Robins, and John Lewis, "Toasts," in *Mother Wit from the Laughing Barrel: Readings in the Interpretation of Afro-American Folklore*, ed. Alan Dundes (New York: Garland, 1968); and Geneva Smitherman, *Talkin' and Testifyin': The Language of Black America* (Boston: Houghton Mifflin, 1977).

104. Henry Louis Gates Jr., *Figures in Black: Words, Signs, and the Racial Self* (New York: Oxford University Press, 1987), xvii.

105. Gates, *Figures in Black*, xxi.

106. Ann duCille, *The Coupling Convention: Sex, Text, and Tradition in Black Women's Fiction* (New York: Oxford University Press, 1993), 9.

107. In jazz and black music studies, the topic of white identity and black representation has recently received insightful attention. See, for example, Ingrid Monson, "The Problem of White Hipness: Race, Gender, and Cultural Conceptions in Jazz Historical Discourse," *Journal of the American Musicological Society* 49, no. 3 (1995); Jon Panish, *The Color of Jazz: Race and Representation in Postwar American Culture* (Jackson: University of Mississippi Press, 1997); Ronald M. Radano, "The Writing of the Slave Spirituals," *Critical Inquiry* 22, no. 3 (Spring 1996); and John Gennari, *Blowin' Hot and Cool: Jazz and Its Critics* (Chicago: University of Chicago Press, 2006), which contains relevant previously published essays on the topic.

108. Floyd, *The Power of Black Music*.

109. Floyd, *The Power of Black Music*, 5, 98.

110. Floyd, *The Power of Black Music*, 91.

111. Floyd is not the first to theorize the importance of African cultural memory to African American music. The composer Olly Wilson, for example, has over the years written several important articles about the continuum between African and African American musics. See Wilson, "The Significance of the Relationship Between Afro-American Music and West African Music"; "Black Music

as an Art Form," *Black Music Research Journal* 3 (1984); and "The Heterogeneous Sound Ideal in African-American Music," in *New Perspectives on Music: Essays in Honor of Eileen Southern*, ed. Josephine Wright with Samuel A. Floyd Jr. (Warren, MI: Harmonie Park Press, 1992).

112. Floyd, *The Power of Black Music*, 3.

113. Gaunt, "African-American Women between Hopscotch and Hip-Hop," 278.

114. Gaunt, "African-American Women between Hopscotch and Hip-Hop," 279.

115. See my *Race Music*. While my study takes into account the entire history of black music (this history is central to Floyd's investigation; he traces black music from its roots in Africa to the United States), my primary focus is on the styles appearing around and after World War II. That historical focus allows me to provide a more nuanced, sustained look at events and cultural processes that contributed to the creation, dissemination, and reception of postwar black music. My Afro-poetics framework, however, is more narrowly focused on musical subject matter and "thicker" (in the Geertzian sense) with regard to its treatment of postwar black music's various modes of use and reception.

116. See, for example, Peter Novick, *That Noble Dream: The "Objectivity Question" and the American Historical Profession* (Cambridge: Cambridge University Press, 1988).

117. Ann duCille, "Postcolonialism and Afrocentricity: Discourse and Dat Course," in *The Black Columbiad: Defining Moments in African American Literature and Culture*, ed. Werner Sollars and Maria Diedrich (Cambridge, MA: Harvard University Press, 1994), 30. It should be clear by now that duCille's scholarship has been critical to my thinking on the issues I have raised. In her work here, discourse is the postcolonial scholarship that has become one of academia's most respected trends of late. "Dat-course" comprises Afrocentricity, which she distinguishes from African American studies.

118. Patricia J. Williams, "On Being the Object of Property," *Signs* 14, no. 1 (1988): 5.

119. See José E. Limón, "Representation, Ethnicity, and the Precursory Ethnography: Notes of a Native Anthropologist," in *Recapturing Anthropology: Working in the Present*, ed. Richard G. Fox (Santa Fe, NM: School of American Research Press, 1991), and *Dancing with the Devil: Society and Cultural Poetics in Mexican-American South Texas* (Madison: University of Wisconsin Press, 1994); and Virginia Giglio, *Southern Cheyenne Women's Songs* (Norman: University of Oklahoma Press, 1994). I thank Timothy D. Taylor for suggesting that I look at Limón's work; it has greatly influenced my thinking on the personal in ethnography and historiography.

120. Limón, "Representation, Ethnicity, and the Precursory Ethnography," 116.

121. Limón studies male humor and meat consumption, popular dancing, a women's devil legend, and literary fiction.

122. Limón, *Dancing with the Devil*, 12.

123. Limón, *Dancing with the Devil*, 13; See also Clifford Geertz, "Thick Description," in *The Interpretation of Cultures* (New York: Basic Books, 1973); Stephen Greenblatt, *Renaissance Self-Fashioning: From More to Shakespeare* (Chicago: University of Chicago Press, 1980), *Shakespeare Negotiations: The Circulation of Social Energy in Renaissance England* (Los Angeles: University of California Press, 1988), and "Toward a Poetics of Culture," in *The New Historicism*, ed. H. Aram Vesser (London: Routledge, 1989).

124. Limón, *Dancing with the Devil*, 14.

125. Limón, *Dancing with the Devil*, 12.

126. For an innovative approach to understanding the value of black women's fiction and autobiography for ethnography and meaning, see Lorna McDaniel, "'Gifts of Power': The Black Woman Writer as Ethnographer," in *New Directions: Readings in African Diaspora Music* 1, no. 1 (Wilmington, DE: Adama, 1997).

127. Toni Morrison, "Home," in *The House That Race Built: Black Americans, U.S. Terrain*, ed. Wahneema Lubiano (New York: Pantheon Books, 1997), 5.

128. Ann duCille, "The Occult of True Black Womanhood."

129. Morrison, "Home," 11.

130. My comments were directed at the many genres of music in which the composer William Grant Still wrote during the early part of his career. I mentioned casually to a Still scholar that his output reminded me of the trickster figure because of the many "voices" in his compositional output. These observations were evidently repeated to the lions and, before I knew it, one of them pounced with all four feet! It was a very disconcerting experience.

131. See duCille, "The Occult of True Black Womanhood." My notion of confessional discourse as a narrative strategy was critiqued from two points during a session at the 1999 American Musicological Society conference at which I gave a paper based on the present chapter. One respondent questioned whether the value of the confessional mode was solely contingent on the craft or quality of the writing. More "objective" narrative strategies are equally dependent on the skill of the writer to "convince" a reader. Other scholars wondered whether the field of ethnomusicology has already provided a model for this kind of work. While it may be true that ethnomusicology has in many respects been a more self-reflexive enterprise than musicology, the former has not produced a voluminous body of work in black music inquiry treating this particular issue. An excellent and useful collection of essays on new directions in ethnomusicological fieldwork and ethnography, Gregory F. Barz and Timothy J. Cooley, eds., *Shadows in the Field: New Perspectives for Fieldwork in Ethnomusicology* (New York: Oxford University Press, 1997), barely mentions African American music.

CHAPTER 3. THE POT LIQUOR PRINCIPLE

1. By using the term "the black experience" I do not mean to suggest that a monolithic racial experience among African Americans can be identified. What I mean here is that the sum total of these varied experiences has a contour and thrust that can be discussed and theorized even as we recognize differences within the group.

2. Wahneema Lubiano, ed., *The House That Race Built: Black Americans, U.S. Terrain* (New York: Pantheon Books, 1997), vii.

3. Richard Leppert and Susan McClary, eds., *Music and Society: The Politics of Composition, Performance, and Reception* (Cambridge: Cambridge University Press, 1987), xii.

4. See *Black Music Research Journal* 11, no. 2 (1991) for one of the first efforts to pull together scholarship of this kind devoted to black music specifically.

5. For more on this issue, see my "Who Hears Here? Black Music, Critical Bias, and the Musicological Skin Trade," *Musical Quarterly* 85, no. 1 (Spring 2001).

6. Katherine Bergeron and Philip V. Bohlman, *Disciplining Music: Musicology and Its Canons* (Chicago: University of Chicago Press, 1992); Philip Brett, Elizabeth Wood, and Gary C. Thomas, eds., *Queering the Pitch: The New Gay and Lesbian Musicology* (New York: Routledge, 1994); Susan C. Cook and Judy S. Tsou, eds., *Cecilia Reclaimed: Feminist Perspectives on Gender and Music* (Urbana: University of Illinois Press, 1994); and Ruth A. Solie, ed., *Musicology and Difference: Gender and Sexuality in Music Scholarship* (Berkeley: University of California Press, 1993). Important exceptions to the Euro-focus of the music studies anthologies are Ingrid Monson, ed., *The African Diaspora: A Musical Perspective* (New York: Garland Publishing, 2000), and Ronald Radano and Philip V. Bohlman, eds., *Music and the Racial Imagination* (Chicago: University of Chicago Press, 2000).

7. Brett, Wood, and Thomas, *Queering the Pitch*, 10.

8. For more on this method of criticism, see my *Race Music: Black Cultures from Bebop to Hip-Hop* (Berkeley: University of California Press, 2003).

9. Samuel A. Floyd Jr., *The Power of Black Music: Interpreting Its History from Africa to the United States* (New York: Oxford University Press, 1995). For representative examples of Radano's articles, see his "Soul Texts and the Blackness of Folk," *Modernism/modernity* 2, no. 1 (1995), and "Denoting Difference: The Writing of the Slave Spirituals," *Critical Inquiry* 22, no. 3 (Spring 1996). See also Ronald Radano, *Lying Up a Nation: Race and Black Music* (Chicago: University of Chicago Press, 2003.

10. Radano and Bohlman, *Music and the Racial Imagination*, 5. My colleague Timothy Rommen suggested to me that all three categories are

discursive. In future uses of these categories I will use his terminology: "theoretical" race in place of discursive race.

11. Marcia J. Citron, "Feminist Approaches to Musicology," in *Cecilia Reclaimed: Feminist Perspectives on Gender and Music,* ed. Susan C. Cook and Judy S. Tsou (Urbana: University of Illinois Press), 25.

CHAPTER 4. SECRETS, LIES, AND TRANSCRIPTIONS

1. Jon Cruz, *Culture on the Margins: The Black Spiritual and the Rise of American Cultural Interpretation* (Princeton, NJ: Princeton University Press, 1999), 3.

2. Tukufu Zuberi, *Thicker Than Blood: How Racial Statistics Lie* (Minneapolis: University of Minnesota Press, 2001).

3. Zuberi, *Thicker Than Blood.*

4. For more on race and genre, see David Brackett, "Questions of Genre in Black Popular Music," *Black Music Research Journal* 25, no. 1/2 (Spring–Fall 2005).

5. Shelly Fisher Fishkin, "Interrogating 'Whiteness,' Complicating 'Blackness': Remapping American Culture," *American Quarterly* 47, no. 3 (1995).

6. Robin D. G. Kelley, *Yo' Mama's Disfunktional! Fighting the Culture Wars in Urban America* (Boston: Beacon Press, 1997).

7. Cruz, *Culture on the Margins,* 3.

8. Cruz, *Culture on the Margins,* 25.

9. James Monroe Trotter, *Music and Some Highly Musical People* (New York: Charles T. Dillingham, 1881). See also Guthrie P. Ramsey Jr, "Cosmopolitan or Provincial? Ideology in Early Black Music Historiography, 1867–1940," *Black Music Research Journal* 16, no. 1 (1996).

10. Gary Tomlinson, "Musicology, Anthropology, History," in *The Cultural Study of Music: A Critical Introduction,* ed. Martin Clayton, Trevor Herbert, and Richard Middleton (New York: Routledge, 2003), 31.

11. Tomlinson, "Musicology, Anthropology, History," 33.

12. Tomlinson, "Musicology, Anthropology, History," 32.

13. Tomlinson, "Musicology, Anthropology, History," 34.

14. Tomlinson, "Musicology, Anthropology, History," 39.

15. Ronald Radano, *Lying up a Nation: Race and Black Music* (Chicago: University of Chicago Press, 2003), 3.

16. Radano, *Lying up a Nation,* 47.

17. Radano, *Lying up a Nation,* 42.

18. For an example of this interdisciplinary scholarship, see Robert G. O'Meally, Brent Hayes Edwards, and Farah Jasmine Griffin, *Uptown Conversations: The New Jazz Studies* (New York: Columbia University Press, 2004).

19. Eric Porter, *What Is This Thing Called Jazz? African American Musicians as Artists, Critics, and Activists* (Berkeley: University of California Press, 2002).

20. Porter, *What Is This Thing Called Jazz?*

21. Porter, *What Is This Thing Called Jazz?*, 18.

22. On the term "Afro-modernism," see Guthrie P. Ramsey Jr., *Race Music: Black Cultures from Bebop to Hip-Hop* (Berkeley: University of California Press, 2003).

23. Paul Allen Anderson, *Deep River: Music and Memory in Harlem Renaissance Thought* (Durham, NC: Duke University Press, 2001).

24. Anderson, *Deep River*, 8.

25. Anderson, *Deep River*, 134.

26. Mark Katz, *Capturing Sound: How Technology Has Changed Music* (Berkeley: University of California Press, 2004), 78.

27. Katz, *Capturing Sound*, 79.

28. Katz, *Capturing Sound*, 15.

29. I first wrote about this in "The Pot Liquor Principle: Developing a Black Music Criticism in American Music Studies," *American Music* 22, no. 2 (2004).

CHAPTER 5. MUZING NEW HOODS, MAKING NEW IDENTITIES

1. Ralph Ellison, *Shadow and Act* (New York: Vintage Books, 1972), 275.

2. *Do the Right Thing*, written and directed by Spike Lee (Universal City Studios, 1989) and *Love Jones*, written and directed by Theodore Witcher (New Line, 1997).

3. Robin D. G. Kelley, *Yo' Mama's Disfunktional! Fighting the Culture Wars in Urban America* (Boston: Beacon Press, 1997), 46.

4. Kelley, *Yo' Mama's Disfunktional!*, 44.

5. Henry Louis Gates Jr., "Must Buppiehood Cost Homeboy His Soul?," *New York Times*, March 1, 1992, 12–13.

6. Gates, "Must Buppiehood Cost Homeboy His Soul?," 12

7. Gates, "Must Buppiehood Cost Homeboy His Soul?," 13.

8. Michele Wallace, "*Boyz N the Hood* and *Jungle Fever*," in *Black Popular Culture*, ed. Gina Dent (Seattle: Bay Press, 1992), 123.

9. Valerie Smith, "The Documentary Impulse in Contemporary African American Film," in *Black Popular Culture*, ed. Gina Dent (Seattle: Bay Press, 1992), 58.

10. Lisa Kennedy, "The Body in Question," in *Black Popular Culture*, ed. Gina Dent (Seattle: Bay Press, 1992), 110.

11. Claudia Gorbman, *Unheard Melodies: Narrative Film Music* (Bloomington: Indiana University Press, 1987), 6.

12. Anahid Kassabian, *Hearing Film: Tracking Identifications in Contemporary Hollywood Film Music* (New York: Routledge, 2001), 1.

13. Kassabian, *Hearing Film*, 2.

14. Gorbman, *Unheard Melodies*, 4.

15. *In This Our Life*, directed by John Houston and with a score by Max Steiner (1942).

16. Kassabian, *Hearing Film*, 3.

17. Kassabian, *Hearing Film*, 3.

18. Kassabian, *Hearing Film*, 44–45.

19. S. Craig Watkins, *Representing: Hip Hop Culture and the Production of Black Cinema* (Chicago: University of Chicago Press, 1998), 108.

20. The original score is played by the Natural Spiritual Orchestra, William Lee, conductor. The ensemble is organized as a string orchestra and jazz combo. It features Branford Marsalis, Terence Blanchard, Kenny Barron, Jeff Watts, and other noted jazz musicians.

21. Victoria E. Johnson, "Polyphony and Cultural Expression: Interpreting Musical Traditions in *Do the Right Thing*," in *Spike Lee's* Do the Right Thing, ed. Mark A. Reid (Cambridge: Cambridge University Press, 1997), 52.

22. Gorbman, *Unheard Melodies*, 3.

23. Watkins, *Representing*, 233.

CHAPTER 6. AFRO-MODERNISM AND MUSIC

1. Farah Jasmine Griffin, *Harlem Nocturne: Women Artists and Progressive Politics During World War II* (New York: Basic Civitas, 2013), 16–17.

2. Fredara Hadley, "George Russell's 'The Concept'—A Small Act of Resistance," Musiqology.com, accessed January 27, 2022, https://musiqology.com/blog/2014/03/10/george-russells-the-concept-a-small-act-of-resistance/.

3. Olive Jones and George Russell, "A New Theory for Jazz," *Black Perspective in Music* 2, no. 1 (Spring 1974): 63.

4. Jones and Russell, "A New Theory for Jazz," 67.

5. Jones and Russell, "A New Theory for Jazz," 68.

6. Jones and Russell, "A New Theory for Jazz," 72.

7. Salim Washington, "'Don't Let the Devil (Make You) Lose Your Joy': A Look at Late Coltrane," in *John Coltrane and Black America's Quest for Freedom*, ed. Leonard L. Brown (New York: Oxford University Press, 2010), 214.

8. Salim Washington, "'All the Things You Could Be by Now': Charles Mingus Presents Charles Mingus and the Limits of Avant-Garde Jazz," in *Uptown Conversations: The New Jazz Studies*, ed. Robert G. O'Meally, Brent Hayes Edwards, and Farah Jasmine Griffin (New York: Columbia University Press, 2004), 32.

9. Robert Walser, ed., *Keeping Time: Readings in Jazz History* (New York: Oxford University Press, 1999), 225.

10. Walser, *Keeping Time,* 254.

11. Tammy K. Kernodle, "Freedom is a Constant Struggle: Alice Coltrane and the Redefining of the Jazz Avant-Garde," in *John Coltrane and Black America's Quest for Freedom,* ed. Leonard L. Brown (New York: Oxford University Press, 2010), 78.

12. Kernodle, "Freedom is a Constant Struggle," 74.

13. Kernodle, "Freedom is a Constant Struggle," 88.

14. Kernodle, "Freedom is a Constant Struggle," 85.

15. Kernodle, "Freedom is a Constant Struggle," 96.

16. Griffin, *Harlem Nocturne,* 165.

17. Griffin, *Harlem Nocturne,* 166.

18. Griffin, *Harlem Nocturne,* 164.

19. Griffin, *Harlem Nocturne,* 185.

20. Tammy L. Kernodle, *Soul on Soul: The Life and Music of Mary Lou Williams* (Boston: Northeastern University Press, 2004), 199–200.

21. Kernodle, *Soul on Soul,* 201.

22. Griffin, *Harlem Nocturne,* 164.

23. Steve Waksman, *Instruments of Desire: The Electric Guitar and the Shaping of the Musical Experience* (Cambridge, MA: Harvard University Press, 1999), 115.

24. Gayle Wald, *Shout, Sister, Shout! The Untold Story of Rock-and-Roll Trailblazer Sister Rosetta Tharpe* (Boston: Beacon Press, 2007), 73.

25. Wald, *Shout, Sister, Shout!,* 73.

26. "Composer Ulysses Kay Dies at 78," *Arizona Daily Star,* May 31, 1995.

27. The Black Music Caucus was organized in 1972 by two hundred black musicians who had gathered at a biennial meeting of the Music Educators National Conference to "protest their exclusion from MENC divisional and national Planning sessions and programs." Now called the National Association for the Study and Performance of African American Music (NASPAAM), the organization continues to exist as a "non-profit professional organization whose members are dedicated to promoting, performing, and preserving all facets of African American music." The NASPAAM website is www.naspaam.org. The reader should take note that the MENC superseded the Music Supervisors National Conference, which was founded in 1907 and led by Frances Elliott Clark. She was subsequently hired by the Victor Talking Machine Company in Camden, New Jersey, to head its new Educational Department. This department was responsible for producing and publishing educational guides that would help teachers select appropriate music for classroom listening.

28. Helen Walker-Hill, *From Spirituals to Symphonies: African-American Women Composers and their Music* (Westport, CT: Greenwood Press, 2002), 225.

29. Walker-Hill, *From Spirituals to Symphonies,* 219.

30. Although Moore did not seek a long-term teaching post at a university, she and her husband Kermit were hired by the esteemed Dorothy Maynor to teach at the Harlem School of the Arts, which had been established in 1964. Maynor was the only African American to be included in the Music Educators National Conference symposium in 1967, "Music in American Society." At this symposium participants discussed the trend of multicultural curricula and whether the field of music education should consider becoming multicultural in scope. The proceedings of this symposium were published in the November 1967 issue of the *Music Educators Journal,* along with photographs of all thirty-one participants. Within five years of this publication, the Black Music Caucus was formed.

31. Eileen Southern, *The Music of Black Americans: A History,* 3rd edition (New York: W. W. Norton, 1997), 555.

32. Walker-Hill, *From Spirituals to Symphonies,* 232.

CHAPTER 8. BLUES AND THE ETHNOGRAPHIC TRUTH

1. Ann duCille, "Phallus(ies) of Interpretation: Toward Engendering the Black Critical 'I,'" *Callaloo* 16, no. 3 (Summer 1993): 560.

2. DuCille, "Phallus(ies) of Interpretation," 571.

3. Among the most influential works that discuss African American music's conceptual approaches by linking, on the formal level, many of the various styles and genres in a "blues matrix" (to borrow a term from literary critic Houston Baker) are Samuel A. Floyd Jr., *The Power of Black Music: Interpreting Its History from Africa to the United States* (New York: Oxford University Press, 1995); Portia K. Maultsby, "Africanisms in African American Music," in *Africanisms in American Culture,* ed. Joseph E. Holloway (Bloomington: Indiana University Press, 1990); and Olly Wilson, "The Heterogenous Sound Ideal in African-American Music," in *Signifyin(g), Sanctifyin', and Slam Dunking: A Reader in African American Expressive Culture,* ed. Gena Dagel Caponi (Amherst: University of Massachusetts Press, 1999). Wilson provides an excellent overview of scholarship on Black expressive culture, especially music. Phillip Tagg, "Open Letter: 'Black Music,' 'Afro-American Music' and 'European Music,'" *Popular Music* 8 (October 1989), offers a critique of scholarship that assumes the existence of an African American music tradition.

4. See Evelyn Brooks Higginbotham, "Rethinking Vernacular Culture: Black Religion and Race Records in the 1920s and 1930s," in *The House that Race Built: Black Americans, U.S. Terrain,* ed. Wahneema Lubiano (New York: Pantheon Books, 1997); and Ronald M. Radano, "Soul Texts and the Blackness of Folk," *Modernism/Modernity* 2, no. 1 (1999).

5. Ann duCille, "Blues Notes on Black Sexuality: Sex and the Texts of Jessie Fauset and Nella Larsen," *Journal of the History of Sexuality* 3, no. 3 (1993): 419–20.

6. This chapter is drawn from my book *Race Music: Black Cultures from Bebop to Hip-Hop* (Berkeley: University of California Press, 2003), in which I explore some of the social energies that circulated in mass-mediated and live music making in post–World War II African American music. *Race Music* is primarily a discussion about musical interpretation and criticism.

7. James Clifford, *The Predicament of Culture: Twentieth-Century Ethnography, Literature, and Art* (Cambridge, MA: Harvard University Press, 1988), 9.

8. See Clifford, *The Predicament of Culture*, and James Clifford and George E. Marcus, eds., *Writing Culture: The Poetics and Politics of Ethnography* (Berkeley: University of California Press, 1986).

9. See Gregory F. Barz and Timothy J. Cooley, eds., *Shadows in the Field: New Perspectives for Fieldwork in Ethnomusicology* (New York: Oxford University Press, 1997).

10. Floyd, *The Power of Black Music*, 8.

11. See Jose Limón, *Dancing with the Devil: Society and Cultural Poetics in Mexican-American South Texas* (Madison: University of Wisconsin Press, 1994).

12. Dizzy Gillespie and Al Frazer, *To Be or Not to Bop* (Garden City, NY: Doubleday, 1979), 201 (quoted in Lewis Porter and Michael Ullman with Edward Hazell, *Jazz: From Its Origins to the Present* [Englewood Cliffs, NJ: Prentice-Hall, 1993], 185). See also George Lipsitz, *Rainbow at Midnight: Labor and Culture in the 1940s* (Urbana: University of Illinois Press, 1994). For an overview of the social and cultural changes in postwar America, see Lary May, "Introduction," in *Recasting America: Culture and Politics in the Age of the Cold War*, ed. Lary May (Chicago: University of Chicago Press, 1989). For discussions on the relationship of bebop to postwar American society, see LeRoi Jones, *Blues People: Negro Music in White America* (New York: William Morrow, 1963); Robin D. G. Kelley, *Race Rebels: Culture, Politics, and the Black Working Class* (New York: Free Press, 1994); Eric Lott, "Double V, Double-Time: Bebop's Politics of Style," *Callaloo* 11 (1988); and Leslie B. Rout Jr., "Reflections on the Evolution of Postwar Jazz," in *The Black Aesthetic*, ed. Addison Gayle Jr. (New York: Anchor Books, 1971).

13. See Acklyn Lynch, *Nightmare Overhanging Darkly: Essays on African-American Culture and Resistance* (Chicago: Third World Press, 1993), who offers an informative overview of artistic developments among Black writers and musicians during the 1940s.

14. These developments in the marketing of Black music registered the dramatic economic and social shifts in other realms of African American culture. Black social critic Harold Cruse discusses some of the economic, ideological, and

cultural restlessness present in wartime Harlem, for example: "Harlem in 1940 was just beginning to emerge from the depths of the Great Depression and it seethed with the currents of many conflicting beliefs and ideologies. It was the year in which Richard Wright reached the high point of fame with his *Native Son* and was often seen in Harlem at lectures. The American Negro Theater, a professional experimental group, was preparing to make its 1941 debut as a permanent Harlem institution. The Federal Theatre Project had been abolished in 1939 and the echoes of that disaster were still being heard in Harlem's cultural circles. Everything in Harlem seemed to be in a state of flux for reasons that I was not then able to fully appreciate." Harold Cruse, *The Crisis of the Negro Intellectual: From Its Origins to the Present* (New York: William Morrow, 1967), 3.

15. Russell Sanjek and David Sanjek, *American Popular Music Business in the 20th Century* (New York: Oxford University Press, 1991).

16. George Lipsitz, *Time Passages: Collective Memory and American Popular Culture* (Minneapolis: University of Minnesota Press, 1990). Lipsitz wrote, "Blacks left the South in large numbers during the 1940s, and during the war years alone 750,000 whites moved to Los Angeles and more than 200,000 moved to Detroit" (116–17).

17. For an excellent essay on the relationship among the rapidly changing worlds of postwar science, literature, medicine, and music, see Charles Hamm, "Changing Patterns in Society and Music: The U.S. Since World War II," in *Contemporary Music and Music Cultures*, ed. Charles Hamm, Bruno Nettl, and Ronald Byrnside (Englewood Cliffs, NJ: Prentice-Hall, 1975).

18. This aspect of my project builds on the groundbreaking work of cultural critic Farah Jasmine Griffin, who recently argued that the African American migration narrative represents a dominant site of African American cultural production. My attention to the relationship of family narrative and musical meaning confirms her observations. Farah Jasmine Griffin, *Who Set You Flowin'? The African-American Migration Narrative* (New York: Oxford University Press, 1995).

19. Sherry B. Ortner, "Resistance and the Problem of Ethnographic Refusal," *Comparative Studies in Society and History* 37, no. 1 (1995): 173. Ortner's definition of the ethnographic stance is instructive: "Ethnography of course means many things. Minimally, however, it has always meant the attempt to understand another life world using the self—as much of it as possible—as the instrument of knowing." For more on ethnography and popular music, see Sara Cohen, "Ethnography and Popular Music Studies," *Popular Music* 12 (1993).

20. Ortner, "Resistance and the Problem of Ethnographic Refusal."

21. Cedric Robinson, *Black Movements in America* (New York: Routledge, 1997), 123.

22. Jannette L. Dates and William Barlow, eds., *Split Image: African-Americans in the Mass Media* (Washington, DC: Howard University Press, 1990).

23. Tera Hunter, *To 'Joy My Freedom: Southern Black Women's Lives and Labors after the Civil War* (Cambridge, MA: Harvard University Press, 1997), 169. See also Lawrence W. Levine, *Black Culture and Black Consciousness: Afro-American Folk Thought from Slavery to Freedom* (New York: Oxford University Press, 1977).

24. Hans A. Baer and Merrill Singer, *African-American Religion in the Twentieth Century: Varieties of Protest and Accommodation* (Knoxville: University of Tennessee Press, 1992), 3.

25. Four Jumps of Jive, "It's Just the Blues," composed by Richard Jones and Jimmy Gilmore (New York: Mercury Records, 1945).

26. See Willie Dixon with Don Snowden, *I Am the Blues: The Willie Dixon Story* (New York: Da Capo Press, 1989); and Jim O'Neal, "It's Just the Blues," in *The Mercury Blues and Rhythm Story, 1945–1955*, liner notes (New York: Mercury Records, 314–528–292–2). Both Willie Dixon and Richard M. Jones had worked in gospel settings as well; see Horace Clarence Boyer, *How Sweet the Sound: The Golden Age of Gospel* (Washington, DC: Elliott & Clark, 1995), 37. For useful descriptions of the various musical styles designated by the term "rhythm and blues," see William Barlow and Cheryl Finley, *From Swing to Soul: An Illustrated History of African-American Popular Music from 1930 to 1960* (Washington, DC: Elliot & Clark, 1994); and Charlie Gillett, *The Sound of the City: The Rise of Rock and Roll* (New York: Pantheon Books, 1983).

27. O'Neal, "It's Just the Blues."

28. See Kevin K. Gaines, *Uplifting the Race: Black Leadership, Politics, and Culture in the Twentieth Century* (Chapel Hill: University of North Carolina Press, 1996); Griffin, *Who Set You Flowin'?;* Evelyn Brooks Higginbotham, *Righteous Discontent: The Women's Movement in the Black Baptist Church, 1880–1920* (Cambridge, MA: Harvard University Press, 1993); and Lawrence W. Levine, "The Concept of the New Negro and the Realities of Black Culture," in *The Unpredictable Past: Explorations in American Cultural History* (New York: Oxford University Press, 1993).

CHAPTER 10. A NEW KIND OF BLUE

1. Nate Chinen, "The Corner of Jazz and Hip-Hop," *New York Times*, February 24, 2012, www.nytimes.com/2012/02/26/arts/music/robert-glasper-experiment-to-release-black-radio.html.

2. Scott DeVeaux, "'Nice Work If You Can Get It': Thelonious Monk and Popular Song," *Black Music Research Journal* 19, no. 2 (Autumn 1999): 172.

3. Mark Anthony Neal, "Liberating *Black Radio:* The Robert Glasper Experiment," *Huffington Post,* March 9, 2012, www.huffingtonpost.com/mark-anthony-neal/black-radio-album-review_b_1326449.html.

CHAPTER 11. FREE JAZZ AND THE PRICE OF
BLACK MUSICAL ABSTRACTION

1. Eddie S. Glaude Jr., "Black Power Revisited," in *Is It Nation Time? Contemporary Essays on Black Power and Black Nationalism*, ed. Eddie S. Glaude (Chicago: University of Chicago Press, 2002), 1.

2. For varied treatments of this music and its history, see LeRoi Jones, *Black Music* (New York: William Morrow and Company, 1967); Ekkehard Jost, *Free Jazz* (New York: Da Capo Press, 1994); Robin D. G. Kelley, "Dig They Freedom: Meditations of History and the Black Avant-Garde," *Lenox Avenue: A Journal of Interartistic Activity* 3 (1997); Frank Kovsky, *Black Nationalism and the Revolution in Music* (New York: Pathfinder, 1970); George Lewis, "Experimental Music in Black and White: The AACM in New York, 1970–1985," in *Uptown Conversation: The New Jazz Studies*, ed. Robert O'Meally, Brent Hayes Edwards, and Farah Jasmine Griffin (New York: Columbia University Press, 2004); David Litweiler, *The Freedom Principle: Jazz After 1958* (New York: DaCapo Press, 1990); Ronald M. Radano, *New Musical Figurations: Anthony Braxton's Cultural Critique* (Chicago: University of Chicago Press, 1993); David G. Such, *Avant-Garde Jazz Musicians Performing "Out There"* (Iowa City: University of Iowa Press, 1993); and Salim Washington, "'All the Things You Could Be by Now': Charles Mingus Presents Charles Mingus and the Limits of Avant-Garde Jazz," in *Uptown Conversations: The New Jazz Studies*, ed. Robert G. O'Meally, Brent Hayes Edwards, and Farah Jasmine Griffin (New York: Columbia University Press, 2004).

3. Lorenzo Thomas, "Ascension: Music and the Black Arts Movement," *Jazz Among the Discourses*, ed. Krin Gabbard (Durham, NC: Duke University Press, 1995).

4. Robert Farris Thompson, *Flash of the Spirit: African and Afro-American Art and Philosophy* (New York: Vintage Books, 1983).

5. Albert J. Raboteau, *Slave Religion: The "Invisible Institution" in the Antebellum South* (New York: Oxford University Press, 1978), 4.

6. Thomas, "Ascension," 262.

7. See, for example Houston A. Baker Jr., *Afro-American Poetics: Revisions of Harlem and the Black Aesthetic* (Madison: University of Wisconsin Press, 1981); Houston A. Baker Jr., *Blues, Ideology, and Afro-American Literature: A Vernacular Theory* (Chicago: University of Chicago Press, 1984); Amiri Baraka, "'The Blues Aesthetic and the Black Aesthetic': Aesthetics as the Continuing Political History of a Culture," *Black Music Research Journal* 11 (Fall 1991); J. Martin Favor, "'Ain't Nothin' Like the Real Thing Baby': Trey Ellis's Search For New Black Voices," *Callaloo* 16 (Summer 1993); George Lipsitz, "Listening to Learn and Learning to Listen: Popular Culture, Cultural Theory, and American Studies," *American Quarterly* 42 (December 1990); Portia Maultsby, "Africanisms in

African-American Music," in *Africanisms in American Culture*, ed. Joseph E. Holloway (Bloomington: Indiana University Press, 1990); Portia Maultsby, "Africanisms Retained in the Spiritual Tradition," in *International Musicological Society, Berkeley 1977*, ed. Daniel Heartz and Bonnie Wade (Basel: Bärenreiter, 1981); Richard J. Powell, ed., *The Blues Aesthetic: Black Culture and Modernism* (Washington, DC: Washington Project for the Arts, 1989); Greg Tate, "Cult-Nats Meet Freaky-Deke: The Return of the Black Aesthetic," *Village Voice Literary Supplement* (December 1986), 7; Craig Hansen Warner; *Playing the Changes: From Afro-Modernism to the Jazz Impulse* (Urbana: University of Illinois Press, 1994).

8. For comprehensive bibliographic treatment of this material, see Eileen Southern and Josephine Wright, eds., *African-American Traditions in Song, Sermon, Tale, and Dance, 1600s–1920: An Annotated Bibliography of Literature, Collections, and Artworks* (New York: Greenwood Press, 1990). Also see several sources by Dena Epstein: "African Music in British and French America," *Musical Quarterly* 59 (January 1973); "A White Origin for the Black Spiritual? An Invalid Theory and How it Grew," *American Music* 1 (Summer 1983); "Documenting the History of Black Folk Music in the United States: A Librarian's Odyssey," *Fontes Artis Musicae* 23 (1976); *Sinful Tunes and Spirituals: Black Folk Music to the Civil War* (Urbana: University of Illinois Press, 1977); and "Slave Music in the United States Before 1860 (Part I)," *Notes* 20, 2nd series (Spring 1963).

9. Susan McClary, "Terminal Prestige: The Case of Avant-Garde Composition," *Cultural Critique* 12 (Spring 1989).

10. Henry Louis Gates Jr., *The Signifying Monkey: A Theory of African-American Literary Criticism* (New York: Oxford University Press, 1988), xxiv.

11. McClary, "Terminal Prestige," 64.

12. David Ake, *Jazz Cultures* (Berkeley: University of California Press, 2002).

CHAPTER 12. JACK WHITTEN'S MUSICAL EYE

1. Kellie Jones, ed., *Energy/Experimentation: Black Artists and Abstraction, 1964–1980* (New York: The Studio Museum in Harlem, 2006).

2. Katy Siegel, ed., *Jack Whitten: Notes from the Woodshed* (New York: Hauser & Wirth Publishers, 2018), 380.

3. Richard J. Powell, *Black Art: A Cultural History*, 2nd ed. (London: Thames and Hudson, 2003), 68.

4. Guthrie P. Ramsey Jr., *Race Music: Black Cultures from Bebop to Hip-Hop* (Berkeley: University of California Press, 2003), 100.

5. See, for example, Quincy Jones, *Q: The Autobiography of Quincy Jones* (New York: Doubleday, 2001), 284.

6. See *Jack Whitten: Five Decades of Painting* (San Diego, CA: Museum of Contemporary Art, 2015), particularly Kathryn Kanjo's "Facing Abstraction" and Robert Storr's "In Conversation with Jack Whitten," for insights into Whitten's formative years as an artist and activist.

7. Guthrie P. Ramsey Jr., "Free Jazz and the Price of Black Musical Abstraction," in *Energy/Experimentation: Black Artists and Abstraction, 1964–1980*, ed., Kellie Jones (New York: The Studio Museum in Harlem, 2006), 73. For varied treatments of this music and its history, see LeRoi Jones, *Black Music* (New York: William Morrow and Company, 1967); Ekkehard Jost, *Free Jazz* (New York: Da Capo Press, 1994); Robin D. G. Kelley, "Dig They Freedom: Meditations of History and the Black Avant-Garde," *Lenox Avenue: A Journal of Interartistic Activity* 3 (1997); Frank Kovsky, *Black Nationalism and the Revolution in Music* (New York: Pathfinder, 1970); George Lewis, "Experimental Music in Black and White: The AACM in New York, 1970–1985," in *Uptown Conversation: The New Jazz Studies*, ed. Robert O'Meally, Brent Hayes Edwards, and Farah Jasmine Griffin (New York: Columbia University, 2004); David Litweiler, *The Freedom Principle: Jazz After 1958* (New York: DaCapo Press, 1990); Ronald M. Radano, *New Musical Figurations: Anthony Braxton's Cultural Critique* (Chicago: University of Chicago Press, 1993); David G. Such, *Avant-Garde Jazz Musicians Performing "Out There"* (Iowa City: University of Iowa Press, 1993); and Salim Washington, "'All the Things You Could Be by Now': Charles Mingus Presents Charles Mingus and the Limits of Avant-Garde Jazz," in *Uptown Conversations: The New Jazz Studies*, ed. Robert G. O'Meally, Brent Hayes Edwards, and Farah Jasmine Griffin (New York: Columbia University Press, 2004).

8. Kellie Jones, "To the Max: Energy and Experimentation," in *Energy/Experimentation*, 23.

9. Siegel, *Jack Whitten*, 15.

10. Storr, "In Conversation with Jack Whitten," 53–54.

11. Jack Whitten, interview by Judith Olch Richards, Archives of American Art, Smithsonian Institute, December 1–3, 2009, 89, www.aaa.si.edu/collections/interviews/oral-history-interview-jack-whitten-15748#overview

12. Siegel, *Jack Whitten*, 410–12.

Index

Afro-modernism, 112, 133–34, 137, 168–71, 174, 180; electric guitar, 147
American Musicological Society, 259–60n1; challenge to exclusionary practices, 12–13; Committee on Cultural Diversity, 12, 45, 261n9; feminist contributions at the 1988 Annual Meeting, 66–67; Phillip Gossett, 43–44
American Negro Academy, 47
Anderson, T. J., 151
Association for the Advancement of Creative Musicians, 201

Baker, Houston, 17, 67; blues matrix, 278n3; generational shift, 263n26
Baraka, Amiri, 7, 52, 59–61, 133, 156, 203, 247; "Jazz and the White Critic," 60–61
bebop, 156, 158–59, 182, 194, 199, 201, 207, 209–10, 240
Birth of a Nation, 117, 124
Black Arts Movement, 200, 204
black church music, 238–39
black criticism: feminist, 56, 120; literary criticism, 64–66
Black Music Caucus of the Music Educators National Conference, 134, 152, 277n27
Black Music Research Journal, 45, 91, 134

black music studies, xiii; historiography, 15–41, 252n4
blackness: identity politics in black music inquiry, 44, 50–68; confessional blackness, 82–84; professional blackness, 79, 84
Black Perspective in Music, 45, 134
black power movement, 14, 53, 56–58, 69, 80, 96, 162, 200, 206
Blue Note label, 148
blues, 164–68, 175–78, 233
Brown, James, 52–56, 69

Carby, Hazel, 162, 269n99
Chess label, 148
Cleage, Pearl, 77–78
Coleman, Ornette, 140–41, 206
Coltrane, Alice, 141–43, 145
Coltrane, John, 139–42, 145, 202, 211–12
Crawford, Richard, 8, 41, 161; cosmopolitan and provincial model, 16–17, 32
Cuney-Hare, Maud, 25, 28; Negro Musicians and Their Music, 24, 28–29, 31–32

Davis, Miles, 69–72
Dent, Gina: Black Popular Culture, 9
Do the Right Thing, 118–19, 124–25, 127, 132; Bill Lee, 125; Public Enemy: "Fight the Power," 125, 127–28

Founded in 1893,
UNIVERSITY OF CALIFORNIA PRESS
publishes bold, progressive books and journals
on topics in the arts, humanities, social sciences,
and natural sciences—with a focus on social
justice issues—that inspire thought and action
among readers worldwide.

The UC PRESS FOUNDATION
raises funds to uphold the press's vital role
as an independent, nonprofit publisher, and
receives philanthropic support from a wide
range of individuals and institutions—and from
committed readers like you. To learn more, visit
ucpress.edu/supportus.